A Beginner's Guide to the Apple

BRUCE PRESLEY

TED DECKEL

DISTRIBUTED BY

 VAN NOSTRAND REINHOLD COMPANY
NEW YORK   CINCINNATI   TORONTO   LONDON   MELBOURNE

First published in 1984

Copyright © 1984
by

ISBN 0-931717-02-7

All rights reserved. No part of this work covered by the copyright may be reproduced or used in any form or by any means—graphics, electronic, or mechanical, including photocopying, recording, taping, or information storage and retrieval systems—without written permission of the publisher, with the exception of programs, which may be entered, stored and executed in a computer system, but not reprinted for publication or resold in any other form. Printed in the United States of America.

Educational orders may be placed by writing or calling:

Van Nostrand Reinhold Inc.
7625 Empire Drive
Attn: Department T
Florence, Kentucky 41042
Telephone 606-525-6600

Van Nostrand Reinhold Company
135 West 50th Street, New York, NY 10020

Macmillan of Canada
Division of Gage Publishing Limited
164 Commander Boulevard
Agincourt, Ontario M1S 3C7, Canada

Van Nostrand Reinhold Australia Pty. Ltd.
480 Latrobe Street
Melbourne, Victoria 3000, Australia

Van Nostrand Reinhold Company Ltd.
Molly Millars Lane
Wokingham, Berkshire, England RG11 2PY

16 15 14 13 12 11 10 9 8 7 6 5 4 3 2

This guide is written and published by Lawrenceville Press, Inc. and is in no way connected with Apple Computer Inc. Apple, Apple II, Apple II Plus, Apple //e, and Applesoft are registered trademarks of Apple Computer Inc. with regard to any computer product.

ACKNOWLEDGMENTS

The publication of this first edition of *A Beginner's Guide to the Apple* represents the latest achievement of Lawrenceville Press in developing curricular materials to assist students in learning to program computers. Written for younger students or for the adult who wants a slower paced text, this book is based on the considerable experience of Ted Deckel has had in teaching middle school students. Both he and I are convinced that a well-structured, concisely written computer text is invaluable in teaching programming to young students.

The production of this manual has involved the cooperation and talents of many individuals. Special thanks are due to Michael Bidwell, Chris Dingle, Fred Nilson, Jonathan Small, John Wang and Greg Zaharchuk, all of whom worked to ensure the clarity and accuracy of each chapter. Gregg Schwinn and Marjorie Vining have produced the graphics, and James Adams has edited the text to ensure that it is both grammatically and stylistically correct. A very special thanks is due to the staffs both at Browne Book Composition Inc. and Heffernan Press, Inc. for their assistance in producing this text.

To all these people I am deeply grateful. Thanks to their combined efforts we have produced what I believe to be one of the finest computer texts available today.

Bruce Presley

TABLE OF CONTENTS

Acknowledgments
Introduction

CHAPTER ONE
Getting Started

Starting Up Your Apple 1-1
    NEW 1-1
    Moving Right and Left 1-1
Immediate Mode 1-2
    PRINT—With Numbers 1-2
    PRINT—With Quotation Marks 1-3
?Syntax Error 1-3
Writing a Program 1-4
    Entering Program Lines 1-4
    RUN—Execute a Program 1-5
    PRINT—in Program Mode 1-6
    LIST—List out a Program 1-7
Correcting Errors 1-8
    Retyping a Line 1-8
    Erase a Whole Line 1-8
    Add a New Line 1-9
Exercises 1-11

CHAPTER TWO
Simple Input and Output

Variables—Representing values 2-1
LET—Assigning a variable its value 2-1
    With Numbers 2-1
    With Strings (Letters & Characters) 2-4
PRINT—Messages and Variables 2-7
INPUT—Take a value in from the keyboard 2-9
    A Number 2-9
    A String (Letters or Characters) 2-11
REENTER 2-12
REM—A remark 2-14
Exercises 2-17

CHAPTER THREE
Working with Data

GO TO—Creating a Loop 3-1
    Using Variable Names in a Loop 3-3
    Counting in a Loop 3-3

        INPUT within a Loop 3-5
        Accumulating a Total 3-6
    READ and **DATA**—Storing data in a program 3-8
        GOTO and READ/DATA 3-10
    PRINT Formatting-Organizing ouput 3-12
    Exercises 3-17

CHAPTER FOUR
Decisions

IF . . . THEN—Making a Decision 4-1
Exended use of IF . . . THEN 4-4
END—The End of a Program 4-5
Flags Signal the Way 4-7
AND & OR—Making IF . . . THEN smarter 4-10
Initializing Variables—Using the correct values 4-13
Exercises 4-19

CHAPTER FIVE
Defined Loops

FOR . . . NEXT—The loop statement 5-1
More FOR . . . NEXT 5-2
STEPS 5-4
    Looping forward by STEPs more than one 5-4
    Looping back from a higher to a lower STEP 5-7
PRINT TAB(X)—More exact PRINT formatting 5-8
Exercises 5-13

CHAPTER SIX
Computer Math

Order of Operations—What the computer does first 6-1
Computer Numbers—Decimal Representation 6-4
INT ( ): **INTegerizing**—Whole Numbers 6-5
RND(1): **RaNDom Numbers** 6-7
    More Useful RaNDom Numbers 6-8
    Choosing Numbers From Range 6-9
Rounding Errors—When the computer is not correct 6-10
Scientific Notation/E Notation 6-11
Rounding Fractions Off 6-12
Exercises 6-17

CHAPTER SEVEN
Graphics and Color

HTAB and **VTAB** 7-1
HOME 7-1
FLASH, **INVERSE** and **NORMAL** 7-3
Low-Resolution Graphics 7-5
    GR and **TEXT** 7-5
    COLOR 7-6
    PLOT 7-6
    HLIN 7-6
    VLIN 7-7
High-Resolution Graphics 7-9

　　　　　　HGR and HGR2 7-9
　　　　　　HCOLOR 7-10
　　　　　　HPLOT 7-10
　　　　Exercises 7-15

CHAPTER EIGHT
Program Planning

Multiple Statement Lines 8-1
The Need for Subroutines 8-2
GOSUB and RETURN—Calling a Subroutine 8-3
　　　Using **GOSUB** and **RETURN** 8-5
ON ... GOSUB—A Special type of branching statement 8-10
ON ... GOTO—Branching without a RETURN 8-12
Program Planning—How to put a program together 8-13
　　　Planning a Real Program 8-14
　　　Putting the Pieces Together 8-16
Debugging—Finding and Fixing the Errors 8-21
　　　Run Time Errors—Errors that halt execution 8-21
　　　Logic Errors—Creating Incorrect Output 8-22
Hand Tracing—Playing Computer 8-23
STOP and CONTinue 8-25
Exercises 8-29

CHAPTER NINE
Nested Loops
and Subscripted
Variables

Nested FOR ... NEXT—A Loop Inside a Loop 9-1
Array Variables 9-4
　　　The Need For Arrays 9-4
　　　Arrays: Variables with Many Boxes 9-6
DIM—Increasing the Length of an Array 9-11
Longer Variable Names 9-14
　　　Reserved Words 9-15
　　　Confusion with BASIC Words 9-15
RESTORE—Using DATA More than Once 9-17
GET—Checking the Keyboard for a Pressed Key 9-18
VAL( )—Change a String Value to a Number 9-21
Conclusion 9-24
Exercises 9-27

Appendix A—Disk Operations A-1
　　　INIT A-1
　　　SAVE A-1
　　　LOAD A-2
　　　CATALOG A-2
　　　RENAME A-3
　　　DELETE A-3
　　　LOCK A-3
　　　UNLOCK A-3

Glossary G-1
Summary of Basic Instructions IS-1
Review Answers R-1
Answers to Odd Numbered Exercises E-1
Index

INTRODUCTION

What is a computer program?

A computer is a machine that accepts information, processes it at a very high speed according to specific instructions and provides the results as new information. The instructions that tell a computer how to process the information are called programs. Programs must be written in a special code, or language, that the computer has been designed to understand. There are hundreds of different languages with names like FORTRAN, BASIC, PASCAL and LOGO. This manual will teach you how to program your microcomputer in BASIC (Beginner's All-purpose Symbolic Instruction Code), a language developed by John Kemeny and Tim Kurtz at Dartmouth College.

Why learn to program?

The first and most obvious reason to learn to program is to get the most out of your microcomputer. If you cannot write your own program, you will have to use commercially available programs, many of which are quite good, but it is unlikely that the people who make this "software" will be able to anticipate all your needs. An ability to program means that you will be able to use the computer efficiently for your own purposes.

Another, and more important, reason for learning to program is the experience it will give you in important problem solving techniques. Learning how to assess the dimensions of a problem, break it down into manageable parts and design a series of operations which will solve it is a skill that will help you in anything you will do. Efficient, logical reasoning is very important, and programming a computer can develop such reasoning rapidly and thoroughly.

Finally, there is an important general reason for learning to program. Computers are a huge influence in our lives today, affecting virtually every industry, and this influence will surely grow. Those who know how to instruct computers can deal with this circumstance confidently; those who cannot will become increasingly dependent on those who can.

GETTING STARTED

1

**PRINT
RUN
LIST
NEW**

**PRINT
RUN
LIST
NEW**

**Starting Up
Your Apple**

*T*o start working on the computer, follow this procedure carefully. First insert a properly formatted diskette into the disk drive and press down the handle of the drive to insure that the diskette is securely in the drive. If you do not have a formatted diskette, Appendix A at the back of this book explains how to make one. Second, turn on the monitor just as you would turn on a television set. Finally, reach back behind the computer and flick the ON-OFF switch to ON. The disk drive will whirr for a few moments, and the red light will come on. You will see a blinking square on the screen signifying that you are ready to begin work.

NEW

The first command that should be typed after the computer is turned on is NEW. Type the letters N, E, and W to spell the word NEW. Then press the RETURN key which is located at the far right of the keyboard. The NEW command clears an area in the computer's memory for you to work in. The RETURN key is always used to enter a command into the computer's memory.

**← and
→ Keys**

These keys, located at the bottom right of the keyboard, are used to move the cursor backwards and forwards on a line.
The → key is used to move the cursor one space to the right. It does not erase anything it passes over.
The ← key is used to move the cursor backwards one space. It does not erase anything it passes over.
Take a look at the following example which displays how the ← key and the → key can be used to correct a mistake.

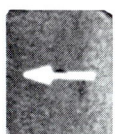

1. Type the following on the computer but do not hit the RETURN key:

    NIW

2. To correct this misspelling, hit the ← key twice so that the cursor is positioned over the letter I. Note that the ← key did not erase the letter W.

    NIW

3. Now type in the correction, the letter E. Note how the I disappears. The screen now looks like this:

    NEW

4. Finally, hit the → key once to restore the cursor to its original position at the end of the word. The screen should look like this:

    NEW

5. Now hit the RETURN key to enter the command into the computer's memory.

Immediate Mode

A computer does nothing without being given instructions. It is possible to have the computer follow an instruction immediately. This is done by typing a BASIC statement and then pressing RETURN; this is called using the computer in immediate mode.

PRINT

PRINT is the BASIC statement used to print numbers, characters and words on the screen.

Using immediate mode, the following example prints the result of a math operation on the screen:

    PRINT 12 + 5   <RETURN>
    17

PRINT followed by a math operation tells the computer to print the result of that operation. Only the result is printed. The math statement is not printed out, and an equal sign does not appear. In immediate mode the computer carries out the operation when the RETURN key is pressed.

In BASIC the following symbols are used for each of the four math operations:

Operation	Sign
Addition	+
Subtraction	−
Multiplication	★
Division	/

The computer can use both numbers and words. To the computer a number is something that can be used in a mathematical calculation. It is something that can be added, subtracted, multiplied or divided. A word or character, on the other hand, cannot be used to do any of those things.

PRINT with Quotation Marks

PRINT followed by quotation marks tells the computer to print whatever appears between the quotation marks. Using immediate mode, the following example prints a message on the screen:

PRINT "MY COMPUTER LIKES ME." <**RETURN**>
MY COMPUTER LIKES ME.

As soon as RETURN is pressed, MY COMPUTER LIKES ME. is printed on the screen. The word PRINT and the quotation marks are not printed.

?SYNTAX ERROR

The computer will only act when it recognizes a command or instruction that is in its language. PRINT is one of the words in the BASIC language. Anytime the computer does not recognize an instruction, it prints an error message and either stops what it is doing or waits until the programmer corrects the error.

One of the most common error messages is the ?SYNTAX ERROR.

PRUNT "I LIKE MY COMPUTER." <**RETURN**>
?SYNTAX ERROR

The computer cannot think for itself. It is not smart enough to know that the programmer meant PRINT. Since PRUNT is not one of the words it understands, the computer displays an error message and halts its attempt to carry out the instruction it was given.

Most BASIC commands can be used in immediate mode. It is best, however, to use immediate mode only for simple calculations and to use programs to perform most tasks.

Review

1. Enter each of the following statements in immediate mode. Predict what the computer will print when RETURN is pressed.

    PRINT 2 + 5
    PRINT 6 − 3
    PRINT 5 * 3
    PRINT 15 / 3

2. Enter the following in immediate mode and predict what the computer will print:

    PRINT "I AM 5 FEET TALL."

3. What will the output of the following be:

    PRLNT "LOOK MA! NO HANDS."

4. Correct the PRINT statement in number 3.

Writing a Program

In order to get a computer to do what you want it to, you must give it instructions. Immediate mode gave the computer instructions one instruction at a time. A program is a series of instructions given to the computer.

A program's instructions are written as a series of lines. Each line of the program must begin with a line number to put the instructions in order. While in immediate mode the computer is given a single instruction without a line number. Program lines are stored in the computer's memory until the computer is given a command to execute the program. The computer will follow the program's instructions by finding the line with the lowest line number and executing the instructions on that line. It will then read the next highest numbered line and execute the instructions on that line. The computer will continue to do this line by line until it reaches the highest numbered line. The following is an example of a program:

    10 PRINT "THIS IS A PROGRAM."
    20 PRINT "INSTRUCTIONS ARE WRITTEN"
    30 PRINT "ON LINES. EACH LINE"
    40 PRINT "HAS A LINE NUMBER."

Entering Program Lines

There are a few simple rules about lines and line numbering. Keep these rules in mind when writing a program:

1. To enter a program line into the computer's memory, press the RETURN key when the line is completed.

    Pressing RETURN is very important even though nothing seems to happen. Once RETURN is pressed the line is stored in the computer's memory until the computer is told to carry out that line's instructions.

    10 PRINT 2 + 2 <RETURN>

2. When writing a program, you should use line numbers that are units of ten. (10, 20, ... 100, 110, 120, etc.). This will leave room to insert nine possible lines between any two lines in case it is necessary to add new lines later.

3. It is not necessary to enter lines in order. Line 20 can be entered first, then line 10 and later line 30. The computer will automatically put the lines in numerical order. Any time a new instruction is to be added to a program, just type the line number, the instruction and press RETURN. The computer will put the line in its proper place in the program.

```
10 PRINT "MATH IS EASY"   <RETURN>
20 PRINT "2 + 2 ="   <RETURN>
15 PRINT "WITH A COMPUTER"   <RETURN>
30 PRINT 2 + 2   <RETURN>
```

4. Do not confuse the capital letter "O" with a zero "0". Use the zero (0) when a number is needed and the letter (O) when a letter is needed.

5. Any whole number from 0 to 63999 can be used as a line number.

6. The NEW command is used to erase the computer's memory. Before entering a program into the computer's memory, a good programmer should type NEW. This will insure that program lines from the program used before will not affect the new program. Be sure that you really want your program erased from the computer's memory when you type NEW. Once it is erased, it is lost forever unless it has been saved on a diskette (See Appendix A for diskette operations).

RUN

The command RUN tells the computer to begin executing the program in its memory. Type the word RUN and press RETURN. The computer will go to the lowest numbered line of the program and follow the instructions that it finds on that line. It then goes on to the next line, and the next, and the next, etc. until it reaches the end of the program. The command RUN is not part of the program.

Program 1.1

Type in this program and then RUN it. Be sure to copy it exactly as it is. Do not forget to press RETURN after each line:

```
10   PRINT "HELLO THERE"
20   PRINT "I AM A FRIENDLY COMPUTER."


]RUN
HELLO THERE
I AM A FRIENDLY COMPUTER.
```

When RUN is typed and RETURN is pressed, the computer begins to execute the program lines that are stored in its memory. The computer begins at line 10. When a line is executed, PRINT works the same as it does in immediate mode. The message HELLO THERE is printed because those characters are between the quotation marks. Line 20 prints the message I AM A FRIENDLY COMPUTER because that is between the quotation marks. The words PRINT and the quotation marks are not shown when the program is executed.

PRINT in Program Mode

When PRINT is used in immediate mode, the instructions are carried out as soon as RETURN is pressed and the results are immediately displayed on the screen. When program lines are typed, the instructions are not carried out until the program is RUN. In a program PRINT followed by a math statement tells the computer to print the result of the calculation when the program line is executed.

Program 1.2

This program uses the PRINT statement to print the result of four mathematical operations:

```
10   PRINT 5 + 3
20   PRINT 5 - 3
30   PRINT 5 * 3
40   PRINT 15 / 3

]RUN
8
2
15
5
```

When line 10 is executed, the computer prints the sum of 5 and 3. Line 20 tells the computer to print the difference between 5 and 3. Line 30 tells the machine to print the product of 5 and 3, and line 40 prints the result of 15 divided by 3. It is not necessary to use an equal sign. The computer will perform the operation and print the result without it.

The command RUN was typed after line 40 was entered to tell the computer to begin executing the instructions of the program. RUN is not part of the program.

Review

5. What will a RUN of the following program print on the screen:

   10 PRINT "MY COMPUTER IS"
   20 PRINT "A CHIP OFF THE OLD"
   30 PRINT "BLOCK!"

6. Predict the results of the following program:

   10 PRINT 123 + 456 + 789
   20 PRINT 27 * 13

It is possible to use PRINT on one line both to display the result of a math operation and to print a message. The rules are simple. Whatever words, numbers or characters are to be printed must be typed within quotation marks. Any math operations that are to be carried out must be typed outside the quotation marks.

Program 1.3

This program shows how to print numbers, words, and characters at the same time:

```
10  PRINT "MATHEMATICS"
20  PRINT "5 * 3 ="
30  PRINT 5 * 3
40  PRINT "5 * 3 = "5 * 3

]RUN
MATHEMATICS
5 * 3 =
15
5 * 3 = 15
```

Line 20 prints 5 * 3 on the screen. It does not print the product of 5 and 3 because the computer understands the 5, the *, and the 3 as characters when they are inside the quotation marks. In line 30, since the 5, * and 3 are not inside the quotation marks, the computer prints the product. Line 40 combines the printing of words and numbers in one PRINT statement. 5 * 3 = appears on the screen because it is inside the quotation marks. 15 comes after the 5 * 3 = because of the 5 * 3 that is after the quotation marks. The computer sees that and prints the product of 5 and 3.

Review

7. What will be the exact output of the following program:

    10 PRINT 4 * 3 "COOKIES MAKE A DOZEN."

8. Predict what this program will print on the screen when it is RUN:

    10 PRINT 5 + 3 "EQUALS" 4 * 2
    20 PRINT "40 +" 5 * 4 "=" 50 + 10

LIST

The LIST command is used to print on the screen the program that is in the computer's memory. For instance, when an error is made and needs to be corrected, LIST shows the program lines. This enables a programmer to see where the mistake is and correct it. Program 1.3 helps demonstrate two ways that LIST can be used:

1. LIST by itself:

    LIST <**RETURN**>
    10 PRINT "MATHEMATICS"
    20 PRINT "5 * 3"
    30 PRINT 5 * 3
    40 PRINT "5 * 3 = " 5 * 3

Typing LIST and then pressing the RETURN key prints the entire program on the screen. It is also possible to LIST a single line of a program.

2. LIST a single line:

>LIST 10 <**RETURN**>
>10 PRINT "MATHEMATICS"

The programmer can now see a single line of the program. This line could be corrected or edited depending on the needs of the programmer.

Review

9. Write a program that prints your name on the screen. RUN it.

>RUN
>TED DECKEL

10. LIST the program. Add a line to the program that says "MY COMPUTER LIKES ME". RUN it.

>RUN
>TED DECKEL
>MY COMPUTER LIKES ME

Correcting Errors

Typing errors or other mistakes in a program can be corrected in several ways. The following examples use Program 1.3:

1. RETYPING A LINE: A program line can be retyped using the same line number.

>LIST 10 <**RETURN**>
>10 PRINT "MATHEMATICS"
>
>READY.
>10 PRINT "MATH MAGIC"
>RUN
>MATH MAGIC
>5 ⋆ 3
> 15
>5 ⋆ 3 = 15

This changes only the output of line 10. Instead of MATHEMATICS, the program now outputs MATH MAGIC. After retyping a line, remember to press <RETURN>.

2. ERASE A WHOLE LINE: An entire line of a program can be erased by typing the line number and pressing RETURN. Using Program 1.3 type:

>20 <**RETURN**>
>30 <**RETURN**>
>RUN
>MAGIC MATH
>5 ⋆ 3 = 15

Getting Started   1-9

Notice that the output of lines 20 and 30 of the original program does not appear. Those lines have been erased.

3. ADDING A NEW LINE: To add a line between other lines of a program, type the new line and press RETURN. The computer will put the line in its proper place. Using Program 1.3 again, a new line can be added:

>   25 PRINT "PRESTO!"
>   RUN
>   MAGIC MATH
>   PRESTO!
>   5 * 3 = 15

Review

11. Type this program into your computer's memory exactly as it is written. After it is typed in, correct the errors by using the methods mentioned above:

>   10 PRUNT "SCREEN EDITING"
>   20 PRINT "CAN BE FN"
>   30 PRINT "IT SAVES WORK."

The program should look like this when it is RUN:

>   RUN
>   SCREEN EDITING
>   CAN BE FUN
>   IT SAVES WORK.

12. Add a new line between lines 20 and 30 so that the program looks like this when RUN:

>   RUN
>   SCREEN EDITING
>   CAN BE FUN
>   AND
>   IT SAVES WORK.

13. Delete lines 10 and 20 so that a RUN produces the following output:

>   RUN
>   AND
>   IT SAVES WORK.

Program 1.4

This program shows how the PRINT statement might be used in a program. Review it carefully:

```
10  PRINT "A COMPUTER IS A USEFUL TOOL"
20  PRINT "IT CAN ADD: 2 + 2 = "2 + 2
30  PRINT "IT CAN SUBTRACT: 4 - 2 = "4 - 2
```

```
40   PRINT "IT CAN MULTIPLY: 2 * 2 = "2 * 2
50   PRINT "IT CAN DIVIDE: 4 / 2 = "4 / 2

]RUN
A COMPUTER IS A USEFUL TOOL
IT CAN ADD: 2 + 2 = 4
IT CAN SUBTRACT: 4 - 2 = 2
IT CAN MULTIPLY: 2 * 2 = 4
IT CAN DIVIDE: 4 / 2 = 2
```

EXERCISES

Exercises

1. Perform each of the following computations on paper. Check your results by using immediate mode on the computer:

    (a) 5 + 16   (b) 33 − 16
    (c) 13 * 3   (d) 239 * 27
    (e) 250 / 5 (f) 999 / 11

2. Write a program that prints the following:

    ```
    RUN
    A
     B
      C
    ABCD
    ```

3. Write a program that draws a rectangle on the screen using the "*" key.

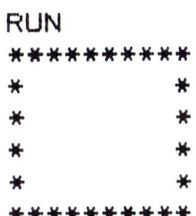

4. Write a program that draws a triangle on the screen.

5. Write a program that draws an arrow on the screen.

Chapter One

6. Write a program that will add the numbers 3, 5 and 7.

   RUN
   3 + 5 + 7 = 15

7. Write a program that will show the product of 275 and 39. A run of the program should look like this:

   RUN
   275 * 39 = 10725

8. Write a program that will divide 1800 by 60.

   RUN
   1800 / 60 = 30

9. In the first week of the season the jogging club ran the following number of miles each day: 2, 3, 5, 3, 5. Write a program to calculate and print the total mileage for the week.

   RUN
   MILEAGE FOR FIRST WEEK IS 18

10. Write a program that will give the length of two ropes, one 25 feet long and the other 72 feet long. The output should look like this:

    RUN
    THE NUMBER OF FEET OF ROPE IS 97

11. There are 5 gerbils, 6 mice and 3 birds in a class zoo. Write a program that lists the animals in the zoo.

    RUN
    OUR CLASS ZOO
    GERBILS: 5
    MICE: 6
    BIRDS: 3

12. Change the class zoo program so that it also prints how many animals there are in all.

> RUN
> OUR CLASS ZOO
> GERBILS: 5
> MICE: 6
> BIRDS: 3
> TOTAL ZOO ANIMALS = 14

13. John has 10 blue marbles and 5 red marbles. His uncle is going to give him 6 more of each kind. Write a program that will show how many of each kind he will have and what his total will be.

> RUN
> RED MARBLES = 11
> BLUE MARBLES = 16
> TOTAL MARBLES = 27

14. Orange juice is $1.99 a half gallon on sale this week. Milk is $.89 a quart. Write a program that displays the following sign:

```
RUN
*********************
*      BIG SALE     *
*                   *
* ORANGE JUICE $1.99 *
* MILK / QUART $ .89 *
*                   *
*********************
```

15. Write a program that will calculate the cost of 2 half gallons of orange juice and the cost of 2 quarts of milk. The program's output should look like this:

> RUN
> ORANGE JUICE $3.98
> MILK $1.78

SIMPLE INPUT AND OUTPUT

2

LET
INPUT
REM

LET
INPUT
REM

Simple Input and Output 2-1

A computer is a data processing machine. This means that numbers, words, letters and symbols can be used by the computer to complete an assigned task. To get any task done a computer must be able to bring the data that it needs into a program. The computer must also be able to move data out of its memory so the data can be printed on the screen, saved on tape or disk, or printed on paper by a printer. The operation of bringing data into a program is called input and the process of getting data out of a program is called output.

Using a PRINT statement to show the result of a math operation, as in PRINT 2 * 2, is one way to bring data out of a program. However, there are many different ways to use data. For example, a programmer often does not want to show the results of a math operation. Instead, the programmer might want to use the result of a calculation in another operation. Many times a programmer needs to use the same number over and over, so constantly retyping the number means more chances to make a mistake. In many situations the data a program needs will be different each time the program is run. To meet the many different situations in which data may be used, BASIC uses "variables." This chapter will explain what a variable is and also how LET and INPUT are used to name variables and assign them a value.

Variables

A variable is a name which is used to represent a value. For example,

$$A = 5$$

The number 5 is given the variable name A. The variable name A can be used in place of the number 5.

To the computer there are two kinds of data: numbers and characters. Therefore, in order to use variables, the computer must be told both the name of the variable and the type of data, either number or character, that the variable stands for.

Because variables stand for a value, they are one of the most useful ways to bring data into a program. Since data can be used in different ways, there are different ways to assign or give a variable its value.

LET with Numbers

The LET statement is one way of assigning a variable name its value. Assigning a variable with LET looks like this:

$$10 \text{ LET } A = 5$$

LET works by telling the computer to set aside a place in its memory called A where the number 5 is stored. The computer's memory is like a post office. Its memory is divided into many boxes. The variable name is the address of the box. When the computer reads a LET statement, it sets aside a box in its memory called A and puts a 5 in it.

A

5

Whenever the computer is told to use A, it will look in the box named A and use the value that A represents.

Variable names can be any single letter, a letter and a single digit or two letters. A, D, A1, D1, AA or DD are all legal variable names. When any of these variable names are used, the computer will expect a number to be assigned to the variable name.

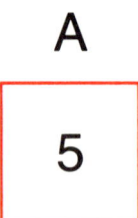

```
10 LET N = 27
20 PRINT N
RUN
27
```

N

The computer will not accept writing the value first and then the variable name. The "=" sign really means "is given the value". Therefore, it is not possible to have "value = variable".

```
10 LET 5 = A
20 PRINT A
RUN
?SYNTAX ERROR IN 10
```

Statements must be written in exactly the way the computer has been programmed to understand them. If a statement is not understood by the computer because it is not in the correct form, the computer stops the program and prints the SYNTAX ERROR message. The computer also tells in what line the error can be found. Then that line can be listed and the error corrected.

Program 2.1   This program shows how variable names are used in a program:

```
10   LET A = 5
20   LET B = 3
30   PRINT A * B

]RUN
15
```

Line 10 puts a 5 in a box named A, and line 20 puts a 3 into the box named B. Line 30 tells the computer to print the product of A and B. It does this by using the value of A and the value of B.

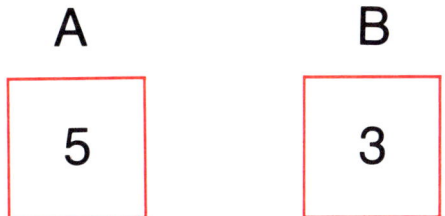

A variable box can only hold one value at a time. If a different number is put in the box, then the first number is erased and lost.

Program 2.2

This program shows how a variable's value is changed when a new value is assigned during a program:

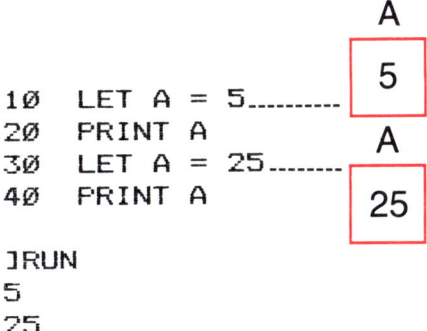

```
10   LET A = 5
20   PRINT A
30   LET A = 25
40   PRINT A

]RUN
5
25
```

When the computer reads line 10, a 5 is stored in the box named A. On line 30, A is changed to 25. The first value of A is erased from the computer's memory and 25 takes its place. Therefore, when the computer prints A for the second time on line 40, it prints 25.

With one exception, a variable is used in the same way that a number is used. This means that a variable can be used to give another variable its value. A variable, however, can never be used as a line number.

Program 2.3

Here one variable is used to give another variable its value.

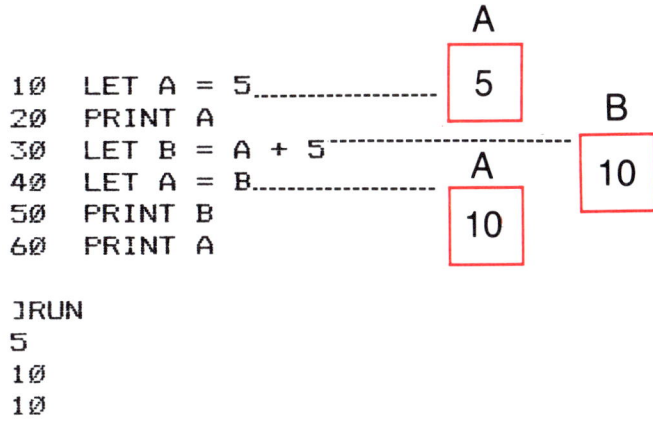

```
10   LET A = 5
20   PRINT A
30   LET B = A + 5
40   LET A = B
50   PRINT B
60   PRINT A

]RUN
5
10
10
```

The variable A is given a value of 5 on line 10. Line 20 prints the value of A on the screen. Then B is given the value of A plus 5, which is 10. Line 40 changes the value that A represents to the value of B, which is 10. Lines 50 and 60 show this by printing the value of B and the new value of A.

Review

1. What will the following program print on the screen?

   10 LET A = 25
   20 PRINT A * 4

2. Write a program that assigns a variable named B a value of 45 and a variable named C a value of 15. Write a program that will produce their difference:

   RUN
   30

3. What will be the output of the following program?

   10 LET A = 20
   20 LET B = A + 10
   30 PRINT B

4. Find the errors in the following program. When you have found them, type the corrected program in and run it.

   10 LET 64 = B
   20 LET 32 = A
   30 LET C = A + B
   40 PRINT C

LET with Characters

A character is any letter, number, punctuation mark or mathematics sign which can be found on the computer's keyboard. For example, A, *, 5 and D are all characters. Even a blank space is a character. A string is a series of characters. These characters are strung together like beads on a necklace to look like a word, number or sequence of symbols.

When a string variable is given a name, the variable name must be followed by a dollar sign ($). A letter, a letter and single digit, or two letters followed by a dollar sign ($) tell the computer that the variable is a string variable. A$, D$, A1$, D5$, AA$ and DD$ are all legal string variable names.

When a string variable is given its value by a LET statement, the characters that make up the string must be enclosed by quotation marks:

   10 LET A$ = "HARRY"

This statement assigns the string HARRY to the variable name A$.

If we think of mail boxes again, the computer will name one of its boxes A$ and place the string HARRY in that box when line 10 is executed.

A$

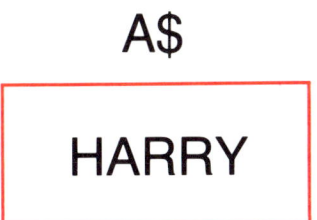

As with numeric variables, it is possible to change the characters that have been given the name A$:

50 LET A$ = "SHERRY"

The value of A$ changes from HARRY to SHERRY when line 50 is executed by the computer.

A$

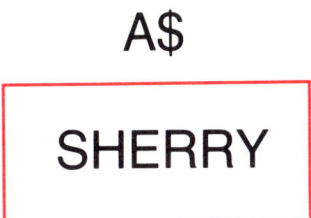

Program 2.4

This program shows a string variable being assigned and then changed:

```
10 LET B$ = "JUDY"
20 PRINT B$
30 LET B$ = "GEORGE"
40 PRINT B$

RUN
JUDY
GEORGE
```

Line 10 makes B$ equal to JUDY. In line 20 JUDY is printed on the screen as the value of B$. Line 30 changes B$ to GEORGE. When line 40 is printed, B$ is GEORGE and that is printed on the screen.

Program 2.5

This program shows what kind of characters can be part of a string:

```
10 LET A$ = "ALPHABET LAND"
20 LET B$ = "+,-;*:/ SYMBOL CENTER"
30 LET C$ = "123456789 NUMBERS TOO"
40 PRINT "WHAT GOES IN A STRING?"
50 PRINT A$
60 PRINT B$
70 PRINT C$
```

```
RUN
WHAT GOES IN A STRING?
ALPHABET LAND
+,-;*:/ SYMBOL CENTER
123456789 NUMBERS TOO
```

Lines 10, 20 and 30 show letters, spaces, numbers and various symbols being assigned to variable names A$, B$ and C$. The strings are then printed out in lines 50, 60 and 70.

When numbers are used as part of a string, they cannot be used mathematically. The computer sees them only as characters. Remember, numbers can be used to perform math operations, but strings cannot.

Program 2.6

This program demonstrates the difference between numbers assigned to a string variable name and numbers assigned to a numeric variable name:

```
10   LET A$ = "5"
20   LET B$ = "10"
30   LET C = 5
40   LET D = 10
50   PRINT A$ + B$
60   PRINT C + D
70   PRINT B$ + A$
80   PRINT D + C

]RUN
510
15
105
15
```

In line 50 the plus sign tells the computer to add A$ to B$. The dollar sign ($) tells the machine that they are not numeric variable names but character strings, so it attaches B$ to A$. This causes the machine to print 510 on the screen. In line 60, C and D are numbers so they can be added, and 15 is printed on the screen. Line 70 puts B$ first and then attaches A$ to it so that 105 is printed. Adding 10 and 5 gives the same answer as adding 5 and 10, and 15 is printed by line 80.

Review

5. What will be the output of the following program?

```
10 LET M2$ = "BROKE"
20 LET M1$ = "GO FOR "
30 PRINT M1$ + M2$
```

Note the blank space at the end of "GO FOR " is needed to place a space before "BROKE" when it is printed.

6. Find the errors in the following program. What will the corrected program print on the screen?

```
10 LET A$ = COMPUTER
20 LET 64 = B
20 PRINT A$
40 PRUNT B
```

PRINT Messages and Variables

Variable names can be combined with PRINT messages. This lets a programmer display on the screen the value a variable name stands for and a message that the variable might be a part of. Both the values of numeric and string variable names can be combined with PRINT messages.

It is important to note that in printing variables, a numeric variable and a string variable have no leading or trailing spaces. Any spaces that are needed must be provided by the programmer.

Program 2.7

Look at the way spacing is done when a PRINT message and a variable are used together:

```
10  LET A = 5
20  PRINT "GIVE ME "A
30  LET A$ = "FIVE"
40  PRINT "GIVE ME "A$

]RUN
GIVE ME 5
GIVE ME FIVE
```

In this program the variables become part of a message on the screen. These variables come after a PRINT. To get a space between ME and FIVE in line 40, type a space between the E in ME and the quotation marks.

Program 2.8

In this program the variables come before a PRINT message. Look at where the spaces are placed:

```
10  LET A = 5
20  PRINT A" IS ALIVE"
30  LET A$ = "FIVE"
40  PRINT A$" IS ALIVE"

]RUN
5 IS ALIVE
FIVE IS ALIVE
```

2-8 Chapter Two

Notice how in lines 20 and 40 a space is imbedded before the IS. This will assure the correct spacing when the lines are printed.

Program 2.9

Variables can be placed between parts of a PRINT statement as well:

```
10   LET A = 5
20   LET T = 15
30   PRINT "SUBTRACT "A" FROM THE
        TOTAL"
40   PRINT T" - "A" = "T - A

]RUN
SUBTRACT 5 FROM THE TOTAL
15 - 5 = 10
```

In line 30 the computer prints the word SUBTRACT because SUBTRACT is between the quotation marks. The computer then prints the value of the variable A, which is 5. The next quotation mark tells the computer that another message is part of the statement, so the computer prints the phrase FROM THE TOTAL as part of this statement. On line 40 the computer prints the value assigned to the variable name T and then prints the minus sign because it is inside quotation marks. The value of the variable A is then printed and followed by an equal sign because the equal sign is also within quotation marks. The difference of T and A is then printed.

Program 2.10

Program 2.9 used numbers as part of a PRINT statement. This program places strings between parts of a PRINT statement:

```
10   LET M$ = "GODZILLA"
20   PRINT "SHOOT "M$" NOW!"
30   LET C$ = "TOKYO"
40   PRINT "WILL "M$" CRUSH "C$" AGAIN?"

]RUN
SHOOT GODZILLA NOW!
WILL GODZILLA CRUSH TOKYO AGAIN?
```

Notice the spaces that are left within the quotation marks on lines 20 and 40 to keep the values of variable names M$ and C$ separated from the words in the PRINT statement.

Review

7. Wendy is full of woe. Her program does not work right. Help her out by correcting her mistake:

```
RUN
WONDERFUL WENDYACE COMPUTERPROGRAMMER
LIST
10 LET N$ = "WONDERFUL WENDY"
20 LET P$ = "PROGRAMMER"
30 PRINT N$ "ACE COMPUTER" P$
```

Simple Input and Output 2-9

8. Produce a program that has two variables named X and Y that will have the following output:

>THE PRODUCT OF 25 AND 50 IS 1250
>25 * 50 = 1250

INPUT: a number

Often the data that a program will use to accomplish its task will be different each time the program is run. The INPUT statement is a good way to assign a variable name its value in such a situation. The LET statement, on the other hand, is best used when data will not be different each time the program is run. A savings account provides good examples of these two situations. Each time money is deposited or withdrawn from an account the amount is likely to be different, but the amount of interest that the bank pays will not change often. Therefore, the rate of interest is best brought into the program with a LET statement while a deposit or withdrawal is best entered with an INPUT statement.

To use an INPUT statement, type the word INPUT and the variable name that will be assigned a value:

>10 INPUT A

When the computer reads the INPUT statement, it will print a question mark on the screen. It then waits for data to be typed in on the keyboard. When the RETURN key is pressed, the computer reads the data and assigns it to a variable name.

>10 INPUT A
>20 PRINT A
>RUN
>? 45 <**RETURN**>
>45

Until RETURN is pressed, the computer waits for more data. When RETURN is pressed, the computer sets aside a box in its memory,

>A
>
>┌────┐
>│ 45 │
>└────┘

names the box A and puts a 45 in the box as the value of the variable named A.

Program 2.11

The following program shows how a number is assigned to a variable name with an INPUT statement:

```
10   INPUT N
20   PRINT "5 * "N
30   PRINT 5 * N

]RUN            <RETURN>
? 5
5 * 5
25
```

When the computer reads the INPUT in line 10, it prints a question mark and waits for the data to be typed and the RETURN key to be pressed. When the 5 is typed and RETURN pressed, the computer sets aside a box in its memory and names it N.

N

5

A 5 is placed in the box as the value of variable N. When lines 20 and 30 are read, the computer uses 5 as the value of variable name N.

To halt the program while the computer is waiting for INPUT, hold down the CONTROL and C keys together. Then press the RETURN key.

Do not use commas when entering large numbers. A comma will cause the computer to print an EXTRA IGNORED error:

```
10   INPUT A
20   INPUT B
30   PRINT A
40   PRINT B

]RUN
? 4,500
?EXTRA IGNORED
? 4500
4
4500
```

When the computer printed the value of the variable name A, it printed a 4. The 500, which is to the right of the comma, was ignored. When 4500 was entered for variable name B, the computer did not ignore any of the digits because there was no comma.

Review

9. Write a program that will use INPUT to assign values to two variables named A and B. After assigning the variables a value, have the computer calculate their sum. A run of the program might look like this:

$$\text{RUN}$$
$$?\ 45$$
$$?\ 10$$
$$45 + 10 = 55$$

10. Write a program that uses INPUT to assign a variable its value and then multiplies that value by 10:

$$\text{RUN}$$
$$?\ 27$$
$$10 \star 27 = 270$$

INPUT: a string

An INPUT statement can also be used to assign a string of characters a variable name. For example:

        10 INPUT A$

Letters, symbols or numbers can be used to give the variable name A$ a value because a string can have any character in it that can be typed in from the keyboard. Numbers can be made part of a string, but they cannot be used as numbers in a mathematical operation since the computer thinks of them as symbols rather than numbers.

Program 2.12

This program waits for a string variable name to be given its value when the characters are typed in from the keyboard:

```
10   INPUT A$
20   PRINT "THIS IS WHAT YOU TYPED"
30   PRINT A$

]RUN
?COMPUTING IS FUN
THIS IS WHAT YOU TYPED
COMPUTING IS FUN
```

Line 10 tells the computer to set aside a box in its memory named A$. The computer then waits for data to be typed in from the keyboard. When RETURN is pressed, the characters that have been typed are put in the box and the box given the variable name A$.

A$

COMPUTING IS FUN

Since the characters typed are COMPUTING IS FUN, the variable name A$ is assigned those characters. When line 30 is executed, the computer prints the variable named A$. Therefore, the computer prints COMPUTING IS FUN.

Review

11. Write a program that uses INPUT to enter your name as a variable named N$. The program should then say HI! to you. A RUN should look like this if your name is Barbara:

```
RUN
? BARBARA
HI! BARBARA
```

REENTER

If a letter or word is typed by mistake when the computer is expecting a number, the computer will print a REENTER error message:

```
10 INPUT N
20 PRINT "5 *" N "=" 5 * N
RUN
? FIVE
?REENTER
? 5
5 * 5 = 25
```

The REENTER message does not mean to start the program over again. The computer prints this error message and waits for the proper INPUT. Any data that is not a number will cause a REENTER error message because the computer was expecting a number. That means no dollar sign ($) or any other symbols can be part of an INPUT if the computer is expecting a number. When the computer is expecting a string variable name to be given its value, a REENTER error will not be displayed because the computer can accept any characters as part of a string. However, the computer will not be able to use those characters as numbers since they are part of a string.

To prevent the REENTER error and to keep from confusing the person using the program, it is good programming style to display a message that tells what kind of data the computer is expecting. A message can be made part of an INPUT statement by combining the INPUT with quotation marks:

10 INPUT "TYPE YOUR NAME"; N$

A semicolon (;) must follow the quotation marks that end the message. If a semicolon does not separate the quotation marks and the variable name, a SYNTAX ERROR will halt the program.

Program 2.13

This program shows how a message can be made part of an INPUT statement:

```
10  INPUT "TYPE A NUMBER: ";N
20  PRINT "THE NUMBER IS "N

]RUN
TYPE A NUMBER: 25
THE NUMBER IS 25
```

The quotation marks after INPUT allow a message to be printed on the screen. A semicolon comes between the quotation marks and the variable name. An INPUT statement like the one in line 10 is less likely to cause a REENTER warning because the user is told what type of input the computer is expecting.

Program 2.14

This program shows how the computer can be made to display dollar signs by using quotation marks with INPUT:

```
10  PRINT "WHAT IS $5 + $2.75"
20  INPUT "TYPE YOUR ANSWER $";A
30  PRINT "DOES YOUR ANSWER MATCH MINE?"
40  PRINT "MINE $7.75"
50  PRINT "YOURS $"A

]RUN
WHAT IS $5 + $2.75
TYPE YOUR ANSWER $7.75
DOES YOUR ANSWER MATCH MINE?
MINE $7.75
YOURS $7.75
```

The last character within the quotation marks on line 20 is a dollar sign. When the program is run, this dollar sign makes the number that the computer is expecting look like a dollar amount. Since the computer assigns only the number to the variable name A, there is no REENTER error. In line 50 another dollar sign at the end of the PRINT message makes the variable name A look like a dollar amount again.

Review

12. Write a program in which you input a value for a variable named N. Have the computer calculate the value of variable N plus 12 and variable N times 12. The output should look like this:

>   RUN
>   TYPE A NUMBER? 5
>   12 + 5 = 17
>   12 * 5 = 60

13. Write a program that allows you to input your name and a friend's name. The output should look like this:

>   RUN
>   WHAT IS YOUR NAME? TED
>   WHAT IS YOUR FRIEND'S NAME? BRIAN
>   BRIAN IS A FRIEND OF TED

REM

The REM statement is used in the body of a program to let the programmer explain what the program is doing. These remarks will not be read by the computer when the program is RUN. Everything to the right of the REM will be ignored. For example:

>   30 REM CALCULATE AREA OF A RECTANGLE

will be displayed only when the program is listed. It is good programming style to use REM statements throughout a program to explain what different parts of a program do. Also, another programmer should be able to read and understand a well-written program without difficulty, and REM statements help to make this possible.

Program 2.15

This program shows how the major topics covered in this chapter might be used together in a single program. Review it carefully:

```
10  REM   CALCULATE THE AREA OF A RECTANGLE
20  LET F$ = "RECTANGLE"
30  PRINT "THE AREA OF A "F$" EQUALS"
40  PRINT "THE LENGTH TIMES THE WIDTH."
50  INPUT "TYPE THE LENGTH: ";L
60  INPUT "TYPE THE WIDTH: ";W
70  LET A = L * W
80  PRINT "THE AREA = "A" SQUARE FEET."

]RUN
THE AREA OF A RECTANGLE EQUALS
THE LENGTH TIMES THE WIDTH.
TYPE THE LENGTH: 75
TYPE THE WIDTH: 25
THE AREA = 1875 SQUARE FEET.
```

- **Line 10:** A REMark to explain what the program is about.
- **Line 20:** LET assigns a string variable named F$ the word RECTANGLE.
- **Line 30:** Variable F$ is used as part of a PRINT message.
- **Lines 50-60:** INPUT is used to assign the variable names L and W their values.
- **Line 70:** LET is used to calculate and assign the value of variable A.

EXERCISES

1. What will a run of the following program print on the screen?

    10 LET A = 3
    20 PRINT " THE VALUE OF A IS"
    30 PRINT A

2. What will the following program print?

    10 LET R1$ = "RED"
    20 LET R2$ = "ROSES"
    30 PRINT R2$ " ARE " R1$

3. What are the values of A and B that the following will print?

    10 LET A = 10
    20 LET B = A + 15
    30 LET A = B
    40 PRINT A
    50 PRINT B

4. Write a program that will assign the numbers 33, 15 and 27 to variables named A, B and C. Have the program calculate the sum of these numbers.

    RUN
    33 + 15 + 27 = 75

5. Write a program that will assign two variables the values 275 and 39 and then calculate the product of those numbers. A run of the program should look like this:

    RUN
    275 ★ 39 = 10725

6. Predict the output of the following program. Check the answer by running the program:

    10 LET P$ = "TOTAL PRICE"
    20 LET P = .89
    30 PRINT P$ "= $" P ★ 3

7. What is the exact output for the following program?

   10 LET A = 3
   20 PRINT " THE VALUE OF B "
   30 LET B = A * 4
   40 PRINT B

8. Write a program that will allow a string A$ to be entered with an INPUT. Then have the computer print the string followed by KEEPS THE DOCTOR AWAY.

   RUN
   WHAT KEEPS THE DOCTOR AWAY? AN APPLE A DAY
   AN APPLE A DAY KEEPS THE DOCTOR AWAY.

9. Using an INPUT statement, write a program that will ask how many packages of gum are wanted and will then output the total cost at $.35 a package.

   RUN
   HOW MANY PACKS OF GUM? 5
   THAT WILL BE $1.75

10. Write a program that will ask for three words: a noun, a verb and another noun. Have the program output them on one line as a sentence.

    RUN
    TYPE A NOUN? HARRY HACKER
    TYPE A VERB? BYTES
    TYPE ANOTHER NOUN? BITS

    HARRY HACKER BYTES BITS.

11. Write a program in which the price (P) in cents of a loaf of bread and the number of loaves bought are entered from the keyboard. The total spent for bread is to be printed in dollars and cents.

    RUN
    PRICE OF BREAD $? .99
    NUMBER OF LOAVES ? 3
    COST $2.97

12. A piece of pizza normally contains 375 calories. A boy jogging one mile uses about 100 calories. Write a program that asks him how many pieces he ate and then tells how far he must run to burn up the calories he took in.

    ```
    RUN
    HOW MANY PIECES DID YOU EAT? 4
    YOU MUST RUN 15 MILES.
    ```

13. Use the computer to calculate your library fines. From the keyboard, enter the number of books you borrowed and how many days they were late. The fine is $.10 a day.

    ```
    RUN
    HOW MANY BOOKS? 3
    HOW MANY DAYS OVER DUE? 3
    FINES ARE $.90
    ```

14. Write a program that sets one variable name equal to "**********" and another variable name equal to "*   *". Then, use those variables to draw the following figure:

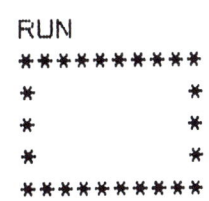

    ```
    RUN
    **********
    *        *
    *        *
    *        *
    **********
    ```

15. Use the computer as a cash register. Write a program that asks for the amount owed and the amount of money offered in payment. Have the computer tell what change should be returned. Do not forget to have the computer say thank you.

    ```
    RUN
    AMOUNT OWED $? 5.79
    AMOUNT PAID $? 10
    YOUR CHANGE $ 4.21
    THANK YOU
    ```

WORKING WITH DATA 3

GO TO READ DATA

GO TO READ DATA

GO TO READ DATA

Unlike humans, computers do not become bored or tired when they are told to do simple tasks over and over again. Computers will also do these tasks quickly and accurately. This chapter will explain how these capabilities are used to read large amounts of stored information called data with the READ and DATA statements. The chapter will also explain how the GOTO statement can be used to tell the computer to follow the same instructions over and over again.

GOTO

The GOTO statement tells the computer to go to a specific line in a program. The computer then follows the instructions that are on that line just as if it had come to that line by following the normal sequence of line numbers.

The correct form for the GOTO statement is the words GOTO followed by the line number that the computer is to go to.

40 GOTO 10

will send the program from line 40 back to line 10. If there is no line with the number specified, the computer will halt the program and print an UN-DEF'D STATEMENT ERROR message. UNDEF'D is an abbreviation for undefined, which means the computer has not been told something that it needs to know.

Program 3.1

The GOTO statement in this program tells the computer to continue printing the same message on the screen until CONTROL-C is pressed.

```
10  PRINT "COMPUTING IS FUN!"
20  GOTO 10

]RUN
COMPUTING IS FUN!
COMPUTING IS FUN!
COMPUTING IS FUN!
COMPUTING IS FUN!
COMPUTING IS FUN!

BREAK IN 20
```

The GOTO statement in line 20 creates a loop. The program continues going from line 20 back to line 10 again and again. Each time line 10 is repeated, the computer prints the message COMPUTING IS FUN! This program is a good example of the tirelessness of a computer.

The computer will continue to repeat this loop until either CONTROL-C is pressed or the computer is switched off.

When the computer finishes a PRINT statement, the cursor is moved down to the next line and over to the left margin. Using a semicolon (;) as the last character of a PRINT statement tells the computer to keep the cursor where it is and to print in the next space to the right.

Program 3.2

This program uses a GOTO statement and a semicolon at the end of the PRINT statement to fill the screen with output:

```
10   PRINT " GO FOR IT!";
20   GOTO 10
```

```
]RUN
 GO FOR IT! GO FOR IT! GO FOR IT! GO FO
R IT! GO FOR IT! GO FOR IT! GO FOR IT!
 GO FOR IT! GO FOR IT! GO FOR IT! GO FO
R IT! GO FOR IT! GO FOR IT! GO FOR IT!
 GO FOR IT! GO FOR IT! GO FOR IT! GO FO
R IT! GO FOR IT! GO FOR IT! GO FOR IT!
 GO FOR IT! GO FOR IT! GO FOR IT! GO FO
R IT! GO FOR IT! GO FOR IT! GO FOR IT!
 GO FOR IT! GO FOR IT! GO FOR IT! GO FO
R IT! GO FOR IT! GO FOR IT! GO FOR IT!
 GO FOR IT! GO FOR IT! GO FOR IT! GO FO
R IT! GO FOR IT! GO FOR IT! GO FOR IT!
 GO FOR IT! GO FOR
BREAK IN 20
```

Line 20 again creates a loop. Line 10 is repeated over and over, but each time the computer finishes printing GO FOR IT! it does not drop down and print the next GO FOR IT! on a new line. Instead, the printing continues in the next available space.

Review

1. Write a program that will print your name over and over down the left side of the screen until the machine is halted by pressing CONTROL-C.

2. Predict the output of the following program. Then type it in and run it:

```
10 PRINT "*** **";
20 GO TO 10
```

Using Variable Names in a Loop

Each time a variable name is given a new value, the old value is lost forever. For example, if variable name A has been given a value

A

| 12 |

of 12 and later the variable name A becomes equal to 24, the original value of variable A, which was 12, will be lost forever.

A

| 24 |

Counting in a Loop

One way of using the ability of variables to change their values is to have the computer count with a statement called a "counter." A counter looks like this:

10 LET C = C + 1

When a variable name is assigned its value, the equal sign really means "is given the value." Therefore, this statement means "C is given the value C+1." Each time the computer reads line 10 the value of C will be increased by one. Therefore, the variable name C counts by 1.

Program 3.3

In this program a "counter" increases its value by one each time a loop is repeated:

```
10   LET C = C + 1
20   PRINT C
30   GOTO 10

]RUN
1
2
3
4
5
6

BREAK IN 20
```

Whenever a program is begun with a RUN command, all variable names have a value of 0 until they are given a value. Therefore, on line 10, variable name C becomes 1 because its starting value was 0, and 0+1 is 1. When the loop repeats line 10 for a second time, variable name C becomes 2 because its value is 1, and 1+1 is 2. Each time the loop is repeated variable name C becomes equal to its current value plus 1.

C
0

C
1

C
2

A counter does not have to count by 1. If line 30 were replaced by

10 LET C = C + 5

the program would count by fives.

```
]RUN
5
10
15
20
25

BREAK IN 20
```

RUN initializes the value of all variable names to 0 when the program begins. Line 10 now counts by 5 since the value of C is increased by 5 each time line 10 is repeated. A counter can count by any amount a programmer tells the computer to count by.

C
0

C
5

C
10

Review

3. Write a program that counts by 2. A run of the program should look like this:

```
RUN
2
4
6
8
10
BREAK IN 10
```

INPUT within a Loop

The INPUT statement can also be used within a loop to give variable names a value. Each time the INPUT statement is executed, the old value of the variable name will be replaced by the new value that is typed in at the keyboard.

Program 3.4

This program uses a GOTO statement to print the product of 5 and a number that is typed in as input from the keyboard. Use CONTROL-C and RETURN to halt the program:

```
10   INPUT "TYPE A NUMBER ? ";N
20   LET P = 5 * N
30   PRINT "5 * "N" = "P
40   GOTO 10

]RUN
TYPE A NUMBER ? 5
5 * 5 = 25
TYPE A NUMBER ? 6
5 * 6 = 30
TYPE A NUMBER ? 7
5 * 7 = 35
TYPE A NUMBER ?
BREAK IN 10
```

The GOTO statement in line 40 creates the loop. Each time line 10 is repeated, the variable name N is given a new value by the user. This means that variable P in line 20, which calculates the product of 5 and the variable name N, will also be given a new value each time the loop is repeated.

Review

4. Write a program in which you input a value for a variable named N. Have the computer calculate the value of variable N plus 12 and variable N times 12. The output should look like this:

```
RUN
WHAT IS N? 12
12 + 12 = 24
12 * 12 = 144
WHAT IS N? 5
12 + 5 = 17
12 * 5 = 60
WHAT IS N?
```

5. Write a program that allows you to input your name and a friend's name. The output should look like this:

```
RUN
WHAT IS YOUR NAME? TED
WHAT IS YOUR FRIEND'S NAME? BRIAN
TED IS A FRIEND OF BRIAN
WHAT IS YOUR NAME? BILL
WHAT IS YOUR FRIEND'S NAME? JUDY
BILL IS A FRIEND OF JUDY
WHAT IS YOUR NAME?
```

Accumulating a Total

Each time an INPUT is repeated the old value of the variable name is lost, but the computer can be told to keep a total of those values. This is done by using a special type of counter called an "accumulator". This adds the old value of the variable name to the variable name that is storing the total of all the previous inputs.

$$20 \text{ LET } T = T + N$$

will work very much like a counter. Each time line 20 is repeated the value of variable name T is increased by the value of variable name N. A counter, such as the one in Program 3.3, always changes its value by the same amount. It counts by 1 or 2 or whatever the programmer tells the computer to count by. Therefore, the counter always changes its value by that amount. An accumulator, on the other hand, uses a variable name to change its value. Therefore, an accumulator can change its value by a different amount each time the loop is repeated.

Program 3.5

This program shows how the individual prices of a number of books can be totaled using an accumulator:

```
10  INPUT "ENTER THE PRICE OF A BOOK $";C
20  LET T = T + C
30  PRINT "THE TOTAL COST SO FAR = $"T
40  PRINT
50  GOTO 10

]RUN
ENTER THE PRICE OF A BOOK $3.50
THE TOTAL COST SO FAR = $3.5

ENTER THE PRICE OF A BOOK $2.55
THE TOTAL COST SO FAR = $6.05

ENTER THE PRICE OF A BOOK $3.76
THE TOTAL COST SO FAR = $9.81

ENTER THE PRICE OF A BOOK $

BREAK IN 10
```

Line 10 inputs a value for variable name C. On line 20 the value of variable T becomes equal to the old value of variable T plus the value of variable C. The first value of variable C is 3.5, so variable name T becomes equal to 0 + 3.5. Note how the computer drops the 0 in 3.50 even though the 0 was entered as input on line 10. That 0 is not needed to express the value of the number so the computer drops it. The second time the loop is repeated variable name C is given a new value of 2.55, and the original value of variable C, which was 3.5, is erased. This new value of variable name C is then added to the old value of variable T, which becomes 6.05 (3.5 + 2.55). Each time the loop is repeated the values of variables T and C are changed. The PRINT on line 40 helps make the program easier to understand as it is running, which is always good programming style.

There is no reason why the computer cannot count backwards. The computer can be told to subtract rather than add each time it repeats a statement.

$$10 \text{ LET } T = T - C$$

will subtract the value of variable name C from variable name T each time this line is read.

Program 3.6

This program displays the balance of a savings account. The computer then subtracts the amount that is entered as input and displays the new balance:

```
10   LET T = 100
20   PRINT "CURRENT BALANCE = $"T
30   INPUT "AMOUNT TO SUBTRACT = $";A
40   LET T = T - A
50   PRINT
60   GOTO 20

]RUN
CURRENT BALANCE = $100
AMOUNT TO SUBTRACT = $15

CURRENT BALANCE = $85
AMOUNT TO SUBTRACT = $3

CURRENT BALANCE = $82
AMOUNT TO SUBTRACT = $

BREAK IN 30
```

- **Line 10:** Assigns the value 100 to the variable name T.
- **Line 20:** Shows the user the present value of variable T.
- **Line 30:** Inputs the amount to be withdrawn and assigns that value to variable name A.
- **Line 40:** Changes the value of variable T by subtracting the value of variable A from the current value of variable T.

The first time line 40 was executed, variable T had a value of 100 and variable A had a value of 15. The new value of variable T therefore became 85, which is 100 − 15.

- **Line 60:** GOTO 20 returns the program to line 20 to print the new value of variable T.

The program does not loop back to line 10 because this would set the value of variable T back to 100. The loop them repeats lines 20, 30, 40, 50 and 60 until CONTROL-C and RETURN halt the program. Each time the loop is repeated, variable A is given a new value and the value of variable T is changed by subtracting the value of variable A from the value of variable T.

Review

6. Predict the output and the results of this program if you ran 2 miles Monday, 3 Tuesday, 3 Wednesday, 2 Thursday and 5 Friday. Type the program in and run it to check your prediction.

```
10    PRINT "MILEAGE CALCULATOR"
20    PRINT "ENTER MILES RUN EACH DAY."
30    INPUT "ONE DAY'S MILEAGE: ";D
40    LET T = T + D
50    PRINT "TOTAL MILES = "T
60    PRINT
70    GOTO 30
```

7. Harry Hacker began with $5 of his allowance money. This program keeps telling Harry that he has more allowance left than he actually has in his pocket. Help "poor" Harry out and correct the program for him:

```
10    PRINT "ALLOWANCE CALCULATOR"
20    LET A = 5
30    INPUT "AMOUNT SPENT $";S
40    LET A = A - S
50    PRINT "AMOUNT LEFT $";A
60    PRINT
70    GOTO 20
```

READ & DATA

Another way to assign a value to a variable is to use the READ and DATA statements. These two statements work together as a team to assign data. One of them cannot be used without the other in the program to help it out.

READ and DATA are useful because they store data within a program. The data need not be re-entered each time a program is run. This means that an INPUT statement or LET statement is not needed to enter the data. The data is entered once in a DATA statement and then stored as part of the program.

Program 3.7

This program shows how to use READ to assign a value to a variable name:

```
10    READ A
20    PRINT "THE NUMBER IS "A
30    DATA   125

]RUN
THE NUMBER IS 125
```

READ A in line 10 tells the computer to set aside a box in its memory for a variable named A. The computer then assigns the variable A the first value it finds in a DATA statement. The first DATA statement it finds is on line 30, and it contains the number 125. Therefore, the number 125 is placed in the computer's memory as the value of variable A.

Working with Data 3-9

When a READ is used to name a numeric variable, the computer will only accept numbers. Any symbols used with the numbers will cause an error message that will halt the program. Therefore, data like $2.75, or 2'6" for 2 feet 6 inches will not work as numeric variables.

Dollar signs, letters of the alphabet and any other characters can be read using READ and DATA if the computer is told to read a string variable:

10 READ A$

Program 3.8

This program assigns strings a value by using READ and DATA:

```
10   READ A$
20   READ B$
30   PRINT "THE FORCE IS WITH "A$"."
40   PRINT "THE EVIL "B$" WANTS HIM."
50   DATA  LUKE SKYWALKER
60   DATA  DARTH VADER

]RUN
THE FORCE IS WITH LUKE SKYWALKER.
THE EVIL DARTH VADER WANTS HIM.
```

The force is with Luke because his name is in the first DATA statement that the computer found. The computer begins looking for data at the lowest line number. It will use the data that it finds first. Once a piece of data has been read, the computer goes on to the next piece of data that it finds. When line 20 reads B$, the next DATA statement is at line 60, so variable name B$ is assigned the string of characters DARTH VADER.

DATA statements can be placed anywhere in a program, but it is good programming style to put all DATA statements together in one place. Usually DATA statements are placed at the end of a program.

When more than one variable in a program is assigned a value by READ and DATA statements, the data must be separated. Program 3.8 used two DATA statements to keep the data separated. Commas can also be used to separate data items:

10 READ A,B
20 DATA 5,8

The comma tells the computer that the first piece of data to be read is the number 5, and the second piece of data is the number 8. It is possible to have many pieces of data in one DATA statement as long as they are separated by commas.

Program 3.9

This program shows how commas are used to separate data:

```
10   READ A
20   READ B
30   LET P = A * B
40   PRINT A" * "B" = "P
50   DATA  125, 25

]RUN
125 * 25 = 3125
```

Variable name A is assigned the value 125 because the first piece of data found is the number 125. In line 20 variable name B is assigned the value 25 because it is the second piece of data in the DATA statement. The comma tells the computer that 125 and 25 are separate pieces of data.

Review

8. Write a program that reads two numbers, variable names X and Y, from DATA statements. The program should set variable X = 5 and variable Y = 3 and then print their difference:

    RUN
    5 − 3 = 2

9. Write a program that reads the name of your favorite snack and your favorite drink from data statements. The output of the program should look like this:

    RUN
    A HAMBURGER IS MY FAVORITE SNACK
    A COKE IS MY FAVORITE DRINK

GOTO and READ/DATA

The GOTO statement is useful when it is used with READ and DATA in a program. The GOTO can be used to make a loop that reads data piece by piece until all the data in the program has been read. However, when the computer is told to READ data and all the data in DATA statements has been read, the computer prints an OUT OF DATA ERROR and halts the program. The computer will not go back to the first DATA statement by itself and start over again.

It is important that the data be kept in the proper sequence by the use of commas or new DATA statements. The data must match the variable names that will read it. If the computer is told to READ a numeric variable and the next piece of data is a string, the computer will halt the program with a SYNTAX ERROR message:

    10 READ N, A$
    20 DATA HELLO, 007
    RUN
    ?SYNTAX ERROR IN 20

Line 20 does not appear to have an error in it, but the error is still there. The error is caused by READ N in line 10. The variable name N is telling the computer to look for a number as the next piece of data, but the computer finds a string instead. This confuses the computer, so it prints a SYNTAX ERROR IN 20 message and halts the program. To correct the error change either the order of the data in the DATA statement:

    10 READ N, A$
    20 DATA 007, HELLO

or the order in which the variables are read in the READ statement:

10 READ A$, N
20 DATA HELLO, 007

Program 3.10

This program reads a list of candies and their prices from data statements:

```
10  READ C$,P
20  PRINT "CANDY: "C$
30  PRINT "PRICE $"P
40  PRINT
50  GOTO 10
60  DATA   HUBBA BUBBA,.35,HERSHEY BAR,.45
70  DATA   SWEET TARTS,.25

]RUN
CANDY: HUBBA BUBBA
PRICE $.35

CANDY: HERSHEY BAR
PRICE $.45

CANDY: SWEET TARTS
PRICE $.25

?OUT OF DATA ERROR IN 10
```

- **Line 10:** Two variables are read using one READ statement by separating the two variables with a comma.

Line 10 reads data from the DATA statement at line 60. The first piece of data read, HUBBA BUBBA, is assigned to variable name C$, and variable name P is assigned .35 as its value.

- **Line 20:** Prints the name of the candy that was just read.
- **Line 30:** The dollar sign ($) in the PRINT statement tells the program user that the numbers displayed are money figures.

The DATA statements cannot contain a dollar sign as part of a number, but they can contain a decimal point.

- **Line 40:** The PRINT puts a blank line on the screen for easier reading.
- **Line 50:** GOTO 10 sends the computer back to line 10 where it reads a new value for variable name C$, HERSHEY BAR, and a new value for variable P, .45.

These new values are then printed by lines 20 and 30, and the GOTO 10 sends the computer back to read SWEET TARTS and .25 as the next data to be used. When the GOTO sends the computer back to 10 for a fourth time, there is no more data to read. Since all the DATA has been read, the computer prints an OUT OF DATA ERROR message and halts the program.

Review

10. Write a program that reads a list of favorite sports teams and outputs that list to the screen.

    RUN
    MY FAVORITIES TEAMS:
    BOSTON RED SOX
    NEW ENGLAND PATRIOTS
    NEW YORK GIANTS

    ?OUT OF DATA ERROR IN 10

11. Write a program that reads the even numbers from 1 to 10 from data statements and then prints the numbers on the screen.

    RUN
    2
    4
    6
    8
    10

    ?OUT OF DATA IN 10

12. Harry Hacker had typed in the following program. See if you can show him who's the better programmer. Predict what his program will do when it is run. (Hint: are there any errors?)

    ```
    10 PRINT "SECRET AGENT FILE"
    20 PRINT
    30 READ N, N$
    40 PRINT N, N$
    50 GOTO 30
    60 DATA JAMES BOND, 007, MAXWELL SMART, 36,
           MRS. SMART, 99
    ```

PRINT Formatting

How data is displayed on the screen is an important part of good programming. The most important data will be of little use if the data is not usefully displayed on the screen. One way to tell the computer how to print data on the screen is to use commas and semicolons. When they are used as part of a print statement, outside of quotation marks, these punctuation marks are format instructions. This means they give the computer special instructions about where data should be printed on the screen.

Commas are used in PRINT statements to tell the computer to move the cursor to one of the three print zones that divide the screen. Since the Apple can print 40 characters on a single line, a line is divided into three print zones. The first two of these zones have 16 spaces while the third has 8 spaces.

```
10 LET A$= "*"
20 PRINT A$, A$, A$
RUN
 *              *              *
```

Each time the computer reads a comma in line 20, the cursor is moved to the first space of the next print zone before it prints the next asterisk (*) character on the screen.

The semicolon, on the other hand, is used to tell the computer to print in the next space to the right on the screen:

```
10 LET A$ = "*"
20 PRINT A$; A$; A$; A$
RUN
****
```

Each time the computer read a semicolon, it printed an asterisk in the next space to the right on the screen.

Program 3.11

This program shows where the print zones are on the screen. It also shows the differences between commas and semicolons in a PRINT statement:

```
10   PRINT "111111111111111122222222222222223333333"
20   PRINT "*","*","*"
30   LET A$ = "*"
40   PRINT A$,A$,A$
50   PRINT A$;A$;A$
60   LET B = 25
70   PRINT A$;B
80   PRINT A$,B
90   PRINT B;A$;
100  PRINT B

]RUN
111111111111111122222222222222223333333
*              *              *
*              *              *
***
*25
*                            25
25*25
```

- **Line 10:** Prints a 1, 2 or 3 in each space of the corresponding print zone.
- **Line 20:** Uses a comma to print an asterisk at the beginning of each of the three print zones.
- **Line 40:** Prints variable A$, an asterisk, in the first space of each zone because of the comma that follows each variable A$.

- **Line 50:** Prints three asterisks in a row because the semicolons that separate the variables tell the computer to print in the next available space.
- **Line 70:** Prints the asterisk and then 25 because these are the values that the variables A$ and B represent.
- **Line 80:** The asterisk and 25 are separated by ten spaces because of the comma between variable name A$ and variable name B.

Lines 40, 50, 70 and 80 show the proper use of commas and semicolons to tell the computer how to display the value of variable names when they are used in a print statement.

Program 3.12

This program shows how commas and semicolons are used to format a table for output to the screen. The program reads sets of names, grades and averages and then arranges the output in a table on the screen:

```
10   PRINT "NAMES","GRADES","AVERAGE"
20   READ N$,G1,G2
30   PRINT
40   LET T = G1 + G2
50   LET A = T / 2
60   PRINT N$,G1;" ";G2,A
70   GOTO 20
80   DATA   J. JONES,90,87
90   DATA   M. SMITH,74,98
100  DATA   T. TURKEY,53,76

]RUN
NAMES             GRADES              AVERAGE

J. JONES          90 87                88.5

M. SMITH          74 98                86

T. TURKEY         53 76                64.5

?OUT OF DATA ERROR IN 20
```

The READ in line 20 reads in data from the DATA lines. The commas in line 20 and lines 80, 90 and 100 are being used to organize this input operation. They keep the variables and the data separated so the computer gives each variable its proper value.

On the other hand, the commas on line 10 and the commas and semicolons on line 60 organize the data for output on the screen. Look carefully at the output produced by line 10. The label G R A D E S begins on the 11th space of the line because of the comma after N A M E. AVERAGE starts at the beginning of the third print zone. When semicolons are used instead of commas as in line 60, the output begins in the next space on the line. The PRINT on line 30 is used to place a blank line between the heading and each line of output.

Lines 40 and 50 compute the average grade for each student by dividing the total points by the number of tests. Therefore, on line 40 variable T calculates the total number of points earned on the three tests by adding G1, G2 and G3. Then the average, variable A, is calculated by dividing the value of variable T by 3 which is the number of tests taken.

Review

13. What will the output of this program be?

    ```
    10   PRINT "*** **","****"," ***";
    20   PRINT " ###"
    ```

14. Use commas and semicolons to output the following table. Use READ to input the data from data statements:

MONSTER	DESCRIPTION
GODZILLA	GREEN SCALY UGLY
KING KONG	BIG BROWN HAIRY

Program 3.13

This program uses the major programming statements and techniques described in this chapter, which the reader should be familiar with. It also shows how they might be used together in a single program:

```
10   PRINT "GRADE AVERAGER"
20   READ S$
30   PRINT "SUBJECT: "S$
40   READ S
50   LET Q = Q + 1
60   LET T = T + S
70   LET A = T / Q
80   PRINT "QUIZ # "Q,S" AVERAGE = "A
90   GOTO 40
100  DATA  MATH,80,92,85,70,83

]RUN
GRADE AVERAGER
SUBJECT: MATH
QUIZ # 1          80 AVERAGE = 80
QUIZ # 2          92 AVERAGE = 86
QUIZ # 3          85 AVERAGE = 85.6666667
QUIZ # 4          70 AVERAGE = 81.75
QUIZ # 5          83 AVERAGE = 82

?OUT OF DATA ERROR IN 40
```

- **Line 20:** Assigns a string variable its value by using READ and DATA statements.
- **Line 40:** Assigns a numeric variable its value by using READ and DATA statements.

- **Line 50:** A counter that tallies the number of quiz grades read.
- **Line 60:** An accumulator that records the total points earned as each grade is read.
- **Line 70:** Calculates the average for that quiz and the previous quizzes.
- **Line 80:** Uses a comma after variable name Q to format the output on the screen.
- **Line 90:** GOTO 40 creates a loop that will read the data piece by piece until it is all read.
- **Line 100:** A DATA statement with each piece of data separated by a comma.

EXERCISES

1. Write a program that counts by threes until the program is halted by pressing CONTROL-C. The program's output should look like this:

   RUN
   3
   6
   9
   12
   15

   BREAK IN 10

2. Make a change to the previous program so that the output of the program runs across the screen:

   RUN
   3 6 9 12 15 18 21 24 27 30 33
   36 39 42 45 48 51 54 57 60 63
   66

   BREAK IN 20

3. Write a program that will calculate the multiples of 5. Have the program print out the results as a times table:

   RUN
   5 * 1 = 5   5 * 2 = 10
   5 * 3 = 15   5 * 4 = 20
   5 * 5 = 25   5 * 6 = 30

   BREAK IN 30

4. Joe Kolodnigork's little brother wants Joe to turn the computer into a magic adding machine. Help Joe out by writing a program that takes in a number as input and then prints the sum of that number and all the previous numbers. A run of the program should look something like this:

   RUN
   TYPE IN A NUMBER? 17
   THE SUM OF ALL NUMBERS TYPED IS 17

   TYPE IN A NUMBER? 13
   THE SUM OF ALL NUMBERS TYPED IS 30

   TYPE IN A NUMBER?

5. Joe's little brother keeps bugging him to make the computer do more "magic." If Joe can't make the computer subtract numbers from 1550 and keep track of the difference, his brother will probably drive him crazy. In his panic, Joe has turned to you for help in writing this program.

```
RUN
THE STARTING AMOUNT IS 1550
SUBTRACT? 35

NEW AMOUNT IS 1515
SUBTRACT?
```

6. Your little cousin Sue is having trouble understanding the difference between adding numbers and multiplying them. Write a program that lists the addition facts table for the number 4 in one column and the multiplication facts table for 4 in the next column. Use the X instead of the * as a multiplication sign in the output, so that Sue will not be confused:

```
RUN
4 + 0 = 4         4 × 0 = 0
4 + 1 = 5         4 × 1 = 4

BREAK IN 10
```

7. Write the output of the following program and check by running the program:

```
10 READ N
20 PRINT N
30 GOTO 10
40 DATA 10, 20, 30, 40, 50
```

8. Write the output and check by running the program:

   > 10 READ A$
   > 20 PRINT A$
   > 30 GOTO 10
   > 40 DATA S, I, X, 6

9. What will be the output of the following program before an OUT OF DATA ERROR IN 10 occurs?

   > 10 READ A, B
   > 20 READ B
   > 30 PRINT A + B
   > 40 GOTO 10
   > 50 DATA 15, 25, 20, 35, 30, 35, 12, 1, 5
   > 60 DATA 21, 45, 55

10. Joe Kolodnigork has loused up again. Here is a program of his which he says "mysteriously doesn't work." Give Joe a hand and correct this monstrosity for him so that the output looks like the following:

    > THE SUM IS 20
    > THE SUM IS 14
    >
    > ?OUT OF DATA ERROR IN 10
    >
    > 10 READ A, B
    > 20 PRINT THE SUM IS A + B
    > 30 GOTO 10
    > 40 DATA 12, 8; 2 * 5, 5

11. Write a program that READs from DATA statements a list of names and grades on a recent computer quiz and prints them.

    > RUN
    > NAME: JOE KOLODNIGORK
    > GRADE: 79
    >
    > NAME: H. HACKER
    > GRADE: 99
    >
    > NAME: T. TURKEY
    > GRADE: 55
    >
    > ?OUT OF DATA ERROR IN 10

12. There was an election at the Pac-Man Memorial School. Write a program that READs from DATA statements the names of the candidates and the number of votes they received. The program should print the number of votes in a column 25 spaces away from the left margin.

```
RUN
CANDIDATES                          VOTES

SID SLOTH                            210
D. KONG                              232
DARTH VADER                            1
MS. PAC                              566

?OUT OF DATA ERROR IN 20
```

13. Self-proclaimed computer whiz Harry Hacker has typed the following gibberish in immediate mode. He challenges anyone to guess the output correctly before he presses the RETURN key. Put Harry in his place and correctly predict the answer.

    PRINT "AAA"; 111, 222; "BBB", "333";"   ";16−3 ★ 2

14. Use the computer to keep track of your Christmas list. The computer should list: whom you bought something for, what it was and how much it cost. Store the information in DATA statements:

```
RUN
PRESENT FOR             COST              PRESENT

MOM                     $ 25              SWEATER
DAD                     $ 15              BOOK
ROVER                   $ 3.99            BONE
TEACHER                 $ 2.99            CANDY
BROTHER                 $ .59             PEN

?OUT OF DATA ERROR IN 20
```

15. The area of a rectangle is calculated by multiplying the length by the width. This gives an answer in square units (feet, inches, yards, centimeters, meters, etc.). Read the lengths, widths and type of units for three rectangles from DATA statements. Have the computer calculate the area and then output the area in the proper square units:

```
LENGTH 5 INCHES
WIDTH 4 INCHES
AREA = 20 SQUARE INCHES

LENGTH 6 CENTIMETERS
WIDTH 10 CENTIMETERS
AREA = 60 SQUARE CENTIMETERS

LENGTH 15 METERS
WIDTH 5 METERS
AREA = 75 SQUARE METERS

?OUT OF DATA ERROR IN 10
```

DECISIONS 4

**IF...THEN
END
AND
OR**

**IF...THEN
END
AND
OR**

In Chapters 2 and 3 the statements presented allow a program to input and output data. The computer can then carry out routine calculations with that data. Though useful, these actions do not take advantage of the higher capabilities of the computer. As a machine, a computer is said to be intelligent while a calculator is not. The computer is intelligent because it can be programmed to make decisions and the calculator cannot. Being able to make decisions means that a computer can evaluate data by making comparisons. For example, the computer can decide which of two numbers is larger or smaller and then take a specific action. This chapter presents the IF... THEN statement which allows the computer to make decisions.

IF... THEN

The IF... THEN statement is a conditional statement. We humans use conditional statements in our thinking all the time. If it rains then wear your raincoat, is an example of a condition. When the condition is true, you carry out the specified response, which is to wear your raincoat. If the condition is false, then you go on about your business and the raincoat is ignored. The computer responds in the same way to the condition described in an IF... THEN statement. This means the action the computer is instructed to take will be taken only when the condition is found to be true.

The statements that have been introduced so far (PRINT, GOTO, INPUT, etc.) are unconditional statements. Unconditional statements are executed whenever they are read by the computer.

The easiest way to describe a condition to a computer is to have it make a comparison using an IF... THEN statement in the form:

IF <condition> THEN <line number>

In the condition part of the statement a comparison is made. If the comparison is true, then the computer will go to the named line number. If the comparison is false, the computer ignores the line number and goes on to the next line of the program.

By using one of the symbols shown below, two quantities can be compared. To make such a comparison, place one of these symbols between the quantities that are to be compared:

SYMBOL	MEANING
=	equal to
>	greater than
<	less than
>=	greater than or equal to
<=	less than or equal to
<>	not equal to

An example of an IF... THEN statement is:

20 IF X > 5 THEN 60

When the condition in line 20, X is greater than 5, is true, the computer goes to line 60. When the condition is false, as when X is less than or equal to 5, the computer goes on to the next line of the program.

Program 4.1

This program decides whether the value entered as a variable named X is the solution to the equation 2 * X = 6. The computer decides which of two messages should be printed.

```
10   INPUT "TYPE A NUMBER: ";X
20   IF 2 * X = 6 THEN 50
30   PRINT X" IS NOT THE SOLUTION"
40   GOTO 10
50   PRINT X" IS THE SOLUTION"

]RUN
TYPE A NUMBER: 2
2 IS NOT THE SOLUTION
TYPE A NUMBER: 4
4 IS NOT THE SOLUTION
TYPE A NUMBER: 3
3 IS THE SOLUTION
```

The computer makes its decision on line 20. When the condition is true, it jumps to line 50 and prints "IS THE SOLUTION". When the condition is false, the computer moves on to line 30 and prints "IS NOT THE SOLUTION". Note the necessity of line 40. Without line 40 the program would print "IS THE SOLUTION" even when the value of variable X is not the solution. When the value of variable X is the solution, the order in which the line numbers are executed is 10, 20, 50. When variable X is not the solution, the sequence of line numbers is 10, 20, 30, 40, 10.

The IF... THEN statement can also compare letters of the alphabet as strings. When strings are compared, the greater than (>), less than (<) and equal to (=) symbols are used to refer to alphabetical order rather than numerical order. The following examples show how strings are compared using an IF... THEN statement:

10 IF A$ < B$ THEN 50
20 IF A$ > "M" THEN 50
30 IF N$ = "SUPERMAN" THEN 100

Strings can be compared as variable names or as the actual letters or characters. When the actual letters or characters are used, they must be used within quotation marks.

Program 4.2

The following program decides whether variable A$ is alphabetically before, the same, or after variable B$:

```
10  PRINT
20  INPUT "TYPE A WORD: ";A$
30  INPUT "TYPE ANOTHER WORD: ";B$
40  IF A$ = B$ THEN 80
50  IF A$ > B$ THEN 100
60  PRINT A$" IS BEFORE "B$
70  GOTO 10
80  PRINT A$" EQUALS "B$
90  GOTO 10
100  PRINT A$" IS AFTER "B$
110  GOTO 10

]RUN

TYPE A WORD: SKY
TYPE ANOTHER WORD: BLUE
SKY IS AFTER BLUE

TYPE A WORD: RAT
TYPE ANOTHER WORD: SNAKE
RAT IS BEFORE SNAKE

TYPE A WORD: COMPUTER
TYPE ANOTHER WORD: COMPUTER
COMPUTER EQUALS COMPUTER

TYPE A WORD:
```

If variable names A$ and B$ are equal, line 40 sends the computer to line 80. Line 50 causes a jump to line 100 if variable name A$ comes after variable name B$ in the alphabet. Line 60 is reached only when variable name A$ is before variable name B$. Since all the other possibilities have already been checked in lines 40 and 50, an IF . . . THEN is not necessary. The PRINT in line 10 keeps a blank line between sets of comparisons to make them easier to read.

Review

1. Write a program that allows a string to be entered as input. If the string is the password, "AVIATRIX", have the computer print "YOU'RE THE BOSS". Otherwise have it print "SORRY CHARLIE".

   RUN
   ENTER PASSWORD PLEASE? DUMBO
   SORRY CHARLIE

   ENTER PASSWORD PLEASE? AVIATRIX
   YOU'RE THE BOSS

2. Allow a number with the variable name N to be entered as input. When the value of variable N is greater than 25 have the computer print "TOO LARGE". When the value of variable N is less than 25 have it print "TOO SMALL". When the value of variable N equals 25 have it print "JUST RIGHT".

```
                            RUN
                            TYPE A NUMBER? 17
                            TOO SMALL

                            TYPE A NUMBER? 47
                            TOO LARGE

                            TYPE A NUMBER? 25
                            JUST RIGHT

                            TYPE A NUMBER?
```

Extended Use of IF ... THEN

The simplest form of the IF ... THEN statement has been given as:

IF <condition> THEN <line number>

The IF ... THEN statement may also be used with a BASIC instruction following THEN. The statement after THEN will be executed by the computer only when the condition is true. Using other BASIC instructions in an IF ... THEN statement makes this statement more flexible. This is particularly useful in reducing the number of GOTOs. Using too many GOTOs is not good programming style. They can make a program difficult to read and very hard to correct when the program does not work properly. The form is:

IF <condition> THEN <instruction>

The following examples show how IF ... THEN may be used with other BASIC statements:

```
IF X < > 0 THEN PRINT X
IF N > 1 THEN PRINT "IT IS LARGER THAN ONE"
IF R <= 0 THEN LET R = X + 2
```

Program 4.3

This program uses PRINT to print messages based upon a number, variable name N, that is taken in as input:

```
10  INPUT "ENTER A NUMBER? ";N
20  IF N * 5 < = 100 THEN  PRINT "TOO SMALL"
30  IF N * 5 > 100 THEN  PRINT "ON TARGET"
40  PRINT "TRY ANOTHER"
50  GOTO 10
]RUN
ENTER A NUMBER? 10
TOO SMALL
TRY ANOTHER
ENTER A NUMBER? 20
TOO SMALL
TRY ANOTHER
ENTER A NUMBER? 23
ON TARGET
TRY ANOTHER
ENTER A NUMBER?
```

The value of variable N is entered from the keyboard as input. Line 20 then compares the value of variable N multiplied by 5 to 100. When the result of variable N times 5 is less than or equal to 100 (N * 5 <= 100), the computer outputs "TOO SMALL". Because line 30 will always be reached, an IF ... THEN on line 30 makes sure that "ON TARGET" is printed only when the value of variable N meets the condition variable N times 5 is greater than 100 (N * 5 > 100). By using PRINT in the IF ... THEN statements, GOTOs are not needed to send the computer to the line where the message will be printed, and then to send the computer back to a line in the main part of the program.

END

The END statement is used to halt the run of a program. It can be used with the IF ... THEN statement or it can be used by itself. For example,

80 END

will cause the run of a program to stop when line 80 is reached. It is possible to have more than one END statement in a program. When used with an IF ... THEN statement, an END statement can halt a program when a condition is true.

Program 4.4

This program uses the END statement to halt the run of a program after the name KERMIT is entered:

```
10  PRINT "WE'RE LOOKING FOR THE FROG."
20  PRINT
30  INPUT "WHAT'S YOUR NAME? ";N$
40  IF N$ = "KERMIT" THEN  END
50  PRINT "MOVE OVER "N$
60  GOTO 10

]RUN
WE'RE LOOKING FOR THE FROG.

WHAT'S YOUR NAME? GONZO
MOVE OVER GONZO
WE'RE LOOKING FOR THE FROG.

WHAT'S YOUR NAME? KERMIT
```

Line 10 prints a message that explains what the program is doing. Then a PRINT puts a blank line after the message of line 10. The INPUT on line 30 prints a message WHAT'S YOUR NAME? and waits for variable N$ to be entered. The IF N$ = "KERMIT" on line 40 checks to see if the name entered is KERMIT. When N$ equals KERMIT the program is halted by the END statement. If any other name is entered for N$, the program goes on to line 40 where MOVE OVER is printed, and the program is sent back to line 10.

Another important use of the END statement is to keep parts of a program separated. A programmer may want certain lines to be read by the computer only if a condition is true. The END statement can be placed above these lines so that they will only be read when the computer is sent there by a GOTO.

Program 4.5

This program uses an END statement to improve Program 4.4 by separating the program into a main section and a section that is read only when a condition is true:

```
10   PRINT "WE'RE LOOKING FOR THE FROG."
20   PRINT
30   INPUT "WHAT'S YOUR NAME? ";N$
40   IF N$ = "KERMIT" THEN 100
50   PRINT "MOVE OVER "N$
60   INPUT "TRY ANOTHER NAME? ";A$
70   IF A$ = "YES" THEN 10
80   END
100  PRINT "OH! KERMY!"

]RUN
WE'RE LOOKING FOR THE FROG.

WHAT'S YOUR NAME? MIKEY
MOVE OVER MIKEY
TRY ANOTHER NAME? YES
WE'RE LOOKING FOR THE FROG.

WHAT'S YOUR NAME? KERMIT
OH! KERMY!
```

Lines 10 through 80 are the main section of the program. Line 100 and any lines that might come after it cannot be reached by the computer unless the computer is told to go to those lines. The END in line 80 prevents the computer from accidentally reading a higher line just because the computer wants to keep going on to the next higher line number.

Review

3. Write a program that allows the user to enter two numbers and then prints the numbers in descending order:

>   RUN
>   ENTER FIRST NUMBER? 27
>   ENTER SECOND NUMBER? 32
>   32
>   27
>   ENTER FIRST NUMBER?

4. Write a program that allows two names to be entered and then outputs the names in alphabetical order. The program should then ask if the user wants to enter two more names. If the user does not want to continue, the program should show that it is no longer running:

```
RUN
ENTER A LAST NAME? SMITH
ENTER ANOTHER NAME? JONES
JONES
SMITH

TWO MORE NAMES TO COMPARE? NO
BYE.
```

Flags Signal the Way

Flags have a long and interesting history. They have been used by people for many centuries to identify armies and countries. Before the invention of radio, flags were also used as signaling devices. Using flag signals, messages were sent from ship to ship, or from hilltop to hilltop. Computer programmers also use flags to signal the computer.

A computer flag is not a large colorful piece of cloth however. A computer flag uses an IF . . . THEN statement to look for a signal that a condition the programmer wants the computer to wait for is now true. When the computer sees this signal, it carries out new instructions. For instance, a flag can be used to keep the computer from halting a program with an OUT OF DATA ERROR.

Program 4.6

Fearless Fred loves movie monsters and has compiled a Hall of Shame of his favorites. His program will check the name you enter to see if it is on his list. END OF LIST is used as a flag to prevent an OUT OF DATA ERROR from halting the program when all the names have been read:

```
10   PRINT "WHO IS THE BEST MOVIE MONSTER"
20   INPUT "OF ALL TIME? ";M$
30   PRINT
40   PRINT "THE HALL OF SHAME:"
50   PRINT
60   READ L$
70   IF L$ = "END OF LIST" THEN 120
80   PRINT L$;
90   IF L$ = M$ THEN  PRINT " IS ON MY LIST TOO!";
100  PRINT
110  GOTO 60
120  PRINT
130  PRINT "A REAL BAD BUNCH"
140  END
200  DATA GODZILLA, JABBA THE HUT, JAWS, KING KONG
210  DATA DRACULA, FRANKENSTEIN, WOLFMAN, THE THING
220  DATA  END OF LIST

]RUN
WHO IS THE BEST MOVIE MONSTER
OF ALL TIME? JAWS

THE HALL OF SHAME:

GODZILLA
JABBA THE HUT
```

```
JAWS IS ON MY LIST TOO!
KING KONG
DRACULA
FRANKENSTEIN
WOLFMAN
THE THING

A REAL BAD BUNCH
```

- **Lines 10-20:** The program user assigns variable M$ the name of a famous movie monster.
- **Lines 30-50:** Two blank lines make the title HALL OF SHAME stand out more noticeably.
- **Line 60:** The next name stored in the data statements is read and its value assigned to variable L$.
- **Line 70:** Checks to see if variable L$ is the flag. If variable L$ is not the flag END OF LIST then the computer goes on to the next line. When variable L$ is the flag END OF LIST, this signals that all the data has been read, so the program branches to line 120.
- **Line 80:** Prints the name that was just read as L$ on the screen. The semicolon at the end of the statement holds the cursor on that line in case the condition in line 90 is true.
- **Line 90:** Compares the name that is the current value of variable L$ to the name entered on line 20 as variable M$. When the names are the same, the computer prints the message IS ON MY LIST TOO! next to the monster's name. A blank space is the first character of the message. The semicolon at the end of the statement tells the computer to take the same action after executing this statement that it took after executing line 80.
- **Line 100:** Cancels the semicolons on lines 80 and 90 so that the next name read will be printed on a new line.
- **Line 110:** Sends the computer back to line 60 to read the next name on the list.
- **Line 120-130:** These lines are executed only after the flag signals that all data has been read. A blank line is printed and the message A REAL BAD BUNCH.
- **Line 140:** Though an END statement is not necessary here, using an END is good programming style because it helps to show the structure of the program.
- **Lines 200-210:** These DATA statements store the names of the monsters.
- **Line 220:** The flag that signals the end of the data.

When the flag on line 70 is "raised," the instructions to the computer are changed. The computer jumps out of the loop, which stops the computer from reading data. This allows the computer to print the message on line 130 without an OUT OF DATA ERROR message halting the program.

    The idea that the computer must be told to look for specific conditions is an important one in programming. Flags are an example of that idea, but there are many other situations where the programmer must use the IF . . . THEN statement to tell the computer to look for specific conditions. For instance, a counter can be used to tell the computer to change its instructions when a certain number or total is reached. Also, data can be checked when it is brought into the program to prevent improper data from affecting the program.

Program 4.7

This program uses a counter to signal the computer that a task has been done a specified number of times:

```
10  PRINT "THE COUNT DOWN BEGINS."
20  LET C = 10
30  PRINT C
40  LET C = C - 1
50  IF C = 0 THEN 70
60  GOTO 30
70  PRINT "BLAST OFF!"

]RUN
THE COUNT DOWN BEGINS.
10
9
8
7
6
5
4
3
2
1
BLAST OFF!
```

This program loops back and forth between lines 30 and 60 until the counter on line 50 reaches a value of 0. The program begins by assigning the variable C a value of 10. Line 30 then prints the current value of variable name C. Line 40 decreases the value of variable C by one each time the loop is repeated. Line 50 looks for the signal that the condition has been reached. When variable C has a value of 0, this produces a true result to the condition IF C = 0 on line 50. This signals the computer to leave the loop by going to line 70 where the BLAST OFF! message is printed.

Program 4.8

This program checks the numbers that are entered as data to make sure that they are within the range of numbers that is needed:

```
10  INPUT "TYPE A NUMBER BETWEEN 5 AND 10 ? ";N
20  IF N > 10 THEN 10
30  IF N < 5 THEN 10
40  PRINT "IN RANGE"
50  PRINT "THAT'S NOT STRANGE."

]RUN
TYPE A NUMBER BETWEEN 5 AND 10 ? 4
TYPE A NUMBER BETWEEN 5 AND 10 ? 11
TYPE A NUMBER BETWEEN 5 AND 10 ? 7
IN RANGE
THAT'S NOT STRANGE.
```

Lines 20 and 30 check the value of variable N. When the value of variable N produces a true result to either of these conditions, the computer goes back to line 10 to input a number. When both conditions are false, the value of N

4-10   Chapter Four

is between 5 and 10, so the computer prints the IN RANGE message.

Checking data to make sure that it is correct is good programming style. A user might enter incorrect data and cause the program to halt, or the data might cause the program to work improperly. A good programmer practices "preventive medicine" and checks the data before the program is allowed to continue.

Review

5. Write a program that counts from 1 to 10 and prints "ALL DONE." when the counting is completed:

>   RUN
>   1 2 3 4 5 6 7 8 9 10
>   ALL DONE.

6. Read the numbers 26, 37, 42, 65, 89, 234, and 567 from data statements. Have the computer add them and print their sum when all have been read. Use −99 as a flag.

>   RUN
>   THE SUM IS 1060

Making IF ... THEN Smarter: AND & OR

AND and OR are used with an IF ... THEN statement to join two or more comparisons together as one condition. AND and OR combine comparisons differently to decide whether a condition is true or false. Because of this, the decisions that a program makes can be more complex.

AND: When AND is used to join comparisons, *all* comparisons must be true for the condition to be true. For example,

>   20 IF X > 5 AND Y = 3 THEN 50

will send the computer to line 50 only when *both* comparisons are true. The value of variable name X must be greater than 5 while the value of variable name Y must also equal 3.

OR: When OR is used to join comparisons, the condition will be true when *any one or all* comparisons are true. The condition is false when all comparisons are false. For example,

>   20 IF X > 5 OR Y = 3 THEN 50

will send the computer to line 50 if *one or both* of the comparisons is true. That means the jump to line 50 will be made when the value of variable X is greater than 5, when variable Y = 3 or when both of these are true. When *both* comparisons are *false,* the move to line 50 will not be made.

Program 4.9

A problem for spies is that they have to remember so many code words. This program uses OR to help James Bond get the message that is meant only for him. The use of OR allows the computer to decide whether the names or words entered from the keyboard are acceptable before the user is allowed to go on with the program:

```
10   INPUT "WHO ARE YOU? ";N$
20   IF N$ = "JAMES BOND" OR N$ = "007" OR N$ = "BOND" THEN 60
30   PRINT "THIS MISSION IS NOT FOR YOU!"
40   PRINT
50   GOTO 10
60   PRINT "THESE ORDERS ARE FOR YOUR EYES ONLY!"
70   INPUT "ARE YOU ALONE? ";A$
80   IF A$ = "YES" OR A$ = "TRUE" THEN 110
90   PRINT "TRY LATER"
100  GOTO 10
110  PRINT "DOCTOR ZHIVAGO HAS ESCAPED."
120  PRINT "YOUR MISSION IS TO RETURN HIM TO PRISON."

]RUN
WHO ARE YOU? MAXWELL SMART
THIS MISSION IS NOT FOR YOU!

WHO ARE YOU? 007
THESE ORDERS ARE FOR YOUR EYES ONLY!
ARE YOU ALONE? NO
TRY LATER
WHO ARE YOU? JAMES BOND
THESE ORDERS ARE FOR YOUR EYES ONLY!
ARE YOU ALONE? YES
DOCTOR ZHIVAGO HAS ESCAPED.
YOUR MISSION IS TO RETURN HIM TO PRISON.
```

- **Line 10:** A name is entered as variable N$
- **Line 20:** The name entered as variable N$ is compared to the three code words: "JAMES BOND", "007" or BOND". If variable N$ is the same as one of them, the condition is true, so the program branches to line 60.
- **Line 30:** When the condition in line 20 is false, THIS MESSAGE IS NOT FOR YOU is printed.
- **Lines 40-50:** A blank line is printed and then the computer returns to line 10 to input a new name.
- **Line 60:** Prints a warning message.
- **Line 70:** Inputs a response to the question ARE YOU ALONE?
- **Line 80:** The OR connecting the comparisons on line 80 allows an answer of either YES or TRUE to send the program to line 110.
- **Lines 90-100:** When the condition on line 80 is false, a warning message is printed, and the program returns to line 10 to begin the questioning again.
- **Lines 110-120:** The mission is revealed.

Program 4.10 This program uses AND to decide what letter grade a quiz score should receive.

```
10   INPUT "WHAT WAS YOUR LAST QUIZ SCORE? ";S
20   IF S > = 90 THEN   PRINT "A - EXCELLENT"
30   IF S > = 80 AND S < 90 THEN   PRINT "B - GOOD SHOW"
40   IF S > = 70 AND S < 80 THEN   PRINT "C - OKAY!"
50   IF S < 70 THEN   PRINT "BETTER LUCK NEXT TIME."
60   PRINT
70   INPUT "TYPE YES TO ENTER ANOTHER? ";A$
80   IF A$ < > "YES" THEN   END
90   PRINT
100   GOTO 10

]RUN
WHAT WAS YOUR LAST QUIZ SCORE? 82
B - GOOD SHOW

TYPE YES TO ENTER ANOTHER? YES

WHAT WAS YOUR LAST QUIZ SCORE? 93
A - EXCELLENT

TYPE YES TO ENTER ANOTHER? NO
```

- **Line 10:** Uses INPUT to assign a value to variable name S.
- **Line 20:** Checks to see if the value of variable S is greater than 90. When it is, such a value is given an A-EXCELLENT.

This is the first of 4 comparisons that decide what range of numbers the value of variable S falls between. The first and last comparisons do not use AND because they check to see if variable S is greater than or less than a given number.

- **Line 30:** AND is used to set a range.

When 82 was entered as the value of variable S, the condition on line 20 was false but the condition on line 30 was true. The condition was true because 82 is greater than 80 making S >= 80 true and 82 is less than 90 making S < 90 true.

- **Line 40:** Checks in a similar way to make sure that only numbers between 70 and 79 will cause the message to be printed.
- **Line 50:** Does not need an AND but does need an IF...THEN. Without IF S < 70, every score would get a BETTER LUCK NEXT TIME message.

Review

7. Write a program that will allow a number with variable name N to be entered as input. If the number is between 25 and 50 the computer should say that the value of variable N is between those numbers. When the value of variable N is not between 25 and 50, the computer should say that the value of variable N is out of range.

```
RUN
ENTER A NUMBER? 14
    14 IS OUT OF RANGE
ENTER A NUMBER? 34
    34 IS BETWEEN 25 AND 50
ENTER A NUMBER? 50
    50 IS OUT OF RANGE
ENTER A NUMBER?
```

8. Write a program in which the user enters a word as variable name N$. If variable N$ comes alphabetically before GARBAGE or after TRASH, then have the computer print YES. Otherwise have the computer print NO.

```
RUN
TYPE A WORD? REFUSE
NO
TYPE A WORD? FILTH
YES
TYPE A WORD?
```

Initializing Variables

When a program begins, it is often necessary to tell the computer what the beginning or initial value of a variable is. This is called initializing a variable, and good programming means keeping track of the variables that a program uses. During a loop for instance, a counter variable changes its value each time the counter is executed. A programmer can use an IF . . . THEN to tell the computer to start such a loop over again, but unless the programmer tells the computer to set the value of the counter back to its *initial value* when the loop was first executed, the computer will continue counting from the current value of the counter variable.

Program 4.11

Look carefully at the following example:

```
10  PRINT "COUNT FROM 0 TO 9"
20  PRINT C" ";
30  LET C = C + 1
40  IF C < 10 THEN 20
45  PRINT
50  INPUT "COUNT AGAIN? ";A$
60  IF A$ = "YES" THEN 20
```

```
]RUN
COUNT FROM 0 TO 9
0 1 2 3 4 5 6 7 8 9
COUNT AGAIN? YES
10
COUNT AGAIN? NO
```

RUN starts all variables with a value of 0 until the variable is given a value by the program. Therefore, the first time line 20 is executed the value of variable C is 0. The counter on line 30 increases the value of variable C by 1 each time the loop is repeated. When the value of variable C reaches 10, line 40 tells the computer to drop down to line 45. When the word YES is entered as the value of A$, line 60 sends the computer back to line 20 to execute the loop again. When the computer prints the value of variable C on the screen, we see that the value of the counter is still 10. Therefore, line 30 increases the value of variable C to 11. However, the condition on line 40 is still false because 11 is greater than 10, so the computer again drops down to line 45. The program will be able to go back and count from 0 to 9 again only if the value of variable C is set back to 0:

```
60  IF A$ < > "YES" THEN END
70  LET C = 0
80  GOTO 20

]RUN
COUNT FROM 0 TO 9
0 1 2 3 4 5 6 7 8 9
COUNT AGAIN? YES
0 1 2 3 4 5 6 7 8 9
COUNT AGAIN? NO
```

Now, only the word YES will allow the program to continue by dropping down to line 70. When the computer drops down to line 70, it initializes the value of variable C by setting it back to 0 before the program returns to line 20.

When a programmer knows that a section of a program is likely to be repeated, it is good programming style to initialize variables at the start of that section of the program. Doing this will insure that the variables have the correct value each time that section of the program is used. When programs start to get longer than a few lines, it is easy to forget which variables must be initialized before they are used again. By initializing them at the spot where they are used, a programmer is sure that the variables will have the correct value when that section of the program is repeated.

Program 4.12

This program averages the numbers that are entered as input. The program begins by intializing the counter variable and the variable that accumulates the total:

```
10  LET T = 0
20  LET B = 0
30  INPUT "HOW MANY NUMBERS TO AVERAGE? ";C
40  INPUT "ENTER A NUMBER? ";N
50  LET B = B + 1
```

```
60   LET T = T + N
70   IF B = C THEN 90
80   GOTO 40
90   PRINT "THE AVERAGE OF THESE NUMBERS= "T / C
100  INPUT "MORE NUMBERS TO AVERAGE? ";A$
110  IF A$ <  > "YES" THEN   END
120  PRINT
130  GOTO 10

]RUN
HOW MANY NUMBERS TO AVERAGE? 3
ENTER A NUMBER? 25
ENTER A NUMBER? 35
ENTER A NUMBER? 30
THE AVERAGE OF THESE NUMBERS= 30
MORE NUMBERS TO AVERAGE? YES

HOW MANY NUMBERS TO AVERAGE? 2
ENTER A NUMBER? 50
ENTER A NUMBER? 80
THE AVERAGE OF THESE NUMBERS= 65
MORE NUMBERS TO AVERAGE? NO
```

Even though RUN starts the variable names B and T with a value of 0, initializing them before they are used prepares them for use if the loop is repeated later. Variable B counts how many numbers have been entered, and variable T accumulates the total of the numbers that have been entered. When the value of variable B equals the value of variable C, the IF... THEN on line 70 tells the computer that the correct amount of numbers has been entered. The computer then branches to line 90 where the average is calculated. Before this program can be repeated however, variable name B and variable name T must be reset to 0. When the answer to the input on line 100 is YES, the computer branches back to line 10 and initializes variables B and T by setting them back to 0. In the run shown above, if variable B were not reset to 0, then variable B would still have a value of 3 when the computer returned to line 10 to repeat the program. Likewise, variable T would still have a value of 90, and it would begin to keep the total of the second set of numbers by starting with 90. Variable names C and N do not need to be initialized because they are given a new value each time a number is entered as input.

Program 4.13

This program uses the BASIC statements and programming techniques described in this chapter to calculate a batting average for a particular ball game. The reader should be familiar with these statements and techniques and be able to understand how they are used in a program. The REMs explain what each section of the program does:

```
10   PRINT "BATTING AVERAGE CALCULATOR"
20   REM  *** INITIALIZE VARIABLES ***
30   REM  *** B = COUNTER; H = ACCUMULATOR
40   LET B = 0
50   LET H = 0
60   REM  *** ENTER DATA ***
70   PRINT "ENTER DATA FOR THIS GAME"
```

```
80   INPUT "HOW MANY TIMES AT BAT? ";A
90   PRINT "TYPE H FOR A HIT OR N FOR NO HIT"
100  LET B = B + 1
110  INPUT "H OR N? ";B$
120  REM *** CHECK THE DATA ***
130  REM *** ONLY H OR N TO GO ON ***
140  IF B$ = "H" OR B$ = "N" THEN 170
150  PRINT "AN H OR N PLEASE!"
160  GOTO 110
170  IF B$ = "H" THEN  LET H = H + 1
180  REM *** CHECK FOR END OF LOOP ***
190  IF A > B THEN 100
200  REM *** COMPUTE AND SHOW AVERAGE ***
210  LET M = H / A
220  PRINT "YOUR AVERAGE = "M
230  INPUT "YES TO AVERAGE ANOTHER GAME? ";B$
240  IF B$ = "YES" THEN 20

]RUN
BATTING AVERAGE CALCULATOR
ENTER DATA FOR THIS GAME
HOW MANY TIMES AT BAT? 4
TYPE H FOR A HIT OR N FOR NO HIT
H OR N? H
H OR N? H
H OR N? N
H OR N? H
YOUR AVERAGE = .75
YES TO AVERAGE ANOTHER GAME? NO
```

- **Lines 20-50:** *** INITIALIZE VARIABLES ***
  Variable B counts the number of times the player was at bat. Variable H accumulates the total number of hits. If the program is repeated, these variables must be reset to 0.
- **Lines 60-110:** *** ENTER DATA ***
  This section collects the data for the ball game. Variable A stores the number of times the player was at bat. Each time this section of the program is repeated variable B is increased by 1. This variable will be compared to variable A to tell the computer that all the at bats have been counted. String variable B$ is used to see if each at bat was a hit "H" or no hit "N."
- **Lines 120-170:** *** CHECK THE DATA ***
  The computer must be told to check the input for variable B$. This data check will prevent accidental entry of characters other than "H" or "N" that will make the count of variable B inaccurate.
- **Lines 180-190:** *** CHECK FOR END OF LOOP ***
  After the result of each at bat is entered, the computer must check to see if the number of at bats entered equals the number of at bats for this player that was entered as the value of variable A. If variable N is less than variable A, then the loop must be repeated. Otherwise the program can go on to compute the average.

- **Lines 200-240:** ★★★ COMPUTE & SHOW AVERAGE ★★★
    Here, the average is computed and assigned to variable name M. It is printed on the screen, and the player is asked if it is necessary to calculate another average. If the answer is "YES", the computer returns to the INITIALIZE VARIABLES section of the program.

EXERCISES

1. Write a program which asks for a person's age. If the person is 16 years old, have the computer print YOU ARE OLD ENOUGH TO DRIVE A CAR. Otherwise, have the computer indicate how many years the person must wait before being able to drive.

    RUN
    HOW OLD ARE YOU? 16
    YOU ARE OLD ENOUGH TO DRIVE A CAR.
    HOW OLD ARE YOU? 12
    YOU MUST WAIT 4 YEARS TO DRIVE.
    HOW OLD ARE YOU?

2. Tom Terrific wants to help his little brother by writing a program that will test his addition skills. He wants a program that asks for two numbers and then waits for their sum to be entered. If the wrong answer is given, he wants the program to repeat the problem. If the answer is correct, he wants the program to say how good the work was. Show him how it should be done. A RUN should look like this:

    RUN
    TYPE A NUMBER? 10
    TYPE A SMALLER NUMBER? 12
    TOO LARGE TRY AGAIN.
    TYPE A SMALLER NUMBER? 3

    10 − 3 = ? 8
    SORRY TRY AGAIN.
    10 − 3 = ? 7
    VERY GOOD.

3. Write a program which prints six exclamation marks if BIGWOW is entered as X$. Have the program print six question marks for any other input. The program should halt after BIGWOW is entered:

```
RUN
TYPE A WORD? SHAZAM
??????
TYPE A WORD? BIGWOW
!!!!!!
```

4. Allow a word to be entered as a variable named A$. Print a message that variable A$ COMES BEFORE MIDDLE if variable A$ comes before "middle" alphabetically. If variable A$ comes after "middle" have the program print that message.

```
RUN
ENTER A WORD? SNAKE
SNAKE COMES AFTER MIDDLE
ENTER A WORD? CAT
MIDDLE COMES AFTER CAT
ENTER A WORD?
```

5. Joe Kolodnigork wrote a program to keep track of how much money his brother owes him. He does not understand why the program never outputs the amount he is owed. Everytime he runs the program he gets an OUT OF DATA ERROR. The sample RUN is how it should work. Correct his program, type it in and run it:

```
RUN
TOTAL AMOUNT BORROWED = $2.75


10 READ A
20 LET T = T + A
30 GOTO 10
40 PRINT "TOTAL AMOUNT BORROWED = $"; T
50 DATA 1.25, .50, .50, .20, .30
```

6. Use the computer to keep track of your Christmas list. Store the information in DATA statements. Have the computer print out whom you bought something for, what it was, how much each item cost, and the total amount spent so far:

```
RUN
PRESENTS FOR        COST             PRESENT
MOM                 $25              SWEATER
DAD                 $15              BOOK
ROVER               $3.99            BONE
TEACHER             $2.99            CANDY
BROTHER             $.59             PEN

TOTAL COST $47.57
```

7. Use only one PRINT statement to produce the following rectangle.

```
]RUN
**********
**********
**********
**********
**********
```

8. Use a counter and one PRINT statement to print a line of 20 asterisks.

```
]RUN
********************
```

9. Harry Hacker is fed up with the way his friend Matilda messes up his programs by entering bad data in response to inputs. He is going to put a data checking instruction in this program. Between what lines should he put them? Write the new lines for him and add them to his program. The run that follows shows how the program should work when the data is checked:

```
10  PRINT "SPEEDY SUBTRACTION PROGRAM"
20  INPUT "ENTER LARGER NUMBER? ";A
30  INPUT "ENTER SMALLER NUMBER? ";B
40  PRINT A" - "B" = "A - B
50  GOTO 10

]RUN
SPEEDY SUBTRACTION PROGRAM
ENTER LARGER NUMBER? 15
ENTER SMALLER NUMBER? 25

NO WAY!
ENTER THE LARGER NUMBER FIRST!

ENTER LARGER NUMBER?
```

10. Find the error in the following program. Correct the error and type the corrected program in and run it:

```
10  LET N = 100
20  PRINT N;" ";
30  LET N = N - 1
40  IF N = 0 THEN 60
50  GOTO 20
60  PRINT
70  INPUT "DO THIS AGAIN? ";A$
80  IF A$ = "YES" THEN 10
90  PRINT "THAT'S ALL FOLKS!"
```

11. Max's program doesn't work right. He wants it to print YES only if variable L$ is between G and P alphabetically. His problem is that the program prints YES all the time. Can you find the "bug" in Max's program and correct it?

```
10  INPUT "ENTER A LETTER? ";L$
20  IF L$ > "G" OR L$ < "P" THEN 50
30  PRINT "NO"
40  GOTO 10
50  PRINT "YES"
60  GOTO 10

]RUN
ENTER A LETTER? L
YES
ENTER A LETTER?
YES
ENTER A LETTER?
YES
ENTER A LETTER?
```

12. Write a program which allows three names to be entered as variable names A$, B$, and C$. Have the computer print the name that is alphabetically last.

```
RUN
TYPE A NAME? FRED
TYPE ANOTHER NAME? ZORK
TYPE ANOTHER NAME? HARRY
ZORK IS LAST
```

13. Allow a number, variable name X, to be entered as input. Print the message NOT BETWEEN if the value of variable X is either less than 50 or greater than 75. Use only one IF ... THEN statement in your program.

```
RUN
ENTER A NUMBER? 25
NOT BETWEEN
ENTER A NUMBER? 90
NOT BETWEEN
ENTER A NUMBER?
```

14. Program KLUTZ your robot to act as a cash register. It should ask for the total cost, and the amount presented for payment. It should also tell how much change is due or indicate that not enough money was offered, and say THANK YOU COME AGAIN.

```
RUN
ENTER TOTAL COST $ 12.75
ENTER AMOUNT PAID $ 20

CHANGE = $ 7.25
THANK YOU COME AGAIN.

ANOTHER SALE? YES

ENTER TOTAL COST $ 5.10
ENTER AMOUNT PAID $ 4.10
SORRY. THAT'S NOT ENOUGH
ENTER AMOUNT PAID? $ 5.10
CHANGE = $ 0
THANK YOU COME AGAIN.
```

15. Write a program that will draw 25 arrows on the screen. Have the arrows appear to be shooting upward on the screen. An arrow should look like this:

```
RUN
  *
 ***
*****
  *
  *
  *
  *
 ***
 ***
 ***
```

HINT: Use a counter in a loop to check how many have been drawn.

16. Below is a list of various creatures and the weapon necessary to kill each:

CREATURE	WEAPON
Lich	Fire Ball
Mummy	Flaming Torch
Werewolf	Silver Bullet
Vampire	Wooden Stake
Medusa	Sharp Sword
Triffid	Fire Hose

    Using READ and DATA have the computer tell what weapon is used to destroy a specific creature. If the name entered is not on the list have the computer apologize to the user. After the list is read, have the computer wish the hunter good luck:

    ```
    RUN
    WHICH MONSTER TO KILL? VAMPIRE
    WEAPON NEEDED WOODEN STAKE
    GOOD HUNTING!

    RUN
    WHICH MONSTER TO KILL? THE THING
    TOUGH LUCK! NOT ON MY LIST
    GOOD HUNTING!
    ```

17. The Slick Oil Company uses the computer to determine the weekly wage for each of its employees. If the employee works more than 40 hours a week, he or she is paid double the hourly rate for each hour above 40. Write a program that inputs the hours worked and the hourly wage and outputs the wages for the week.

    ```
    RUN
    HOURS WORKED? 45
    HOURLY WAGE $? 10.00
    THE WEEKLY WAGE IS $ 500
    ```

18. The Bored Auto Company did it again. Some of their cars do not work too well because their wheels are not quite round. Cars with model numbers 102, 780, 119, 229, 189, and 195 have this defect. Write a program that allows Bored customers to enter the model number of their car to find out whether or not it is defective.

    ```
    RUN
    ENTER MODEL NUMBER? 125
    NOT A LEMON

    ENTER MODEL NUMBER? 229
    YOU GOT SQUEEZED!
    IT'S A LEMON

    ENTER MODEL NUMBER?
    ```

19. The following table contains employee performance data for the Tippecanoe Typing Company:

EMPLOYEE	PRODUCTION RATING
Howe	92
Oakley	70
Anderson	96
Wolly	88
Goerz	74

Tippecanoe Typing is suffering financial problems and needs to cut its staff. Using READ and DATA statements write a program that will print dismissal notices for any employee whose production rating is below 75.

RUN

DEAR OAKLEY,
    I AM SORRY THAT I MUST FIRE YOU.
YOU HAVE BEEN SUCH A FINE EMPLOYEE
WITH A PRODUCTION RATING OF 70.
    I AM SURE THAT YOU WILL HAVE NO
TROUBLE FINDING ANOTHER JOB.
        SINCERELY,

    SIMON LEE GREE

20. This program is supposed to simulate an adding machine that will allow ten pairs of numbers to be entered and their sums calculated. Can you find the error in this program?

```
10   READ A,B
20   LET T = T + 1
30   IF T = 10 THEN  END
40   PRINT A" + "B" = "A + B
50   GOTO 10
60   DATA   1,5,2,5,3,5,4,5,5,5
70   DATA   6,5,7,5,8,5,9,5,10,5
```

```
]RUN
1 + 5 = 6
2 + 5 = 7
3 + 5 = 8
4 + 5 = 9
5 + 5 = 10
6 + 5 = 11
7 + 5 = 12
8 + 5 = 13
9 + 5 = 14
```

21. Write a program that asks how many times the message TESTING should be printed on the screen. When the correct number of TESTINGs have been printed, have the computer tell the user that the test is over, how many TESTINGs were printed and ask if the user wants to run another test:

```
RUN
HOW MANY TIMES TO PRINT TEST? 5
TESTING
TESTING
TESTING
TESTING
TESTING

TEST OVER. 5 TESTINGS PRINTED
TYPE YES TO RUN ANOTHER TEST? NO
```

DEFINED LOOPS

5

FOR...TO
NEXT
TAB ( )

FOR...TO
NEXT
TAB ( )

FOR...TO
NEXT
TAB ( )

*I*F... THEN statements used with a counter can create loops that will repeat their instructions as many times as a programmer specifies. However, when programs start to get long, this technique can be time consuming and confusing. For example, there may be many loops in a program for which the counter variables must be kept track of and initialized. Also, loops may be set to work with in other loops which means more difficulty in keeping track of the counters. Because the use of loops is such a common practice in programming, BASIC provides us with a set of looping statements. Therefore, when a programmer knows that a loop is needed, the FOR... NEXT statements are usually used.

FOR... NEXT

The FOR... NEXT statements provide a simple way of creating a loop that will be repeated a specific number of times. These statements give the programmer a way of easily telling the computer how many times the loop should be repeated. The general form of the FOR... NEXT statement is:

FOR <variable> = <starting value> TO <ending value>
.
.
.
NEXT <variable>

The *variable* after FOR and NEXT must be the same. The *starting value* tells the computer at what number the loop should begin. The *ending value* tells the computer to end the loop when it reaches this value. A string variable cannot be used as the variable in a FOR... NEXT loop.

In a program, these statements would look like this:

10 FOR J = 1 TO 25
.
.
30 NEXT J

Variable name J will keep track of how many times the loop is repeated. The starting value of variable J is 1 and the value of J that will end the loop is 25.

Program 5.1

Here a FOR...NEXT loop is used to calculate and print the 5 times table from 0 to 10:

```
10   FOR J = 0 TO 10
20   PRINT J" * 5 = "J * 5
30   NEXT J
40   PRINT "FINISHED WITH LOOP"
```

```
]RUN
0 * 5 = 0
1 * 5 = 5
2 * 5 = 10
3 * 5 = 15
4 * 5 = 20
5 * 5 = 25
6 * 5 = 30
7 * 5 = 35
8 * 5 = 40
9 * 5 = 45
10 * 5 = 50
FINISHED WITH LOOP
```

In line 10 the computer is given the information it needs to execute a loop. FOR J = 0 tells the computer that variable name J is the variable that will keep track of the number of times the loop has been repeated, and variable J will start the loop with a value of 0. TO 10 tells the computer to end the loop when the value of variable J is greater than 10. Each time the loop is repeated, the value of variable J increases by 1. Line 20 outputs the times table by printing the current value of J followed by "* 5 =" and the result of variable J multiplied by 5 (J * 5). The NEXT J on line 30 tells the computer to increase the value of variable J by 1. If the value of variable J is less than or equal to 10, the computer repeats lines 20 and 30. When the value of variable J is greater than 10, the computer stops repeating the loop and goes on to line 40.

Review

1. Using a FOR...NEXT loop, write a program that prints the numbers from 1 to 10 on the screen:

```
RUN
1  2  3  4  5  6  7  8  9  10
```

2. Using a FOR...NEXT loop, write a program that prints "LOOP THE LOOP!" 20 times on the screen.

More FOR...NEXT

The FOR...NEXT loop is very flexible. A loop can be described for the computer in several ways. For instance, a FOR...NEXT loop does not need to begin counting at 0 or 1. A programmer can tell the computer to start counting at any number. In fact, the programmer can use a variable to set the starting number of the loop and a variable can also be used to name the end value of the loop:

$$10 \text{ FOR } X = A \text{ TO } Z$$

In this example, variable X will keep track of the number of times the loop has been repeated. The loop will start with the current value of variable A and end when the value of variable X is greater than the value of variable Z.

Program 5.2

The loop variable in this program begins at 100 and ends at 115:

```
10  FOR K = 100 TO 115
20  PRINT K" ";
30  NEXT K
40  PRINT
50  PRINT "LOOP COMPLETED"
```

```
]RUN
100 101 102 103 104 105 106 107 108 109
110 111 112 113 114 115
LOOP COMPLETED
```

The loop begins by giving the variable K a value of 100. When the value of variable K is greater than 115, the loop stops repeating.

Program 5.3

In this program, variable names are used to assign the starting and ending values of the loop:

```
10   INPUT "ENTER STARTING VALUE OF LOOP: ";S
20   INPUT "ENTER END VALUE OF LOOP: ";E
30   IF E < = S THEN 10
40   FOR K = S TO E
50   PRINT K" ";
60   NEXT K
70   PRINT
80   PRINT "LOOP FINISHED."
90   INPUT "AGAIN? ";A$
100  IF A$ = "YES" THEN 10
```

```
]RUN
ENTER STARTING VALUE OF LOOP: 25
ENTER END VALUE OF LOOP: 37
25 26 27 28 29 30 31 32 33 34 35 36 37
LOOP FINISHED.
AGAIN? YES
ENTER STARTING VALUE OF LOOP: 5
ENTER END VALUE OF LOOP: 7
5 6 7
LOOP FINISHED.
AGAIN? NO
```

Variable name K begins the loop at line 40 with a value of 25 because 25 was the value given to variable name S when line 10 was executed. The loop stops repeating when the value of variable K reaches 37 since 37 is the value that was assigned to variable E when line 20 was executed. Line 30 checks the numbers that have been entered for variable S and variable E. This will prevent numbers from being entered that could cause the loop to work improperly. For instance, if the end value, variable E, is less than the starting value, variable S, the loop will only be executed once. PRINT K " "; on line 50 shows us the actual value of variable K each time the loop is repeated. When the loop is started for a second time, the value of variable K is assigned the new valye of variable S and the loop ends when the new value of variable E is reached.

Review

3. Predict the output of the following program. Type the program into your computer and run it to check your prediction:

```
10  FOR W = 5 TO 10
20  LET T = T + W
30  PRINT W" ";
40  NEXT W
50  PRINT
60  PRINT "THE SUM OF ALL NUMBERS
        FROM 5 TO 10"
70  PRINT "IS "T
```

4. Can you find the error in this program? Type it in and correct the error:

```
10  INPUT "NUMBERS TO ADD? ";N
20  FOR J = 1 TO N
30  INPUT "ENTER A NUMBER: ";X
40  LET T = T + X
50  NEXT N
60  PRINT "THE SUM IS "T
```

Looping forward by STEPs

Another way to use a FOR . . . NEXT loop is to have it step or count through the loop by a number other than 1. The STEP instruction tells the computer how many numbers to "step" over in the sequence from the starting number to the end number.

10 FOR J = <start value> TO <end value> STEP <count by>

This loop will increase the value of variable J by the step value each time the loop is repeated. When the starting value is 0 and the end value is 10 with a step of 1, the computer will begin the loop at 0 and step forward by 1 number in the sequence until 10 is reached (1, 2, 3, 4, 6, 7, 8, 9, 10). When the STEP value is 2, the computer will step foward by adding 2 to the last number in the sequence until 10 is reached (2, 4, 6, 8, 10). Because a STEP value of 1 is so common, the STEP 1 can be left out of the loop when it is used. STEP is required whenever a STEP other than 1 is used.

10 FOR J = 0 TO 25 STEP 5

In this example, variable name J is the counter variable. Each time the loop is repeated, the value of variable J will increase by the STEP value of 5 producing 0, 5, 10, 15, 20, 25.

Program 5.4

This program shows the use of a STEP value of 2:

```
10  FOR K = 1 TO 15 STEP 2
20  PRINT K" ";
30  NEXT K
40  PRINT
50  PRINT "DONE"

]RUN
1 3 5 7 9 11 13 15
DONE
```

Line 10 describes the loop to the computer. Variable name K will count the number of times the loop is repeated, and variable K will start with a value of 1. STEP 2 tells the computer to increase the value of variable K by 2 each time the loop is repeated. Line 20 prints the value of variable K. NEXT K on line 30 tells the computer to add the STEP value to variable K and repeats the loop by going back to line 20. When the value of variable K is greater than 15 the computer does not repeat the loop again. The PRINT on line 40 cancels the effect of the semicolon on line 20 there by allowing the message DONE to be printed on the next line at the left margin instead of next to the number 15.

A variable can also be used to assign the STEP value, and a math operation can be performed to set any of the values that are used to describe a loop to the computer. These capabilities make the FOR... NEXT loop even more powerful because of the different ways a programmer can use a loop.

Program 5.5

In this program, both an INPUT and a math operation are used to set the values that describe a loop which prints any multiplication table from 0 to 10:

```
10  PRINT "ENTER THE TIMES TABLE FROM 0 - 10 THAT"
20  INPUT "YOU WANT PRINTED OUT : ";M
30  FOR J = 0 TO 10 * M STEP M
40  PRINT C" * "M" = "J
50  LET C = C + 1
60  NEXT J

]RUN
ENTER THE TIMES TABLE FROM 0 - 10 THAT
YOU WANT PRINTED OUT : 5
0 * 5 = 0
1 * 5 = 5
2 * 5 = 10
3 * 5 = 15
4 * 5 = 20
```

```
 5 * 5 = 25
 6 * 5 = 30
 7 * 5 = 35
 8 * 5 = 40
 9 * 5 = 45
10 * 5 = 50
```

Variable M is used to set the STEP value on line 30. Each time the loop is completed the step value is added to the value of variable J. The end value of the loop is also different for each value of M. The end value must tell the computer to print 10 multiples of the variable M because the times table must show all the factors from 0 to 10. Therefore the end value is calculated by multiplying the value of M by 10 on line 30 (FOR J = 0 to M * 10). On line 40, variable C is used to print out a factor of variable J each time the loop is repeated. Line 50 is the counter that increases the factor used on line 40 by 1 each time the loop is repeated.

When STEP values other than 1 are used, it is quite probable that the counter variable of the loop will never equal the end value of the loop. For example:

```
10  FOR J = 0 TO 10 STEP 4
20  PRINT J" ";
30  NEXT J
40  PRINT
50  PRINT "THE FINAL VALUE OF J = "J

]RUN
0 4 8
THE FINAL VALUE OF J = 12
```

The value of J never equals 10. The value of variable J steps from 8 to 12. Good programmers should be aware of this so that they do not expect the counter variable to always equal the end value of the loop when the loop is completed.

Review

5. Write a program that will allow a number N to be entered. Then use N as a STEP value and print the numbers from 10 to 30.

```
              RUN
              STEP VALUE? 3
              10 13 16 19 22 25 28
```

6. Predict the output of this program, especially the value of variable J that will be printed when M is 5 or when M is 10. Then type the program in and run it

```
10 INPUT "FROM 0 TO 100 BY "; M
20 FOR J = 0 TO 100 STEP M
30 PRINT J;
40 NEXT J
50 PRINT
60 PRINT "LOOP COMPLETED J = " J
```

7. Predict the final value of variable B in the program below. Type in and run the program to check your prediction.

   10 FOR B = 5 * 0 TO 3 * 12 STEP 7
   20 PRINT B;
   30 NEXT B
   40 PRINT
   50 PRINT "THE FINAL VALUE OF B IS " B

From a Higher to a Lower STEP

There is no reason why the computer cannot count backwards in a loop. This is done by making the starting value of the loop higher than the end value of the loop. Whenever the starting value is higher than the end value a STEP instruction *must* be used. The STEP tells the computer how much to *subtract* from the counter variable each time the loop is repeated. For example,

FOR J = 25 TO 1 STEP −1

tells the computer to start this loop with a value of 25 for the counter variable J. The loop will stop when the end value reaches 1. Each time the loop is repeated, the loop will subtract 1 from the value of variable J.

Program 5.6

The following program counts down from 10 to 0 for a rocket ship blast off:

```
10  FOR J = 10 TO 0 STEP - 1
20  PRINT J
30  NEXT J
40  PRINT
50  PRINT "BLAST OFF"

]RUN
10
9
8
7
6
5
4
3
2
1
0

BLAST OFF
```

The starting value of variable J is set at 10, and the loop is set to end when the value of J reaches 0. The STEP −1 tells the computer to take 1 away from the value of variable J each time the loop is repeated. The changes in the value of variable J are shown by the PRINT statement on line 20, which prints the value of variable J during each repetition of the loop. The loop ends when the value of variable J reaches 0.

Program 5.7

Here a loop counts backward from 100 to 20 by STEP −20:

```
10 FOR T = 100 TO 20 STEP -20
20 PRINT T" ";
30 NEXT T
40 PRINT
50 PRINT "LOOP COMPLETED"

]RUN
100 80 60 40 20
LOOP COMPLETED
```

The loop begins by assigning the variable T a starting value of 100. Since the end value of 20 is less than the start value, a STEP instruction is necessary. The STEP −20 tells the computer to take 20 away from the value of T each time the loop is repeated by NEXT T on line 30. Line 20 prints the current value of T each time the loop is executed. When the value of variable T is less than 20 the computer stops repeating the loop and executes lines 40 and 50.

Review

8. Using a FOR ... NEXT loop have the computer print the following:

    RUN
    20 18 16 14 12 10

9. Write a program that will allow a number N to be entered. Then use N as a STEP value and print the numbers from 30 to 0:

    RUN
    STEP VALUE? 5
    30 25 20 15 10 5 0

PRINT TAB (X)

Using TAB with the PRINT statement is another way to format output for printing on the screen. It allows the cursor to be moved to a specific place on a line, unlike the comma that prints in preset print zones or the semicolon that prints in the next available space. The left edge of the screen is TAB(1) and the right edge is TAB(40), which means there are 40 columns on the screen. The number or variable that is inside the parentheses tells the computer how far over from the left margin the cursor should be moved before printing. For example,

PRINT TAB(20) "*"

will place the cursor at the middle of a line and print an asterisk.

Program 5.8

This program shows the printing of information at TAB positions 3, 11 and 17:

```
10   PRINT   TAB( 3);"THIS"
20   PRINT   TAB( 11);"IS"
30   PRINT   TAB( 17);"TAB"
40   PRINT   TAB( 3);"THIS"; TAB( 11);"IS"; TAB( 17);"TAB"

]RUN
  THIS
          IS
                  TAB
  THIS    IS              TAB
```

Lines 10, 20 and 30 print the words THIS IS TAB on three separate lines on the screen. Line 40 shows how the three words can be placed on one line.

Program 5.9

A variable can be used inside the parentheses with TAB. This program uses a variable with TAB to draw a triangle on the screen:

```
10   LET R = 16
20   PRINT  TAB( 10);"*******"
30   FOR J = 11 TO 14
40   PRINT  TAB( J);"*"; TAB( R);"*"
50   NEXT J
60   PRINT  TAB( R);"*"

]RUN
         *******
          *     *
           *    *
            *   *
             *  *
                *
```

Line 10 assigns the variable R a value of 16. On line 20, the TAB(10) draws the top of the triangle 10 spaces from the left margin. Line 30 describes a loop that starts at 11 and ends when variable J reaches a value of 14. These values were chosen because they are values that will also be used in the TAB(J) instruction on line 40. Each time the loop is repeated the cursor will TAB over a number of spaces equal to the value of variable J. To make the left side of the triangle slant, the TAB(J) must start at 11 and increase by 1 each time the loop is repeated until it reaches 14. The right side of the triangle is straight because TAB always counts over from the left margin, and the value of variable R is 16 each time the TAB(R) instruction is executed. TAB does not count from the last place a character was printed. It always counts from the left margin.

The PRINT TAB statement moves the cursor to the right only. It can never move the cursor to the left. If a TAB number is less than the last number TABbed on a line, the cursor will remain where it is and print from there.

```
10 PRINT TAB(10) "##" TAB(15) "##"
20 PRINT TAB(15) "##" TAB(10) "##"
RUN
         ##    ##
               ####
```

In line 10 the cursor moves 10 spaces to the right before printing two "#" characters. Line 20 starts out with the cursor moving 15 spaces to the right where two more "#" characters are printed. The TAB(10) that followed however cannot be done by the computer. The 10 is less than the 15 of the first TAB on that line, so the cursor remains where it is and types two "#" 's.

Review

10. Use PRINT TAB( ) to output the following in the middle of the screen:

    ```
    RUN
                 THIS
                  IS
                 TAB
    ```

11. Predict the output of the following program. Then type the program in and run it to check your prediction.

    ```
    10 FOR J = 1 TO 40
    20 PRINT TAB(J) "-";
    30 NEXT J
    ```

Program 5.10

This program uses the major programming statements and techniques covered in this chapter. It allows the user to pick a word from the sentence THIS IS A SAMPLE OF THE MATERIAL IN CHAPTER FIVE, which will be left out of the sentence when it is printed:

```
10  INPUT "WORD TO SKIP? ";S$
20  FOR W = 1 TO 10
30  READ W$
40  IF W$ = S$ THEN 60
50  PRINT   TAB( W);W$
60  NEXT W
70  PRINT "THAT'S ALL FOLKS!"
80  DATA  THIS,IS,A,SAMPLE,OF,THE
90  DATA  MATERIAL,IN,CHAPTER,FIVE
```

```
]RUN
WORD TO SKIP? CHAPTER
THIS
 IS
  A
   SAMPLE
    OF
     THE
      MATERIAL
       IN
        FIVE
THAT'S ALL FOLKS!
```

- **Line 10:** Assign the word to be skipped to variable S$.
- **Line 20:** Describes the loop that will read the data, search for the word to be skipped, and print the remaining words.
- **Line 30:** Reads a word from the words stored in the data statements and assigns it to variable W$.
- **Line 40:** Compares the value of variable W$ to the value of variable S$. If they are the same, the computer branches to line 60, and therefore does not print the word.
- **Line 50:** Prints the word that is the value of variable W$ when the condition on line 40 is false. TAB(W) prints each word one space further away from the left margin than the last word printed. The variable W is the counter variable for the loop and increases by 1 each time the loop is repeated.
- **Line 60:** Tells the computer that this is the end of the loop and to increase the counter variable by the step value. Because the step value in this program is 1, STEP 1 does not have to be written.
- **Line 70:** Tells the program user that the program has reached its conclusion. An OUT OF DATA ERROR does not halt the program because the loop repeats the READ statement on line 30 ten times, and there are 10 pieces of data stored in the data statements. However, one more attempt to read data would cause the OUT OF DATA ERROR to halt the program.
- **Lines 80-90:** The data that is stored within the program.

EXERCISES

1. Use only one PRINT statement and a FOR...NEXT loop to produce the following rectangle:

    ```
    RUN
    *********
    *********
    *********
    *********
    *********
    *********
    *********
    ```

2. Use one PRINT instruction in a FOR...NEXT loop to print a line of 20 asterisks:

    ```
    RUN
    ********************
    ```

3. Use a FOR...NEXT loop to print a giant letter I as follows:

    ```
    RUN
    *****
     ***
     ***
     ***
     ***
     ***
     ***
    *****
    ```

4. Use a FOR...NEXT loop to draw a box like the following on the screen:

    ```
    RUN
    **********
    *        *
    *        *
    *        *
    *        *
    *        *
    *        *
    **********
    ```

5. Write a program that uses a FOR...NEXT loop to draw and redraw 25 arrows on the screen. The arrows should look as though they are moving up the screen. The arrows should look like this:

```
RUN
    *
   ***
  *****
    *
    *
    *
    *
   ***
   ***
   ***
```

6. Print all the numbers which end in 4 from 4 to 84:

```
RUN
 4   14   24   34   44   54   64   74   84
```

7. Print all of the numbers in the set 10, 13, 16, 19, ... , 94, 97.

8. John Doe's good ol' teacher wants him to write the 7 and 8 times tables from 0 to 12. Use a loop and TAB to output this table for him:

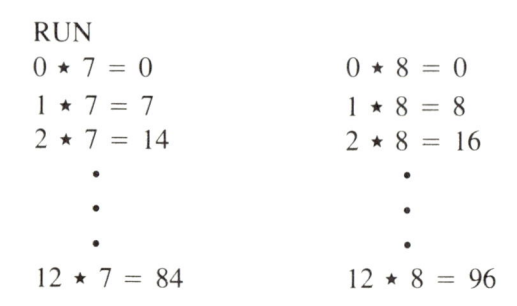

```
RUN
0 * 7 = 0            0 * 8 = 0
1 * 7 = 7            1 * 8 = 8
2 * 7 = 14           2 * 8 = 16
   .                    .
   .                    .
   .                    .
12 * 7 = 84          12 * 8 = 96
```

9. Print this box on the screen 10 spaces away from the left margin:

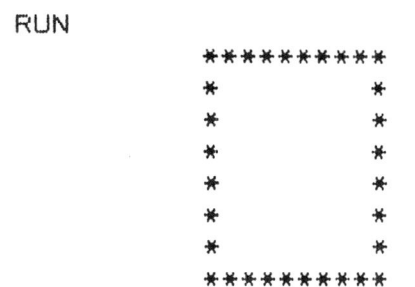

    RUN
    ```
    **********
    *        *
    *        *
    *        *
    *        *
    *        *
    *        *
    *        *
    **********
    ```

10. Write a program that prints the steps of the following stairway design:

    RUN
    ```
    *****
     *****
      *****
       *****
        *****
         *****
    ```

11. Re-write the stairway program so the direction of the steps is reversed:

    RUN
    ```
         *****
        *****
       *****
      *****
     *****
    *****
    ```

12. Write a program which will produce the following table as output:

    RUN

N	N * N	N * N * N
2	4	8
4	16	64
6	36	216
8	64	512
10	100	1000

13. Will the following program reach line 90 and print the total amount or will an OUT OF DATA ERROR halt the program first? What will the output of the program look like? Type the program in and run it to check your answer:

```
10   PRINT "ITEM"; TAB( 20);"COST"
20   PRINT
30   FOR J = 1 TO 5
40   READ I$,C
50   LET T = T + C
60   PRINT I$ TAB( 20)"$ "C
70   NEXT J
80   PRINT "-------------------------------"
90   PRINT "TOTAL COST:" TAB( 20)"$ "T
100  DATA   CANDY,5.59,ICE CREAM,2.55
110  DATA   CAKE,7.65,SODA,2.99
120  DATA   FAVORS,2.99
```

14. Write a program that uses a FOR . . . NEXT loop to read and TAB to list the name, state and term of office of the first 8 Presidents of the U.S.:

RUN

NAME	STATE	TERM
GEORGE WASHINGTON	VIRGINIA	8
JOHN ADAMS	MASSACHUSETTS	4
THOMAS JEFFERSON	VIRGINIA	8
JAMES MADISON	VIRGINIA	8
JAMES MONROE	VIRGINIA	8
JOHN QUINCY ADAMS	MASSACHUSETTS	4
ANDREW JACKSON	SOUTH CAROLINA	8
MARTIN VAN BUREN	NEW YORK	4

15. Use the data from problem 14 above to write a program that will let the user search for a particular President. When that President is found his position (1, 2, 3, 4, 5, etc.), name, state and term of office should be displayed. If his name is not found, then NOT ON THIS LIST should be displayed:

>   RUN
>   THE FIRST 8 PRESIDENTS:
>   DATA FOR WHICH PRESIDENT? JAMES MONROE
>
>   NUMBER: 5
>   NAME: JAMES MONROE
>   STATE: VIRGINIA
>   TERM: 8 YEARS
>
>   RUN
>   THE FIRST 8 PRESIDENTS:
>   WHICH PRESIDENT? WILLIAM TYLER
>
>   WILLIAM TYLER NOT ON THIS LIST.

COMPUTER MATH

6

INT ( )
RND ( )

INT ( )
RND ( )

INT ( )
RND ( )

One of the first things that comes to mind when people think of a computer is mathematics. The word compute itself means to calculate or figure mathematically, and computers are excellent "number crunchers." However, a programmer must still tell the computer which calculations to carry out. This chapter will describe how the computer carries out mathematical operations, and how the computer uses both very large and very small numbers. The chapter will also explain how the computer can be made to pick a random number. Computers are only machines however, and do not understand some of the problems that might arise with numbers, so this chapter will explain some of the situations where the computer's calculations are not accurate and how these inaccuracies can be avoided.

Order of Operations

What value will be assigned to variable A when the computer calculates the following expression?

LET A = 3 + 12 / 3

Will the computer add 3 and 12 and then divide by 3? If it does, the answer will be 5. Or will the computer first divide 12 by 3 and then add 3? If the computer does that, the answer will be 7:

PRINT 3 + 12 / 3
7

The computer divided first and then added 3 to the result because the computer follows a specific order of operations. The computer will always carry out mathematical calculations in the same way. As a programmer you must know in what order math operations will be executed by the computer. Otherwise, you might plan calculations one way, but the computer will do them a different way.

To the computer, reading a math statement is like directing traffic. To do this the math operations have been given an order of priority that tells the computer which operations should be done first, second or third. Also, the computer has been told to read math statements from left to right. Therefore, if operations of equal priority are used in the same statement, the computer will not be confused. It will execute them in order from left to right.

The computer uses the following order of priority when it reads a mathematical expression:

FIRST

Exponents: Any numbers raised to a power, i.e. 2^2, are done first. The up arrow "^" is the symbol used by the computer for raising to a power:

>PRINT 2 + 2 ^ 2
>6

The computer first calculated 2^2, which is 4 (2×2), even though 2+2 appears first when reading from left to right. Then the computer read through the statement again and added 2 to the 4 to get 6 as the final result.

SECOND

Multiplication & Division: Next the computer looks for multiplication or division signs:

>PRINT 2 + 5 * 4 / 2
>12

First the computer reads through this statement looking for an exponent. Since there is none, the computer reads the statement again. On its second reading, the computer looks for multiplication and division signs. Since these signs have a higher priority, the computer ignores the plus sign between the 2 and the 5. When the computer reads the multiplication sign between the 5 and the 4, it executes that multiplication with 20 as the result. The computer then reads the division sign and divides 20 by 2 with a result of 10. Only after all the multiplications and divisions are done does the computer read the statement again and add 2 to 10 to get the final result, which is 12. Remember, when there is more than one operation of the same priority being performed in a statement, the computer does them in order from left to right.

THIRD

Addition and Subtraction: The third time the computer reads an expression it looks for addition and subtraction signs:

>PRINT 3 * 2 + 6
>12

Since multiplication and division are done before addition, the computer first calculates the product of 3 and 2, which is 6. To get the final result, 6 is added to 6 and the result is 12.

When parentheses, "(" and ")", are used, the computer does whatever operations are within the parentheses first. By using parentheses, a programmer can tell the computer to change the order of operations. If a programmer wants 3 added to 12 and the result of that divided by 3, parentheses can be used to tell the computer to follow that order:

>PRINT (3 + 12) / 3
>5

Computer Math   6-3

If parentheses are used within parentheses, the computer will execute the operation within the inner most parentheses first:

$$\text{PRINT } (5 * ((3 + 12)/3))$$
$$25$$

First the computer adds 3 and 12. Then that result is divided by 3. Finally the computer multiplies that by 5. What would the result be if all parentheses were removed?

When the number of left parentheses "(" do not match the number of right parentheses ")", the computer will print a ?SYNTAX ERROR message and halt the program:

```
10 PRINT 5 * ( (5 + 2) * (16 / 4 + 12)
RUN
?SYNTAX ERROR IN 10
```

Program 6.1

Notice how the rules for order of operations are used in this program to insure that all calculations are accurate:

```
10   PRINT  TAB( 8)"WELCOME TO THE STORE"
20   LET J = 1.99
30   LET C = 1.29
40   PRINT
50   PRINT "OUR SPECIALS TODAY ARE:"
60   PRINT "JUICE $ "J" A HALF GALLON"
70   PRINT "CHIPS $ "C" PER BAG"
80   PRINT
90   INPUT "HOW MANY HALF GALLONS? ";G
100  IF G < 0 THEN 90
110  INPUT "HOW MANY BAGS OF CHIPS? ";B
120  IF B < 0 THEN 110
130  LET T = G * J + B * C
140  PRINT
150  PRINT "YOU OWE $ "T

]RUN
        WELCOME TO THE STORE

OUR SPECIALS TODAY ARE:
JUICE $ 1.99 A HALF GALLON
CHIPS $ 1.29 PER BAG

HOW MANY HALF GALLONS? 2
HOW MANY BAGS OF CHIPS? 1

YOU OWE $ 5.27
```

The calculations on line 130 will accurately total the costs and assign that value to variable T. Variable G, the number of half gallons of juice, will be multiplied by variable J, the cost of each half gallon. Then variable B, the number of bags of chips purchased, will be multiplied by variable C, the cost per bag. Only after these calculations have been executed will the computer add the results to get the total cost. To make the order of these operations more obvious and perhaps to be on the safe side, you could have used parentheses to write line 130:

$$130 \text{ LET } T = (G * J) + (B * C)$$

The IF ... THEN statements on lines 100 and 120 check the values of the variables G and B as they are entered. This is to prevent a value less than 0 from being entered. In this situation a value less than 0 would be nonsense, but the computer would not know that. The computer would accept a negative number and carry out the calculations on line 130. Therefore, it is good programming practice to check input when it is entered to avoid bad data by using an IF ... THEN statement. Remember, the computer cannot think. It is the programmer who makes the computer seem to be intelligent.

Review

1. Solve the following by hand using the computer's order of operations. Then check your answers by using immediate mode:

   a. 6 − 9 / 3
   b. 5 * 15 − 5
   c. 3 ∧ 2 + 1
   d. 3 * (5 + 6)
   e. 25 / 5 + 3 * 12
   f. (13 − 3) / (10 / 2)
   g. (2 + 1) ∧ (8 / 4)
   h. 3 * (2 + (5 − 2))

2. Find the error in the following program:

   ```
   10 INPUT "TYPE A NUMBER "; A
   20 INPUT "TYPE ANOTHER NUMBER "; B
   30 LET C = ((A + B) * 2))
   40 PRINT C
   ```

Computer Numbers

Because the computer is a machine, it uses numbers in a way that is best for a machine. Therefore, the computer displays all numbers as decimals including fractions and mixed numbers.

   1125 = one thousand one hundred twenty-five
   1.2 = one and two tenths
   1.25 = one and twenty-five hundredths
   .25 = twenty-five hundredths

The computer's use of decimal numbers is most obvious with division. Any result that is not a whole number will be expressed as a decimal fraction:

PRINT 5 / 2
2.5

The result of 5 divided by 2 is 2 and one half. The computer expresses the answer as a mixed decimal 2.5. Often, the result of a division continues to have a remainder and so the process of division could be repeated again and again:

PRINT 10 / 3
3.33333333

A result like this is called a repeating decimal because 3 will continue to be the result each time the division is repeated. Because the computer is a machine, there is a limit to the size of a number that can be stored in the computer's memory. The computer can store numbers that have up to 9 digits plus a decimal point. Therefore, the computer stopped dividing when the number of digits reached 9.

If the value of a repeating decimal is equal to or greater than 5, the computer will round the last digit off to the next highest digit:

PRINT 10 / 6
1.66666667

Since 6 is greater than 5, the computer rounded the 6 up to a 7 when it reached the ninth digit.

The "/" sign that is used as the computer's division sign is taken from the line that is used to separate the numerator and denominator in a common fraction. However, even when the computer is given numbers to work with that look like common fractions, it will still give its result as a decimal fraction:

PRINT 2/4 + 1/4
.75

Review

3. Use immediate mode to have the computer execute the following operations. Can you predict how the computer will print the results?

   a. 100 / 8
   b. 22 / 7
   c. 5/6 − 1/8
   d. 37 / 2
   e. 11 / 3

INT ( ) =
INTegerizing

An integer is a whole number. The numbers 1, 2, 10 and 100 are all integers. Often, only the integer part of a number is important. For instance, if you have 30 golf balls and you need to know how many dozen you have, only the whole number part of your division result is used because only the number of full dozen is important:

PRINT 30 / 12
2.5

By using the INTeger function, the computer can be told to use only the whole number part of any value. To use the INTeger function write:

$$INT(X)$$

X can be a number, a variable or a mathematical expression like 10/3. The computer looks at the value within the parentheses and then uses only the whole number part of the value:

$$PRINT\ INT(\ 30\ /\ 12\ )$$
$$2$$

INT(X) does not round the number off; instead, it drops any fractional part off. For example:

$$INT(4.769) = 4 \qquad INT(5.9) = 5$$
$$INT(.63) = 0 \qquad INT(12.098) = 12$$

The value that the integer function returns is always smaller than the original value. Therefore, when INT(X) is used with negative numbers, the value returned is always the integer that is one less:

$$INT(-4.769) = -5 \qquad INT(-5.9) = -6$$
$$INT(-.63) = -1 \qquad INT(-12.098) = -13$$

Program 6.2

At work Linda must pack 3 left handed skyhooks in a box. She wrote this program to tell her how many boxes she needs and how many skyhooks will be left over:

```
10   LET N = 3
20   INPUT "ENTER THE NUMBER OF SKYHOOKS? ";H
30   LET B =  INT (H / N)
40   LET L = H - (3 * B)
50   PRINT "BOXES NEEDED: "B
60   PRINT "SKYHOOKS LEFT OVER: "L

]RUN
ENTER THE NUMBER OF SKYHOOKS? 14
BOXES NEEDED: 4
SKYHOOKS LEFT OVER: 2
```

- **Line 10:** Variable name N is assigned the number of hooks per box.
- **Line 20:** Variable name H is assigned the number of hooks.
- **Line 30:** Variable name B is the number of boxes that will be needed. Variable B is assigned the integer value of variable H divided by variable N.

In the example shown, the value of variable H is 14 and the value of variable N is 3. The result of 14/3 is 4.66666667. Therefore, variable B is assigned 4 as its value.

- **Line 40:** Variable name L is assigned the value of the number of hooks left over. This is calculated by subtracting the number of hooks that are in the boxes, (N * B), from the value of variable H, which is the total number of hooks.

In this example, variable H has a value of 14, variable B has a value of 4 and variable N has a value of 3. Therefore, variable L is assigned a value of 2 because 14 − (3 * 4) = 14 − 12, which equals 2.

Review

4. Predict the outcome of the following. Then use immediate mode to check your prediction:

    a. INT(199.99999)   b. INT(22/ 7)
    c. INT(−3.001)   d. INT(.005)
    e. INT (−.999)

RND (1) =
Random Numbers

We pick random numbers in a number of ways. Rolling dice, spinning a spinner, drawing a card from a deck or picking numbers from a hat are some of the ways that people choose a random number. The computer can also be told to pick a random number. Random numbers have many uses, but getting a machine as logical and methodical as a computer to do anything randomly means work for the programmer. To pick a RaNDom number the computer uses the following format:

    PRINT RND(1)
    .21345

The computer always picks a number that has a value that is greater than 0 but less than 1. However, for many uses of numbers, a value that is less than 1 is not very helpful. Therefore, the computer can be told to pick a number that is greater than 1 by using multiplication:

    10 LET A = 10 * RND(1)

This statement tells the computer to pick a number that is greater than 0 and less than 1 and then to multiply that number by 10. The variable name A is then assigned whatever number is picked as its value.

Program 6.3

This program has the computer choose and then print 5 random numbers:

```
10  FOR J = 1 TO 5
20  PRINT 10 * RND (1)
30  NEXT J

]RUN
8.69869877
5.69059111
2.27749396
.630244402
1.98392672
```

There are several things to notice about these numbers. First, the numbers are all decimal fractions. This can be a problem because quite often a programmer wants to use whole numbers such as 1, 2, 3, 4, etc. Second, the computer never picked 10 as one of the numbers, and as many times as this program is run, 10 will never be picked. The computer will not pick 10 because first it picks a number that is less than 1 and only 10 * 1 will cause the computer to output 10 in line 20.

More Useful Random Numbers

By using the integer function, a programmer can tell the computer to pick only whole numbers.

Program 6.4

This program picks 10 random integers by multiplying the RND(1) by 10 and prints them on the screen:

```
10  FOR J = 1 TO 10
20  PRINT  INT (10 * RND (1)),
30  NEXT J

]RUN
0          4          1
8          1          3
3          4          4
3
1
```

The value of each of these integers is between 0 and 9. RND(1) was multiplied by 10 and there are ten possible integers that can be displayed as output (0, 1, 2, 3, 4, 5, 6, 7, 8, 9). It is easy to forget that 0 is a digit. The computer did what it was told. It picked one of 10 integers, but it still could not pick 10 because RND(1) picks a fraction that is greater than 0 and less than 1.

By adding 1 to whatever number the computer picks on line 20, the computer can be told to pick any whole number from 1 to 10:

20 PRINT INT(10 * RND(1) +1)

If 0 is the integer picked, adding 1 will give us a 1 as the final result. If 9 is the integer picked, adding 1 will give us 10 as the final result. When the program is run again, it may pick 10 but it will never pick 0:

```
RUN
3            2            8
10           7            9
2            1            5
4
```

Review

5. Write a program that picks 10 random integers from 1 to 100:

```
RUN
27           42           89
68           17           75
5            53           94
28
```

6. Write a program that picks two random integers from 1 to 25 and then adds them together and prints their result:

```
RUN
17 + 3 = 20
```

Choosing Numbers from a Range

The computer can also be told to pick random numbers that are within a specific range where 1 is not the lowest number. For example, picking numbers that are between 5 and 10, 10 and 20 or 100 and 200 is done by using the following formula. In this formula, the letter A stands for the lowest number in the range, and the letter B stands for the highest number in the range of numbers:

$$INT((B - A + 1) * RND(1) + A)$$

To pick a number that is greater than or equal to 10 and less than or equal to 20, the formula is used to write:

$$LET\ X = INT((11 * RND(1) + 10)$$

To give the variable X its value the computer does four things. First, it picks a number that is greater than 0 but less than 1. Then, that number is multiplied by 11 (20 − 10 + 1). Third, 10 is added to that number. Finally, the variable name X is assigned the integer value of the number that was picked.

Program 6.5

This program creates 3 addition problems by picking two random numbers as addends. The computer then waits for the program user to enter a correct answer:

```
10  FOR J = 1 TO 3
20  LET A = INT (400 * RND (1) + 100)
30  LET B = INT (100 * RND (1) + 1)
40  LET C = A + B
50  PRINT A" + "B" = ";
60  INPUT D
70  IF D = C THEN PRINT "GOOD SHOW!"
80  IF D < > C THEN PRINT "SORRY! TRY AGAIN."
90  PRINT
100 IF D < > C THEN 50
110 NEXT J
120 END

]RUN
162 + 72 =? 234
GOOD SHOW!

419 + 28 =? 447
GOOD SHOW!

404 + 71 =? 476
SORRY! TRY AGAIN.

404 + 71 =? 475
GOOD SHOW!
```

On line 20 the computer assigns variable A the integer value of a number that it chooses from within the range 100 to 499. On line 30 the computer assigns variable B the integer value of a number from within the range 1 to 100. The IF ... THEN statement on line 70 tells the computer whether the answer is right or wrong. The IF ... THEN on line 100 tells the computer to repeat the current problem if the answer was incorrect.

Review

7. Write a program that will output 15 random integers from 10 to 20.

8. Write a program that selects one random integer from 25 to 50 and another from 1 to 25 and outputs their difference:

   RUN
   37 − 17 = 20

Rounding Errors

Like all machines, computers are limited in some of the things they can do. Just as you cannot drive the average family car at 300 miles an hour or get 200 miles to the gallon, you cannot get a computer to do things that as a machine it is not capable of doing. One of these limitations causes the computer to make a slight error in some of its calculations. A good programmer, therefore, must be aware that the results of some calculations can be inaccurate. When this occurs, it is called a rounding error. For example:

PRINT 5.7879 − 5
.787800001

PRINT 7 ∧ 2
49.00000001

The results of these calculations are not accurate. Subtracting 5 from 5.7879 should give .7879 not .787800001. In the second example, 7∧2 should be 49 not 49.0000001. The errors are small and usually will not cause any difficulty. However, a problem can arise when the computer is told to compare values in an IF . . . THEN statement:

IF 7 ∧ 2 = 7 * 7 THEN PRINT "THEY ARE EQUAL"

The computer will not see that these two statements are equivalent. Both 7∧2 and 7 * 7 should have 49 as their result, but 49.0000001 is not equal to 49: therefore, THEY ARE EQUAL will not be printed.

Scientific Notation/ E Notation

As a machine, there are also limits to the size of a number that the computer can store in its memory.

PRINT 123456789 * 123456789
1.52415788E+16

The computer can store numbers that have up to 9 digits plus a decimal point. To work with numbers that have more than 9 digits, the computer rounds off the number and uses scientific notation. Scientific notation uses the code letter E as in 2.934E+7 followed by a sign and a number. If the E is followed by a plus sign, the number must be multiplied by 10 that number of times:

1.52415788E+16 = 15,241,578,800,000,000
                 ‾‾‾‾‾‾‾‾‾‾‾‾‾‾‾‾‾‾‾‾‾‾
                    16 places to the right

A minus sign means multiplying by 1/10 that many times:

3.56768788E−4 = .000356768788
                ‾‾‾‾‾‾‾‾‾‾‾‾‾
                4 places to the left

The minus sign tells us to move the decimal point to the left that many places.

$$2.934E+7 = 29340000.$$
7 places to the right

$$2.934E-7 = .0000002934$$
7 places to the left

$$3.7E+3 = 3700.$$
3 places to the right

$$3.7E-3 = .0037$$
3 places to the left

Though most of the math work that is done in this book does not require E notation, there are times when such numbers will appear and a good programmer must know what these numbers mean.

The computer will accept E notation as a number in any situation where a number can be used. This includes DATA statements. The E in DATA 5.8943E+6 will not cause an error message.

Review

9. Change the following from E notation to standard notation:

   a.) 1.42E−2   b.) 4.321E5
   c.) 4.56231E8   d.) 5E−3
   e.) 6.7087E6   f.) 6.7896E−5

10. What will be the output of the following program? Make your prediction, then type it in to see if you were correct:

```
10 FOR J = 1 TO 3
20 READ A
30 PRINT A
40 NEXT J
50 PRINT "ALL DATA READ"
60 DATA .5E−2, 1.234E+5, 1.984E−5
```

Rounding Fractions Off

A programmer can correct the computer's rounding error by "rounding off." Besides correcting a rounding error, there are many situations where a programmer does not need or want numbers that are carried out to the nearest millionth or billionth. However, the computer does its calculations this way automatically. Therefore, the computer must be given instructions to round numbers off as part of the program.

However, before a programmer can plan the instructions for the computer, the programmer must understand how a procedure is done and why the procedure works the way that it does. In this case, a programmer must know what the "rule" for rounding numbers off is and why the rule works the way it does.

The rule for rounding a number off to a specific decimal place is a simple one:
- If the number to the right of the digit being rounded is 5 or greater, increase the rounded digit by 1.
- If the digit to the right of the rounded digit is less than 5, leave the rounded digit as it is.
- Then drop off any digits to the right of the rounded digit and use only the remaining number.

Therefore, 5.587 rounded to the nearest hundredth is 5.59 because the 7 in the thousandths place is greater than 5. On the other hand, 4.1234 would be rounded to 4.12 because the 3 in the thousandths place is less than 5.

The way that the rule to round a number to a specific decimal place works is also very simple.

- If adding 5 to a digit makes the digit's value equal to or greater than 10, then a 1 is added to the digit to the left.

$$\begin{array}{r} 5.587 \\ + .005 \\ \hline 5.592 \end{array}$$

- If adding 5 to a digit makes the digit's value less than 10, then there is no change in the value of the digit to the left.

$$\begin{array}{r} 4.1234 \\ + .005 \\ \hline 4.1284 \end{array}$$

- Then all digits to the left of the rounded digit are dropped off and only the number to the left is used.

$$\begin{array}{c} 4.1284 \\ 4.12 \end{array}$$

With an understanding of how the rule works, a programmer can now plan instructions that will tell the computer how to carry out this operation.

For example, to instruct the computer to round off 3.786 to the nearest hundredth will require the following steps:

FIRST: Add 5 to the digit in the thousandths place:

```
10 LET A = 3.786 + .005
```

The result of this is 3.791. The digit in the hundredths place has been rounded up by 1, but now the digit to the right of the 9 must be dropped off.

SECOND: Multiply this number by 100. This will move the decimal point over two places to the right:

```
10 LET A = 3.786 + .005
20 LET B = A * 100
```

The computer now has the number 379.1 to work with.

THIRD: Use the integer function to tell the computer to drop off the remaining decimal places:

> 10 LET A = 3.786 + .005
> 20 LET B = INT(A * 100)

This will leave the number 379 for the computer to work with.

FOURTH: Put the decimal point back by multiplying the integer by the value of the place being rounded to. In this example that is the hundredths place, .01:

> 10 LET A = 3.786 + .005
> 20 LET B = INT(A * 100)
> 30 LET C = B * .01

The final result of these calculations is 3.79.

> 40 PRINT C
> RUN
> 3.79

The number 3.786 has been rounded off to the nearest hundredth. These steps can be used to round any number off to any place a programmer wishes. The first two calculations can be combined into one statement, LET B = INT (3.786 + .005) * 100). The last step, however, should remain a separate command. When all three steps are combined in one statement, the rounding error sneaks back in causing the rounded off fraction to be occasionally inaccurate.

Program 6.6

This program rounds off batting averages to the nearest thousandth of a point:

```
10   PRINT "BATTING AVERAGE CALCULATOR"
20   INPUT "ENTER TIMES AT BAT: ";B
30   INPUT "ENTER NUMBER OF HITS: ";H
40   LET T = H / B
50   LET A =  INT (T * 1000 + .5)
60   LET A = A * .001
70   PRINT
80   PRINT "YOUR AVERAGE IS "A

]RUN
BATTING AVERAGE CALCULATOR
ENTER TIMES AT BAT: 12
ENTER NUMBER OF HITS: 4

YOUR AVERAGE IS .333
```

Lines 40, 50 and 60 calculate the batting average and round it off to the thousandth place. Variable T is the average before it is rounded off. On line 50, .0005 is added to the value of variable T to begin the rounding off process. Variable A is assigned the integer value of that result multiplied by 1000, which drops off any fraction that is left over. On line 60, the value of variable A is multiplied by .001 to return the decimal point to its proper place.

Review

11. Write a program that rounds off 25.92 to the nearest tenth.

    RUN
    25.92 TO THE NEAREST TENTH IS 25.9

EXERCISES

1. Perform each of the following computations on paper. Check your results by using immediate mode on the computer:

   a.) 33 − 5 + 16   b.) 3 * 2 + 2 * 3
   c.) 33 − (5 + 16)   d.) 3 * (2 + 2) * (3 + 2)
   e.) (25 + 30) / 25 + 3   f.) ((10 + 5) / 3) + 2 * 15
   g.) 15 / 3 + 2   h.) (10 + 5) / (5 − 2)
   i.) 2 ∧ 3   j.) 2 ∧ (2 + 1)

2. What is the exact output of the following program? Type the program into the computer's memory and run it to check your prediction:

   ```
   10    LET A = 3
   20    PRINT "THE VALUE OF B IS ";
   30    LET B = A + 4 * 4
   40    PRINT B
   ```

3. Linda has a problem with her perimeter program. It is supposed to calculate the distance around a rectangle, but it does not work correctly. Help Linda out by finding the error and then correct the program and type it in to check it:

   ```
   10    INPUT "ENTER WIDTH: ";W
   20    INPUT "ENTER LENGTH: ";L
   30    LET P = 2 * L + W
   40    PRINT "THE PERIMETER IS "P
   ```

4. Write a program to calculate your pay if you receive $3.65 cents an hour. You worked 2 hours Monday, 1.5 hours Tuesday, 0 hours Wednesday, 3.25 hours Thursday and 3 hours Friday. Do all the calculations in one statement.

   ```
   RUN
   SALARY EARNED = $35.7875
   ```

5. Marilyn and Harry Hacker are having an argument. She says her program will tell if any number is an even number. Harry says it will not. You decide and then type it in and test it out:

```
10   PRINT "EVEN NUMBER TESTER"
20   INPUT "ENTER A NUMBER: ";N
30   IF N / 2 =  INT (N / 2) THEN 60
40   PRINT N" IS ODD."
50   GOTO 20
60   PRINT N" IS EVEN."
70   INPUT "ANOTHER NUMBER TO TEST? ";A$
80   IF A$ = "YES" OR A$ = "Y" THEN 20
```

6. Tennis balls are packed three to a can. Write a program that will tell how many cans are needed if the number of balls is entered as input:

   RUN
   ENTER NUMBER OF TENNIS BALLS? 368
   CANS NEEDED = 122

7. There is a problem in Joe Kolodnigork's program. It is supposed to tell how many planes are needed to move all the passengers who have arrived at the airport when each plane holds 256 people. Even Harry Hacker cannot find the "glich" though. They have asked for your help. Sometimes the program comes up with the right answer and sometimes it does not. Below is a run of the program and a listing. Help them out and tell them what is missing:

   ]RUN
   NUMBER OF PASSENGERS 2148
   NUMBER OF PLANES NEEDED 9

   NUMBER OF PASSENGERS 1024
   NUMBER OF PLANES NEEDED 5

   ]LIST

```
10   LET C = 256
20   FOR J = 1 TO 2
30   READ N
40   LET P =  INT (N / C) + 1
50   PRINT "NUMBER OF PASSENGERS "N
60   PRINT "NUMBER OF PLANES NEEDED "P
70   PRINT
80   NEXT J
90   DATA  2148,1024
```

8. Write a program that chooses two random numbers from 1 to 12 and then asks the program user to enter the product:

>   RUN
>   6 * 7 = ?42
>   RIGHT ON!
>
>   3 * 4 = ?

9. Probability is the branch of mathematics that allows us to predict how likely an event is to take place.
   a.) Write a program that simulates the flipping of a coin 100 times. Have the computer count how many heads and how many tails occur and print the results:

>   RUN
>   FLIPPING
>   HEADS = 43
>   TAILS = 57

   b.) Change the program so that the program user tries to guess whether heads or tails wins. Have the computer tell if the guess was correct or not:

>   RUN
>   WHICH WILL WIN HEADS (H) OR TAILS (T)?
>   ENTER YOUR GUESS? H
>
>   FLIPPING
>   HEADS = 49
>   TAILS = 51
>   TAILS WON!
>   YOU PICKED HEADS

10. Write a program that simulates the rolling of two 6 sided dice. Have the program print the result for each die and their total:

>   RUN
>   DIE #1   DIE #2
>   3   5
>   TOTAL
>   8

11. There are 2.54 centimeters in an inch. Write a program that converts inches to centimeters:

>   RUN
>   ENTER THE NUMBER OF INCHES? 10
>   10 INCHES = 25.4 CENTIMETERS

12. Write a program that reads the following test grades from data statements and calculates their average. Round the answer to the nearest tenth of a point:

```
          RUN
          TEST   GRADES              TEST AVERAGE
          88 67 93 62 89 90           81.5
```

13. The area of a right triangle is found by multiplying the product of the base and the height by 1/2 (1/2 * (b * h)). Write a program that enters the base and height in meters as input and calculates the area in square meters:

    ```
    ENTER BASE IN METERS: ? .651
    ENTER HEIGHT IN METERS: ? .956
    AREA = .311178 SQUARE METERS

    ANOTHER TRIANGLE TO COMPUTE?
    ```

14. Each number printed by Lisa's program should be an integer. Correct the "bug" in Lisa's program so that only integers are printed:

    ```
    10  FOR J = 1 TO 10
    20  PRINT J" SQUARED = "J ^ 2
    30  NEXT J

    ]RUN
    1 SQUARED = 1
    2 SQUARED = 4
    3 SQUARED = 9
    4 SQUARED = 16
    5 SQUARED = 25
    6 SQUARED = 36
    7 SQUARED = 49.0000001
    8 SQUARED = 64
    9 SQUARED = 81.0000001
    10 SQUARED = 100
    ```

15. Write a program that calculates the following fractional parts of a meter: ¼, ⅓, ½, ⅝, ⅔, ¾ and ⅞. Round the result off to the nearest thousandth of a meter.

    ```
    RUN
    1/2 OF A METER = .250 METERS
    1/3 OF A METER = .333 METERS

    BREAK IN 20
    ```

7

GRAPHICS AND COLOR

HTAB/VTAB
HOME
FLASH
INVERSE
NORMAL
GR/TEXT
COLOR
PLOT
HLIN/VLIN
HGR/HGR2
HCOLOR
HPLOT

Often, a picture or graphic display is the best way to communicate a message across in a program. On the Apple, graphic displays can be created in three ways. The simplest pictures can be drawn using only cursor control statements and characters enhanced with flash or reverse lettering. More complicated pictures require the use of either low- or high-resolution graphics. A low-resolution mode picture is constructed with small box-like shapes which the user plots on the screen, while high-resolution graphics uses smaller blocks which allow for more detail. Both low- and high-resolution mode pictures can be displayed in a number of colors. This chapter will cover the statements and commands needed to create graphics using each of the three screen modes.

HTAB and VTAB

In an earlier chapter, we saw how we could produce graphic images on the screen using the PRINT TAB statement. A more efficient way of producing the same results is by using the HTAB and VTAB statements.

It is best to visualize the text screen as divided into many small boxes contained in horizontal and vertical rows. Each one of these boxes holds one character of information. On the Apple, these boxes form a grid of 24 vertical positions and 40 horizontal positions.

The VTAB statement allows us to move the cursor to any one of the vertical positions and may have any value between 1 and 24, inclusive. The statements:

```
10 VTAB 10
20 PRINT "*"
```

would print an asterisk 10 rows down on the left side of the screen.

The HTAB statement allows us to move the cursor horizontally along the edge of the screen and may have any value between 1 and 40, inclusive. Adding the statement:

```
15 HTAB 20
```

would now print the asterisk 10 rows down and 20 spaces from the left side of the screen.

HOME

It is often helpful to start with the cursor in the same position on a clear screen. This is accomplished through the use of the HOME statement. For example:

```
10 HOME
```

will erase the screen and move the cursor to the upper-left corner of the screen. It is important to remember that only the screen is being erased, not the contents of memory. Your program will still be in the computer's memory after HOME has been executed.

Program 7.1

This program will randomly place your name 20 times on the screen:

```
10   HOME
20   INPUT "ENTER YOUR NAME: ";N$
30   HOME
40   FOR I = 1 TO 20
50   A = INT ( RND (1) * 20) + 1
60   B = INT ( RND (1) * 20) + 1
70   VTAB A
80   HTAB B
90   PRINT N$
100  NEXT I
110  END
```

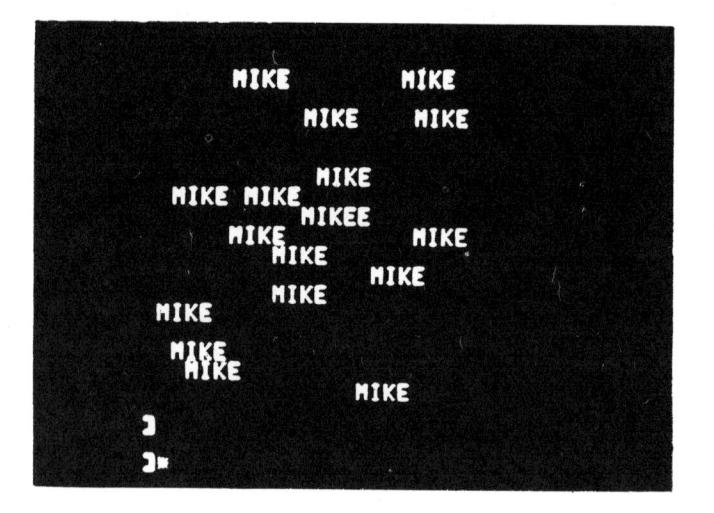

- **Line 10:** Clears the screen of any previous output.
- **Line 20:** Accepts your name as input.
- **Line 30:** Clears the screen and moves the cursor to position (1,1).
- **Line 40:** Initiates the loop which will print your name 20 times.
- **Line 50:** Generates a random number between 1 and 20.
- **Line 60:** Generates a second random number between 1 and 20.
- **Line 70:** Moves the cursor to a line A rows down from the top of the screen.
- **Line 80:** Moves the cursor B spaces from the left side of the screen.
- **Line 90:** Prints your name at the current cursor position.
- **Line 100:** Completes the loop.
- **Line 110:** Ends the program after the name has been printed twenty times.

Graphics and Color   7-3

Review

1. Write a program that will place the word APPLE approximately at the middle of the screen.

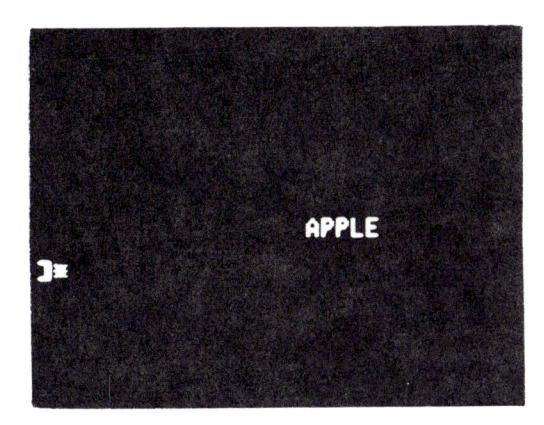

2. Write a program to print an asterisk in each of the four corners of the screen. Use a READ...DATA statement to input your screen positions.

FLASH, INVERSE and NORMAL

The output of a PRINT statement can have one of three characteristics: the output can blink, it can be in inverse, or it can be normal. The FLASH statement causes the output of following PRINT statements to blink on the screen. That is everything printed on the screen after the FLASH statement is executed will blink. The INVERSE statement allows characters to be printed in inverse, much like a photographic negative. Normally, characters appear on the screen in white on a black background. However, with INVERSE, characters can appear in black on a white background, but the white background appears only behind those characters printed. The NORMAL statement cancels the effect that FLASH and INVERSE have on the PRINT statement. Be aware that when INVERSE or

FLASH is used on the Apple IIe computer, lower-case characters (e.g., a-z) will produce unusual results. For example, typing a lower-case T in FLASH mode will produce a blinking digit 4. When using upper-case, there is no such problem.

Program 7.2

This program illustrates the effects of the FLASH, INVERSE and NORMAL statements:

```
10  PRINT "THIS IS NORMAL"
20  FLASH
30  PRINT "THIS IS FLASH"
40  INVERSE
50  PRINT "THIS IS INVERSE"
60  NORMAL
70  PRINT "BACK TO NORMAL AGAIN"
```

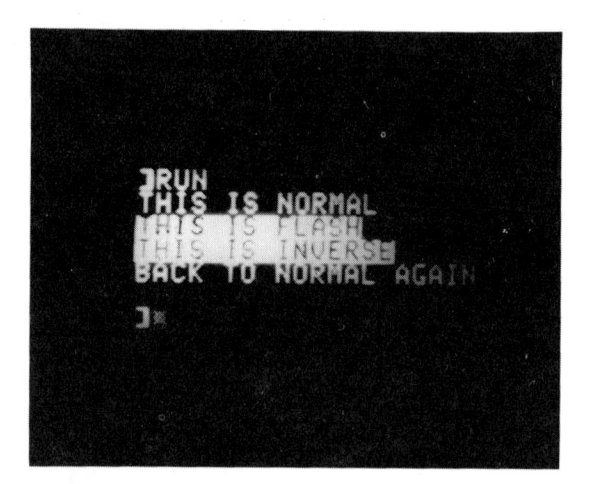

- **Line 10:** Prints the message THIS IS NORMAL.
- **Line 20:** Sets any subsequent PRINT to FLASH.
- **Line 30:** Prints THIS IS FLASH which flashes on and off.
- **Line 40:** Sets any following PRINT to INVERSE, and cancels the FLASH from line 20.
- **Line 50:** Prints THIS IS INVERSE in inverse characters.
- **Line 60:** Sets any following output to PRINT in NORMAL style, canceling the effect of the INVERSE in line 40.
- **Line 70:** Prints BACK TO NORMAL AGAIN.

Review

3. Uncle Bill's Whamburgers is having a special. They are selling a regular whamburger, fries and a drink for $1.39 and need a flashing sign to promote the special. Write a program to help them out.

Graphics and Color 7-5

```
UNCLE BILL'S WHAMBURGERS
     WEEKLY SPECIAL
   REGULAR WHAMBURGER
      FRIES & DRINK

        ONLY $1.39
```

4. Uncle Bill said your sign was good, but the flashing was distracting his customers. What changes must be made so that the sign is in inverse print while the price is still flashing?

LOW-RESOLUTION GRAPHICS

The low-resolution graphics mode divides the screen into an invisible 40 by 40 grid and gives the user a selection of 16 colors which can be used to fill the rectangles in the grid. The valid X and Y values of the grid range between 0 and 39, inclusive, where X is the horizontal coordinate and Y the vertical coordinate. The origin (0,0) of the grid is located in the upper-left corner of the display screen. The grid occupies the top portion of the screen, while the bottom 4 lines of the screen contain a small "text window" for program lines and character output. All of the graphing statements discussed may be used either in immediate mode or in a program.

GR *and* TEXT

In order to enter the low-resolution mode, the programmer must use the GR statement either in immediate mode or in a program. GR will clear the 40 by 40 grid on the user's display in preparation for graphics. For example:

20 GR

erases the screen and prepares the computer to accept low-resolution graphics statements.

In order to leave the low-resolution graphics mode and return to normal mode, use the TEXT statement. If the line

40 TEXT

is typed while you are in low-resolution graphics, the computer is reset to normal mode, but the screen is not completely cleared. The low-resolution graphics currently on the screen will be lost, and the screen will be filled with miscellaneous characters and text. HOME can be used to clear the screen.

COLOR

When plotting points and lines in low-resolution graphics, the programmer can use the COLOR variable. A value between 0 and 15 is assigned to this variable to select one of 16 colors. The COLOR variable is set like any other variable. For example, the line:

120 COLOR = 9

will set the value of the COLOR variable to 9, which represents the color orange. Thereafter, all points plotted will be orange until the value of COLOR is changed. The COLOR variable is set to zero automatically when the GR statement is used. The valid colors are:

0 - Black	4 - Dark Green	8 - Brown	12 - Green
1 - Red	5 - Gray	9 - Orange	13 - Yellow
2 - Dark Blue	6 - Medium Blue	10 - Gray	14 - Aqua
3 - Purple	7 - Light Blue	11 - Pink	15 - White

PLOT

In low-resolution mode, the PLOT statement is used to plot a single brick-shaped area on the screen in the 40 by 40 grid. The color of the brick is determined by the COLOR variable. The statement

20 PLOT X,Y

will plot a brick at the coordinates (X,Y). Remember that the values for X and Y range from 0 to 39.

Program 7.3

The following program will plot 3 red bricks on the screen at the points (12,32), (29,11), and (1,2):

```
10  GR
20  COLOR= 1
30  PLOT 12,32
40  PLOT 29,11
50  PLOT 1,2
```

HLIN

The HLIN statement is used to plot, while in low-resolution mode, a horizontal line of bricks. The statement

30 HLIN X1, X2 AT Y

will plot a horizontal line from point (X1,Y) to (X2,Y). The color of the line will be the last one set by the COLOR variable before the HLIN statement is executed. For example,

30 HLIN 10,30 AT 22

will draw a line from coordinates (10,22) to (30,22). If COLOR = 9 when line 30 is executed, then the line will be orange.

VLIN

The VLIN statement operates similarly to the HLIN statement but produces a vertical line. The statement

$$180 \text{ VLIN Y1, Y2 AT X}$$

will plot a vertical line from point (X,Y1) to (X,Y2). The color of the line will depend on the last setting of the COLOR variable. For example,

$$180 \text{ VLIN 0,29 AT 21}$$

will draw a vertical line from coordinates (21,0) to (21,29). Assuming that COLOR = 1 when line 180 is executed, a red line will be produced.

Program 7.4

This program demonstrates the various statements used in low-resolution graphing:

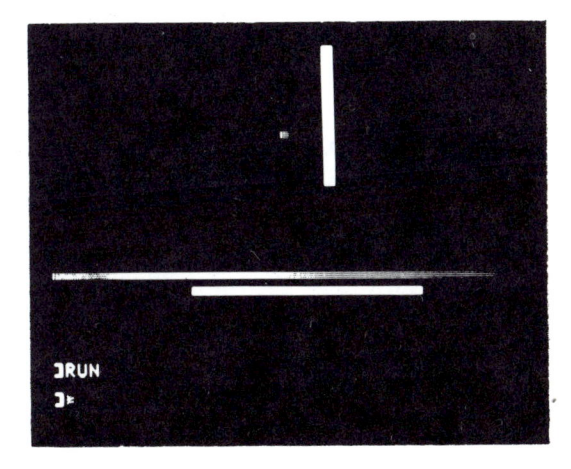

```
10  GR
20  COLOR= 1
30  PLOT 20,12
40  HLIN 0,39 AT 30
50  COLOR= 15
60  HLIN 12,32 AT 32
70  VLIN 1,18 AT 24
```

- **Line 10:** The GR statement prepares the screen for graphing.
- **Line 20:** This line selects the color red.
- **Line 30:** A red brick is PLOTted at location (20,12).
- **Line 40:** A horizontal line is drawn from location (0,30) to (39,30).
- **Line 50:** The COLOR is now changed to white (COLOR=15).
- **Line 60:** A horizontal line is drawn in white from point (12,32) to (32,32).
- **Line 70:** A vertical line is drawn in white from point (24,1) to (24,18).

Program 7.5	This program uses low-resolution graphics to draw a large red X (using PLOT) with a green border around the screen (using HLIN and VLIN).

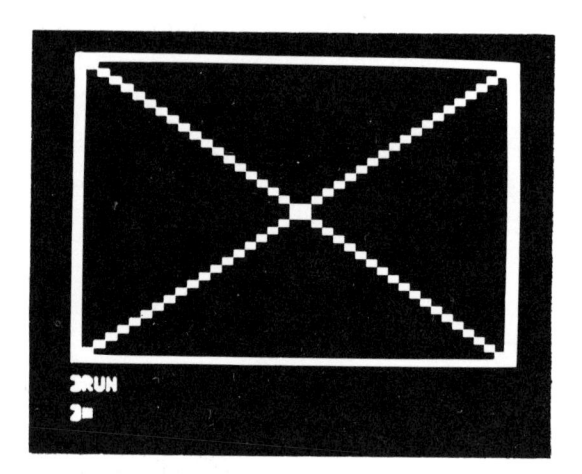

```
10  GR
20  COLOR= 12
30  HLIN 0,39 AT 0
40  HLIN 0,39 AT 39
50  VLIN 0,39 AT 0
60  VLIN 0,39 AT 39
70  REM   Now draw the red "X"
80  COLOR= 1
90  FOR I = 1 TO 38
100   PLOT I,I
110   PLOT 39 - I,I
120   NEXT I
```

- **Line 10:** Prepares the screen for graphing.
- **Line 20:** Sets the COLOR to green (COLOR = 12).
- **Line 30:** Draws a horizontal line at the top of the screen.
- **Line 40:** Draws a horizontal line at the bottom of the screen.
- **Line 50:** Draws a vertical line on the left side of the screen.
- **Line 60:** Draws a vertical line on the right side of the screen.
- **Line 80:** Sets the COLOR to red (COLOR = 1).
- **Line 90:** Initiates loop to draw the "X".
- **Line 100:** Plots a brick to form one diagonal line.
- **Line 110:** Plots the other diagonal line to form the other side of the "X".
- **Line 120:** Completes the loop.

Review

5. Have the computer draw a large, purple letter "L" in the upper-left corner of the low-resolution graphics screen.

Graphics and Color 7-9

6. Have the computer draw a large, orange letter "i" with the dot at the coordinates (14,25).

HIGH-RESOLUTION GRAPHICS

High-resolution graphics enables the user to draw more finely detailed images than those drawn in low-resolution graphics because the display screen is divided into a grid of dots which are smaller and far more numerous than the bricks used in low-resolution graphics. There are two modes used in high-resolution graphics. One uses the entire screen for a 192 by 280 display grid. The other reserves a 4 line text window which reduces the grid to 160 rows by 280 columns. As in low-resolution graphics, the origin (0,0) is located at the upper-left corner of the screen.

HGR and HGR2 The HGR and HGR2 statements are used to switch the display screen into high-resolution graphics mode. The HGR statement reserves a text window at the bottom of the screen, while the HGR2 statement uses the entire screen for graphing. Execution of either statement will clear the high-resolution graphics screen. Valid examples are:

70 HGR

and

45 HGR2

HCOLOR

When plotting in high-resolution graphics, use the HCOLOR variable for color selection. A range of 8 colors is available, numbered 0 to 7, inclusive. For example, the statement

139 HCOLOR = 1

will set the value of the HCOLOR variable to 1, thus selecting the color green. All following graphing will be done in green until the HCOLOR variable is changed. The valid colors for high-resolution graphics are:

| 0 - Black | 2 - Purple | 4 - Black | 6 - Blue |
| 1 - Green | 3 - White 1 | 5 - Red | 7 - White 2 |

Because of the variation in colors produced by different displays, the colors produced may not agree exactly with those in the table.

HPLOT

The HPLOT statement is used for drawing both points and lines in high-resolution graphics. The statement

20 HPLOT X,Y

will draw a single point at the coordinates (X,Y). The X-coordinate can vary from 0 to 279. If HGR is used, the Y-coordinate can vary from 0 to 159. If HGR2 is used it can vary from 0 to 191. The HPLOT statement can be modified to draw lines. The statement

180 HPLOT X1, Y1 TO X2, Y2

draws a line from the point (X1, Y1) to (X2, Y2) whose color is dependent upon the current value of the HCOLOR variable. Several connecting lines can be drawn in a single statement. For example, the statement

210 HPLOT X1, Y1 TO X2, Y2 TO X3, Y3

draws a line from (X1,Y1) to (X2,Y2) and another line from (X2,Y2) to (X3,Y3). The modifier TO can be added to the HPLOT statement as many times as needed except for the restriction that every program line is limited to 239 characters.

If the first set of coordinates after the word HPLOT is omitted, a line is drawn from the last point plotted by a previous HPLOT statement to the point specified after the word TO. The color of the new line will be that of the last point plotted and not the color corresponding to the current value of the HCOLOR variable. An example of this form of HPLOT statement is

40 HPLOT TO X,Y

Because of the way the Apple displays colors, there may be some difficulty with the color of points and vertical lines in high-resolution graphics. This difficulty can be avoided by plotting even numbered colors at points with even numbered X-coordinates, and odd numbered colors at points with odd numbered X-coordinates. For example, to plot a red (HCOLOR = 5) line with an X-coordinate of 21, use the statement

20 HPLOT 21,3 TO 21,12

Should we attempt to plot a red line with an X-coordinate of 22, the statement

20 HPLOT 22,3 TO 22,12

will plot a black line which cannot be seen against the screen's black background.

The only exception to this rule is the color white, HCOLOR = 3 or HCOLOR = 7. It is impossible to draw a single white vertical line or a single white point on the screen. To generate white vertical lines, draw two vertical lines next to each other with either HCOLOR = 3 or HCOLOR = 7.

Also, care must be taken to avoid drawing two differently colored vertical lines next to each other on the screen, since the resulting color will rarely be as intended.

Program 7.6

The following program using high-resolution graphing statements, constructs a green border around the display area and plots a single blue point:

```
10  HGR
20  HCOLOR= 1
30  HPLOT 1,1 TO 279,1 TO 279,159
40  HPLOT    TO 1,159
50  HPLOT    TO 1,1
60  HCOLOR= 6
70  HPLOT 140,80
```

- **Line 10:** Prepares the screen for high-resolution graphing.
- **Line 20:** Sets the color to green.
- **Line 30:** Plots a line across the top of the screen and continues it along the right side.
- **Line 40:** Continuation of the HPLOT statement in line 30 which plots a line along the bottom of the screen.
- **Line 50:** Continuation of the HPLOT statement in line 40 which plots a line along the left side of the screen.
- **Line 60:** Sets the color to blue.
- **Line 70:** Plots a point, in blue, at coordinates (140,80).

Lines 30 through 50 draw the green border around the edge of the display screen. Note that the last point plotted before line 40 was (279,159) at line 30. Therefore, line 40 has the same effect as the statement

40 HPLOT 279,159 TO 1,159

A similar comment applies at line 50. Line 70 plots a single blue point at the center of the screen. Note that if line 30 is changed to

30 HPLOT 1,1 TO 278,1 TO 278,159

the right, vertical side of the border might be black and thus invisible since an attempt has been made to plot an odd numbered color with an even numbered X-coordinate.

Review

7. Using high-resolution mode (HGR) write a program which will draw 500 randomly colored "stars" at random points on the screen. A star consists of a single HPLOT dot. When finished, print the message "STARRY, STARRY NIGHT" in the text window at the bottom of the screen.

8. Create a high-resolution pattern shown below. The top point of the figure is at (0,0) and the bottom right corner of the figure is at (140,140). Note that all lines are straight and are 20 plot positions apart.

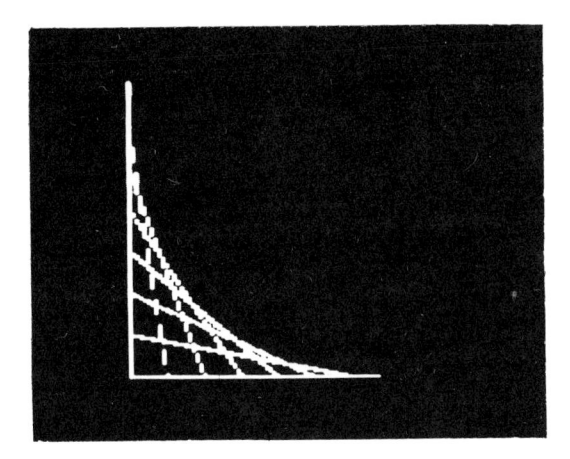

EXERCISES

1. Use HTAB and VTAB to draw an arrowhead of asterisks like the one shown below:

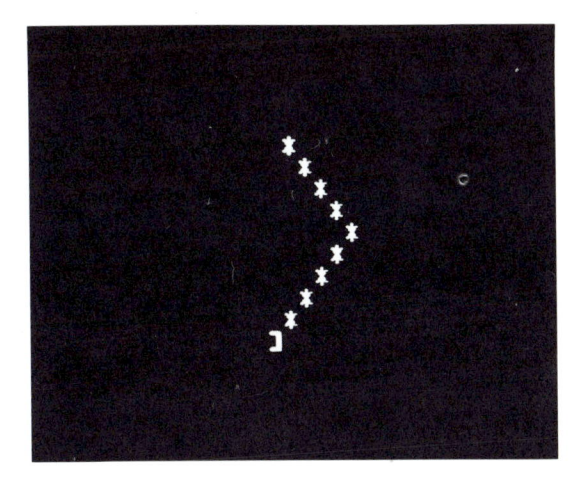

2. Write a program to create "MIKE'S MAGICAL MYSTERY SIGN." First clear the screen, then ask the user to INPUT whether the sign should be in NORMAL, FLASH, or INVERSE mode. Then clear the screen and print the words "MIKE'S MAGICAL MYSTERY SIGN" in the middle of the screen in the specified mode.

3. Using the low-resolution mode, have the computer draw a gray border around the edge of the graphing screen. Make the border 1 "brick" wide.

7-16   *Chapter Seven*

4. Using low-resolution mode, write a program to color the entire screen yellow except for a small, purple square (2 × 2) in the middle.

5. Have the computer draw a test pattern on the screen. This can be done by drawing 16 vertical lines on the screen, one of each color available in the low-resolution graphing mode. Each line should be two bricks wide.

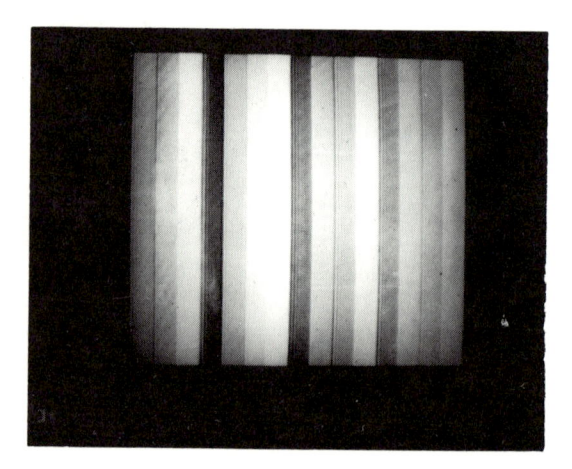

6. Have the computer draw an orange rectangle with its upper-left corner at (3,5). It should be 3 bricks wide and 2 bricks high.

7. Animation can be created by drawing a figure, blacking it out, then redrawing it one position away. Drop a red brick from the top of the screen to the bottom by continually drawing it, blacking it out, and then redrawing it one line lower.

8. Write a program that allows the user to INPUT a horizontal and vertical set of coordinates. Have the computer draw a point at that position in high-resolution mode in a randomly selected color.

9. Have the computer draw horizontal lines, one for each possible color of high-resolution graphics (except HCOLOR = 0). Each color should be separated by a black area, 10 lines wide:

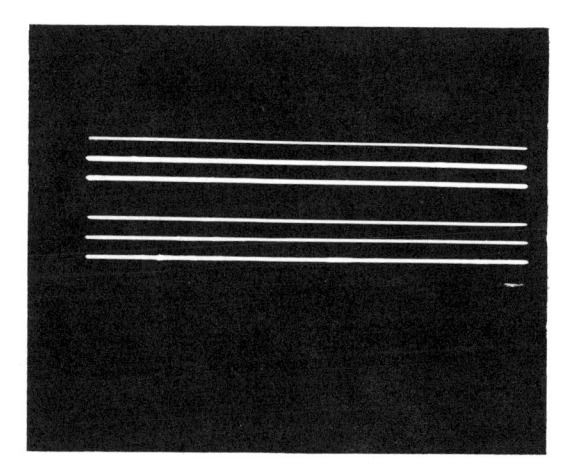

10. Using high-resolution mode, draw a blue, vertical line and a white, horizontal line which intersect at the coordinates (140,80):

11. Have the computer draw a purple right triangle with the corner points at (250,20), (250,110), and (130,110). Use only one HPLOT statement:

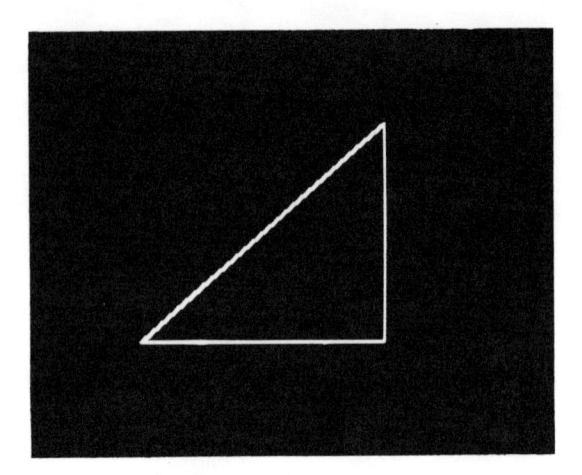

12. In high-resolution mode, draw a green letter "A" with the top at position (40,40) and the lowest point of the left side at (10,130).

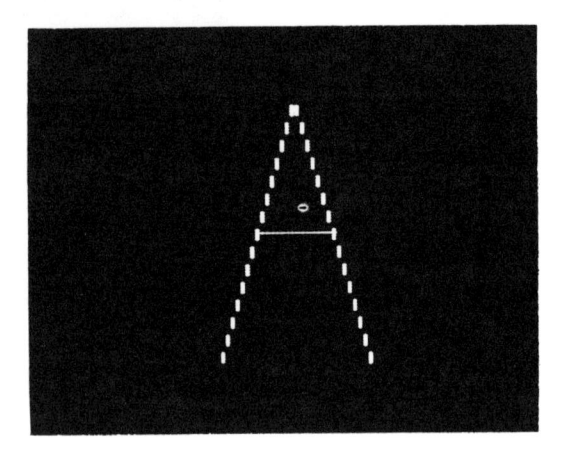

13. Have the computer produce the following logo in high-resolution graphics:

14. Create the following pattern in your choice of colors. The spokes radiate from the following points: (140,0), (140,159), (0,80), and (279,80). There are 28 spokes 10 positions apart radiating from points (140,0) and (140,159) and 20 spokes 8 positions apart radiating from points (0,80) and (279,80). Note: use the HGR screen:

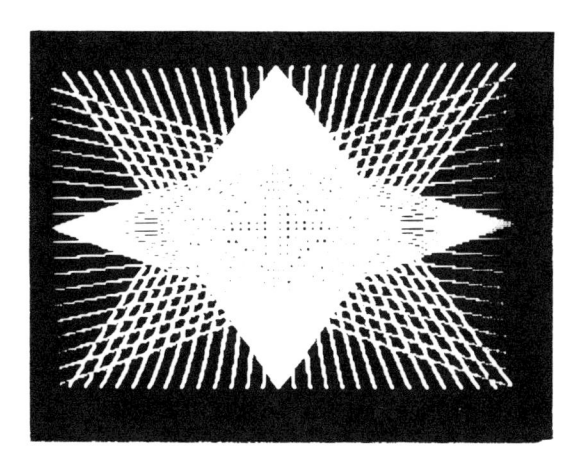

15. Harry Hacker and Joe Kolodnigork need help in designing their new robot, Ted. Help them out by writing a program in high-resolution graphics mode that will draw Ted the robot for them:

PROGRAM PLANNING

8

GOSUB
RETURN
ON...GOSUB...
ON...GOTO...
STOP
CONT

Program Planning

Writing programs that work properly and are well written requires planning and organization. Because the computer must be given many specific instructions in order to carry out even simple tasks, a program can easily become long and complex. Writing a program is much easier if time is first spent planning it. This chapter will explain several BASIC instructions and some techniques which help to simplify lengthy and complex programs. The chapter will also explain some of the ways they are used to find the correct programming errors.

Multiple Statement Lines

One way to simplify programs is to put more than 1 instruction on a line. This is done by using a colon ":" to separate statements. A colon can be used in this way at anytime. However, a line cannot be longer than 239 characters.

The colon is especially useful when it is used with an IF ... THEN statement. For example:

```
50 IF N <= 100 THEN PRINT "TOO SMALL": GOTO 90
```

Remember, the condition must be true for any statements after THEN to be carried out. This includes any and all statements added to a line by the use of the colon.

Program 8.1

Notice how this program is simplified by the use of the colon to place more than one statement on a line:

```
1  REM  A = A RANDOM NUMBER FROM 1 TO 400
2  REM  B = A RANDOM NUMBER FROM 1 TO 100
3  REM  C = THE SUM OF A AND B
4  REM  D = YOUR GUESS
10 FOR J = 1 TO 3
20 LET A =  INT (400 * RND (1) + 1)
30 LET B =  INT (100 * RND (1) + 1)
40 LET C = A + B
50 PRINT : PRINT A" + "B" = ";
60 INPUT D
70 IF D = C THEN  PRINT "GOOD SHOW!": GOTO 90
80 PRINT "SORRY! TRY AGAIN.": GOTO 50
90 NEXT J
```

```
]RUN

8 + 78 = ?86
GOOD SHOW!

221 + 62 = ?293
SORRY! TRY AGAIN.

221 + 62 = ?283
GOOD SHOW!

385 + 55 = ?440
GOOD SHOW.
```

- **Lines 1-4:** REM statements are used to define what each important variable represents. This is a good programming technique that should be used whenever a program is complicated or long.
- **Line 50:** The first PRINT on this line puts a blank line on the screen. This helps to separate the problem from any message that was just printed on the screen and makes the output on the screen easier to read.
- **Line 70:** When the condition on line 70 is true, the computer prints the message GOOD SHOW! The colon allows GOTO 90 to be part of this line. Therefore, the computer goes directly to line 90 after printing this message, skipping over line 80.

With two instructions on line 70, it is much easier to see what the program is supposed to do when a correct answer is entered. Likewise, it is also easier to follow the instructions the computer will execute when an incorrect answer is given if those instructions are on one line.

- **Line 80:** When the condition on line 70 is false, the computer prints the message SORRY! TRY AGAIN. The colon allows GOTO 50 to send the computer back to line 50 so that the problem can be repeated and a new answer entered. Because GOTO 90 was made part of line 70, there is no way that the computer can execute these instructions unless an incorrect answer was entered.
- **Line 90:** NEXT J marks the end of the loop. If J is not greater than 3, the loop will repeat.

The Need For Subroutines

To simplify longer, more complex programs, it is good programming practice to divide programs into sections called subroutines. A subroutine is a section of a program that carries out a specific task. A subroutine can be activated or called from anywhere in the program and are very useful in organizing and writing a program. For instance, by using subroutines a long program can be divided into a main section followed by a series of subroutines. The main section describes the order in which the subroutines will be called while each subroutine is written as if it were a short program that had only a simple task to perform. Another important use of subroutines is to reduce the size of a program by allowing a routine that is used several times to be written only once. Each time the programmer wants the computer to perform that task, the program simply tells the computer to call that subroutine.

GOSUB, RETURN

GOSUB is the instruction that calls a subroutine. The computer is sent to the beginning of a subroutine by:

20 GOSUB <line number>

This tells the computer to go to the line number where the instructions for the subroutine begin. When the subroutine has completed its task, the computer is told to go back to the point in the program from where the subroutine was called:

230 RETURN

The computer will then execute the next statement that follows the GOSUB which called the subroutine. For example:

```
10 . . . . . . . . . .
20 GOSUB 200
30 . . . . . . . . . .
40 . . . . . . . . . .
50 GOSUB 200
60 . . . . . . . . . .
70 END
200 . . . . . . . . . .
210 . . . . . . . . . .
220 . . . . . . . . . .
230 RETURN
```

When line 20 calls the subroutine at line 200, the RETURN on line 230 will send the computer back to line 30. When line 50 calls the subroutine at line 200, the RETURN will send the computer back to line 60. Though GOTO and GOSUB are similar, with GOSUB and RETURN the computer keeps track of where the program should go for its next instruction when the subroutine is finished. With GOTO, the computer does not keep track of where the next statement is.

Usually, subroutines are placed toward the end of a program. Therefore an END, such as the one on line 70 or another instruction like a GOTO is important in order to keep the computer from trying to execute a subroutine without being sent there by a GOSUB. When the computer executes a RETURN statement without having been sent to the subroutine by a GOSUB statement, the following error message will halt the program:

?RETURN WITHOUT GOSUB IN <line number>

To make subroutines stand out as part of the structure of a program it is a good idea to begin each subroutine with a REM statement that describes the subroutine and to follow the last line of the subroutine with a REM that tells which subroutine has been completed. Also, a blank REM or two before each subroutine will make the subroutine stand out even more. It is also a good idea to follow each GOSUB with a REM that names the subroutine that has been called. For example:

8-4 Chapter Eight

```
10.........
20 GOSUB 200 : REM ** NAME OF ROUTINE **
30.........
40.........
50 GOSUB 200 : REM ** NAME OF ROUTINE **
60.........
70 END
180 REM
190 REM
200 REM *** NAME OF ROUTINE ***
210.........
220.........
230.........
240 RETURN
250 REM *** END SUBROUTINE 200 ***
260 REM
270 REM
```

Throughout the remainder of this book, we will use REMs to identify subroutines and to make them a visible part of our program's structure:

Program 8.2

This program needs two numbers. One number is assigned to variable A and another number is assigned to variable B. The numbers are added together and their sum becomes the value of variable C. The program uses the same statement to pick these random numbers by placing the statement in a subroutine and calling the subroutine when a number is needed:

```
1   REM   A = A RANDOM NUMBER FROM 1 TO 100
2   REM   B = A RANDOM NUMBER FROM 1 TO 100
3   REM   C = THE SUM OF A AND B
4   REM   D = YOUR GUESS
5   REM   N = A RANDOM NUMBER FROM 1 TO 100
10  HOME
20  FOR J = 1 TO 3
30  GOSUB 200: REM   * PICK A RANDOM NUMBER *
40  LET A = N
50  GOSUB 200: REM   * PICK A RANDOM NUMBER *
60  LET B = N
70  LET C = A + B
80  PRINT : PRINT A" + "B" = ";
90  INPUT D
100 IF D = C THEN  PRINT "GOOD SHOW!": GOTO 120
110 PRINT "SORRY! TRY AGAIN.": GOTO 80
120 NEXT J
130 END
180 REM
190 REM
200 REM   *** PICK A NUMBER ***
210 LET N =   INT (100 * RND (1) + 1)
220 RETURN
230 REM   *** END OF SUBROUTINE ***
240 REM
250 REM
```

```
]RUN

8 + 78 = ?86
GOOD SHOW!

19 + 98 = ?119
SORRY! TRY AGAIN.

19 + 98 = ?117
GOOD SHOW!

83 + 81 = ?164
GOOD SHOW.
```

- **Line 30:** Calls the subroutine that begins at line 200. The computer goes to line 200 and on line 210 picks a random number and sets the value of variable N equal to that number. The computer then returns to line 40.
- **Line 40:** The computer is told to make variable A equal to the value of variable N.
- **Line 50:** Calls the subroutine at 200 again. Another number is chosen and variable N is assigned that number. This time, the RETURN on line 220 sends the computer back to line 60.
- **Line 60:** Variable B is made equal to the new value of variable N.
- **Lines 200-220:** The subroutine where variable N is assigned a random number between 1 and 100. The RETURN on line 220 will send the computer back to the point in the program where the subroutine was called.

Notice how the subroutine stands out because of the use of REMs. REMs tell the programmer the name of the subroutine that is being called, where the subroutine begins and where it ends. Also, blank REMs place empty lines before and after the subroutine to make it more visible.

Using GOSUB & RETURN

The GOSUB and RETURN statements can be used in many situations. For instance, GOSUB can be used to call a subroutine into operation from an IF . . . THEN statement:

50 IF H = 1 THEN GOSUB 100

The RETURN statement can also be used as part of an IF . . . THEN statement. The IF . . . THEN statement allows a program to RETURN from a subroutine only when a condition is true. Therefore, there may be more than one RETURN statement in a subroutine.

Program 8.3

This program adds graphics to a coin flipping game. The subroutines are executed as a result of IF . . . THEN statements. The symbol for heads will be an asterisk (*), for tails an (O).

```
1  REM  H = NUMBER OF HEADS ("*")
2  REM  T = NUMBER OF TAILS ("O")
3  REM  G$ = YOUR GUESS
4  REM  F = THE NUMBER OF FLIPS
```

```
5   REM   C =  A RANDOM NUMBER; EITHER 1 OR 2
10    HOME
20    PRINT "IN 10 FLIPS, WILL HEADS OR TAILS WIN?"
30    INPUT "TYPE H FOR HEADS OR T FOR TAILS: ";G$
40    IF G$ = "H" OR G$ = "T" THEN 60
50    PRINT : GOTO 20
60    FOR F = 1 TO 10
70    LET C =   INT (2 * RND (1) + 1)
80    IF C = 1 THEN   GOSUB 300: REM    HEADS
90    IF C = 2 THEN   GOSUB 400: REM    TAILS
100   NEXT F
110   PRINT
120   PRINT "THERE WERE "H" HEADS (*) AND "T" TAILS (O)."
130   END
300   REM
310   REM   *** HEADS SUBROUTINE ***
320   REM
330   PRINT "* ";
340   LET H = H + 1
350   RETURN
360   REM   *** END OF HEADS SUBROUTINE ***
400   REM
410   REM   *** TAILS SUBROUTINE ***
420   REM
430   PRINT "O ";
440   LET T = T + 1
450   RETURN
460   REM   *** END OF TAILS SUBROUTINE ***
470   REM

]RUN
IN 10 FLIPS, WILL HEADS OR TAILS WIN?
TYPE H FOR HEADS OR T FOR TAILS: H
O O * O O O O * * O
THERE WERE 3 HEADS (*) AND 7 TAILS (O).
```

- **Lines 10-40:** These lines explain what the program does and input the player's guess as variable G$.
- **Lines 60-100:** A loop that picks either a 1 or a 2 ten times. The IF ... THENs send the program to the correct subroutine. If a 1 is picked the computer goes to the subroutine for heads that begins on line 300. If a 2 is picked the program goes to the subroutine for tails that begins on line 400.
- **Lines 110-120:** These statements cancel the effect of the semicolons that have kept the heads and tails figures on the same line. A summary of the results of the program is then printed on the screen.
- **Line 130:** An END statement that prevents the computer from continuing down to the subroutine at line 300 without being sent there by a GOSUB.

- **Lines 300-350:** Each time a 1 is picked as a random number on line 70 the computer calls this subroutine. Line 330 prints an asterisk on the screen to represent a head and the counter variable H is increased in value by 1 on line 340.
- **Lines 400-450:** Similar to the subroutine at line 300, but this subroutine counts the number of tails. Each time a 2 is picked on line 70, the computer calls this subroutine which prints an O on the screen to represent a tail and then increases the value of variable T by 1.

The use of subroutines in a program like this makes the program much easier to understand because the subroutines allow the program to work from the top down. This means that the program goes from line to line without GOTO statements that jump forward and backward. This sequential order of instructions is an example of good programming style.

It is also possible to call a subroutine into operation from within a another subroutine:

```
10 GOSUB 200 : REM ** SUBROUTINE #1 **
20..........
   ..........
   ..........
   ..........
   ..........
100 END
190 REM
195 REM
200 REM *** SUBROUTINE #1 ***
210 IF A<>B THEN GOSUB 300 : REM ** SUBROUTINE #2 **
220..........
230 RETURN
240 REM *** END SUBROUTINE #1 ***
290 REM
295 REM
300 REM *** SUBROUTINE #2 ***
310..........
330 RETURN
340 REM *** END SUBROUTINE #2 ***
```

When GOSUB 200 on line 10 calls the subroutine at line 200 into operation, the computer goes to line 200 and begins executing the instructions there. If the condition on line 210 is true, the computer will go to line 300 and begin to execute the instructions of that subroutine. When the computer executes the return on line 330, it will return to line 220 because that is the next instruction after the GOSUB that sent the computer to line 300. The computer will not return to line 20 until it executes the RETURN on line 230.

Program 8.4   Jill has written a game program that prints a name near the center of the screen and then randomly takes 50 shots at the name:

```
1   REM   D = LINES DOWN
2   REM   R = SPACES TO THE RIGHT
3   REM   N$ = YOUR NAME
4   REM   M = NUMBER OF LINES TO MOVE DOWN
5   REM   S = NUMBER OF SHOTS
10   HOME
20   INPUT "TYPE YOUR NAME: ";N$
30  D = 12
40  R = 15
50   VTAB 1: HTAB 1
60   GOSUB 300
70   PRINT N$
80   FOR S = 1 TO 50
85   VTAB 1
90   GOSUB 200
100   NEXT S
110   END
200   REM   *** TAKE A RANDOM SHOT ***
210   LET D =  INT (23 *  RND (1) + 1)
220   LET R =  INT (39 *  RND (1) + 1)
230   GOSUB 300
240   PRINT "*"
250   RETURN
260   REM   *** END OF TAKE A RANDOM SHOT SUBROUTINE ***
270   REM
300   REM   *** MOVE CURSOR ***
310   VTAB 1: HTAB 1
320   FOR M = 1 TO D - 1
330   PRINT
340   NEXT M
350   HTAB R
360   RETURN
370   REM   *** END OF MOVE CURSOR SUBROUTINE ***


]RUN
TYPE YOUR NAME: JULIO IGLESIAS
```

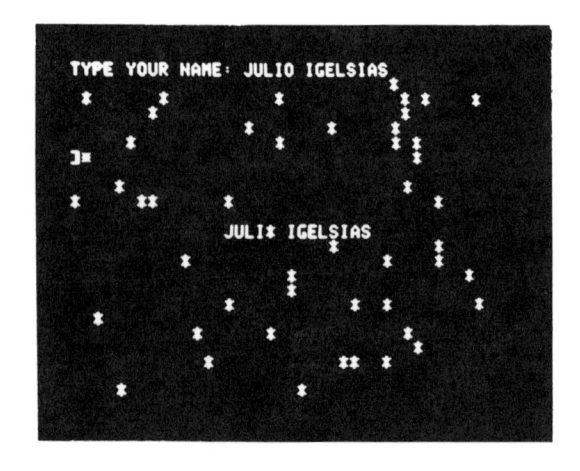

The program begins simply enough by explaining what the variable names stand for and then by clearing the screen and asking for the game player's name. To move the cursor to a point near the center of the screen, a GOSUB statement calls the subroutine at line 300.

- **Line 300:** A REM that explains the purpose of the subroutine.
- **Line 310:** A combination of HTAB 1 and VTAB 1 is used to make sure that each time the cursor is moved it begins its movement from the top of the screen.
- **Lines 320-340:** A PRINT is placed within a loop to move the cursor down a number of lines equal to the value of variable D. However, each time a PRINT statement is executed, the computer moves down one line to the beginning of the next line at the left margin. Therefore, if the loop moving the cursor repeats the PRINT statement 10 times, the cursor will move down 10 lines and then move to the beginning of the next line. This means the cursor will end up at the beginning of the eleventh line down. To take this into account, 1 is subtracted from the value of D on line 320.
- **Line 350:** Once the cursor has been moved down, HTAB R moves the cursor to the right the correct number of spaces.
- **Line 360:** A RETURN that sends the computer back to the point where the subroutine was called.

This routine is called into operation twice. It is called once from the main section of the program and once from another subroutine that begins at line 200. The subroutine at line 200 chooses at random the number of lines down and the number of spaces to the right the cursor is to be moved. Once values for variables D and R have been chosen, the cursor is moved into position by activating the subroutine at line 300. When the cursor has been moved down and to the right the correct number of times, an asterisk character is printed on the screen.

Review

1. Write a program in which names are input and then printed. If DONALD is input, use a subroutine to underline the name:

    RUN
    NAME? MARY
    MARY

    NAME? SUE
    SUE

    NAME? DONALD
    DONALD
    ----

2. Jack wants to jazz up his multiplication review program. He wants to give different rewards for getting the correct answer. He does not want to rewrite the entire program. Help him add a subroutine to this program that will choose one of three statements: GOOD SHOW!, SUPER EFFORT!, or RIGHT ON! Type in the program as it is and add the subroutine to it:

```
10   HOME
20   FOR J = 1 TO 10
30   LET A =   INT (12 *  RND (1) + 1)
40   LET B =   INT (12 *  RND (1) + 1)
50   LET C = A * B
60   PRINT A" * "B" = ";
70   INPUT D
80   IF D = C THEN  PRINT "OKAY"
90   IF D <  > C THEN 60
100   NEXT J
```

ON ... GOSUB

The ON statement is like a special type of IF ... THEN instruction. It allows a program to branch to a number of different subroutines:

50 ON N GOSUB 100, 200, 300, 400

When the value of variable N is 1, the program will branch to the first subroutine listed which begins at line 100. When the value of variable N is 2, it will branch to the second subroutine listed which is at line 200. When variable N is 3, it will go to the third. If the value of variable N is less than 1 or greater than the number of subroutines listed, the program will drop down to the next line. In this example if the value of variable N were 5, the computer would move on to the next line and ignore the GOSUB section of the statement. This statement saves both time and space because it allows a program to branch to a specific subroutine without having to write a long list of IF ... THEN statements.

ON can also be used with an arithmetic expression in place of a variable:

50 ON INT (6 * RND(1) + 1) GOSUB 10, 20, 30, 40, 50, 60

This line will cause the computer to branch to one of six subroutines depending on the random number that is chosen.

Program 8.5

This program uses ON ... GOSUB to deliver a movie review:

```
1    REM   N = YOUR CHOICE OF MOVIE
2    REM   A$ = YOUR CHOICE TO SEE ANOTHER REVIEW
10   HOME
20   PRINT "SELECT A MOVIE REVIEW:"
30   PRINT "1 - STAR WARS"
40   PRINT "2 - THE EMPIRE STRIKES BACK"
50   PRINT "3 - RETURN OF THE JEDI"
60   PRINT : PRINT "CHOOSE THE REVIEW BY NUMBER."
70   INPUT "TYPE 1, 2, OR 3: ";N
80   IF N < 1 OR N > 3 THEN 70
90   PRINT
100   ON N GOSUB 200,300,400
110   PRINT
120   INPUT "ANOTHER REVIEW (YES/NO) ? ";A$
130   IF A$ = "YES" THEN 10
140   END
```

```
180  REM
190  REM
200  REM   *** STAR WARS ***
210  PRINT "LUKE BATTLES THE EMPIRE,"
220  PRINT "RESCUES THE PRINCESS,"
230  PRINT "DESTROYS THE DEATH STAR AND"
240  PRINT "GETS HIS PICTURE ON BURGER KING"
250  PRINT "GLASSES."
260  RETURN
270  REM   *** END STAR WARS ***
280  REM
290  REM
300  REM   *** THE EMPIRE STRIKES BACK ***
310  PRINT "THE REBEL ALLIANCE IS TEMPORARILY"
320  PRINT "SET BACK AND HAN IS CAPTURED"
330  PRINT "AND FROZEN."
340  RETURN
350  REM   *** END EMPIRE STRIKES BACK ***
360  REM
370  REM
400  REM   *** RETURN OF THE JEDI ***
410  PRINT "LUKE LEARNS HIS REAL"
420  PRINT "IDENTITY AND THE EMPIRE IS"
430  PRINT "DEFEATED."
440  RETURN
450  REM   *** END RETURN OF THE JEDI ***

]RUN
SELECT A MOVIE REVIEW:
1 - STAR WARS
2 - THE EMPIRE STRIKES BACK
3 - RETURN OF THE JEDI

CHOOSE THE REVIEW BY NUMBER.
TYPE 1, 2, OR 3: 1

LUKE BATTLES THE EMPIRE,
RESCUES THE PRINCESS,
DESTROYS THE DEATH STAR AND
GETS HIS PICTURE ON BURGER KING
GLASSES.

ANOTHER REVIEW (YES/NO) ? NO
```

This program lists the movie reviews that are stored in three subroutines. The user enters the number for the movie to be reviewed.

Line 80 checks the value of variable N to make sure that it is one of the three numbers listed. Any number greater than 3 or less than 1 would cause the ON N GOSUB statement on line 100 to be ignored. Once the computer reaches line 100, it branches to the subroutine that contains the review that was selected.

ON ... GOTO

The ON instruction may also be used with the GOTO instruction. This form of the ON statement is useful when a program has no need to return to the point where the ON statement called those lines into operation.

      60 ON N GOTO 100, 200, 300

Program 8.6

Jean wrote this program to help her younger sister learn different shapes. The program prints either a rectangle, a triangle, or a diamond:

```
10   HOME
20   ON   INT (3 * RND (1) + 1) GOTO 100,200,300
100  REM  *** RECTANGLE ***
110  PRINT "**********"
120  FOR S = 1 TO 5
130  PRINT "*         *"
140  NEXT S
150  PRINT "**********"
160  END
200  REM  *** TRIANGLE ***
210  PRINT   TAB( 7)"*"
220  FOR L = 6 TO 2 STEP  - 1
230  PRINT   TAB( L)"*"; TAB( 14 - L)"*"
240  NEXT L
250  PRINT "*************"
260  END
300  REM  *** DIAMOND ***
310  PRINT   TAB( 7)"*"
320  FOR L = 6 TO 1 STEP  - 1
330  PRINT   TAB( L)"*"; TAB( 14 - L);"*"
340  NEXT L
350  FOR L = 2 TO 6
360  PRINT   TAB( L)"*"; TAB( 14 - L)"*"
370  NEXT L
380  PRINT   TAB( 7)"*"
390  END
```

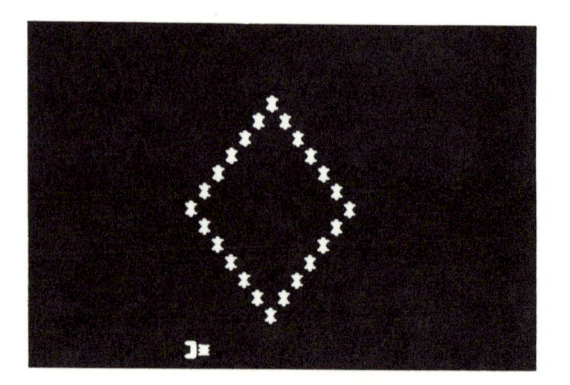

The ON ... GOTO on line 20 waits for the computer to pick a 1, 2 or 3 as random numbers. When the computer picks a 1, the rectangle is drawn. If a 2 is picked, the triangle is drawn, and if a 3 is picked, then the diamond is drawn.

Review

3. Harry Hacker loves Spiderman comics, so Joe Kolodnigork wants to write a program for him that gives Joe's thoughts about such "books". Write a program to show Joe how he can use ON ... GOSUB to print these four comments in response to a user's input.

    IF A = 0 PRINT "SPIDERMAN IS A ZERO!"
        A = 1 PRINT "J. JONA JAMSON IS A GEM."
        A = 2 PRINT "SPIDY IS ALL SPUN OUT."
        A = 3 PRINT "SPIDERS SHOULD BE SQUASHED."

4. Write a program that simulates picking cards from a deck. The computer must pick two random numbers, the first between 1 and 4 and the second between 1 and 13. An ON ... GOTO statement should use the first number to pick each suit. The second represents the card's value within the suit.

```
RUN
CARD 1 IS THE 6 OF HEARTS
CARD 2 IS THE 2 OF SPADES
CARD 3 IS THE 3 OF CLUBS
CARD 4 IS THE 9 OF SPADES
CARD 5 IS THE 1 OF SPADES
```

Program Planning

Now that you are familiar with most of the BASIC commands it is important to spend some time thinking about how these commands are put together to form a program. The first step in writing any program is planning.

The first step in planning is to understand precisely the problem that is to be solved. This is done by analyzing the problem and developing a logical sequence of steps that will lead to its solution. To do this the problem is broken down into smaller parts each of which should be easier to solve. They can then be arranged in a logical sequence that will lead to the completion of the task. Writing a program is like building a house. When the problem of building the house is broken down into smaller tasks, the problem becomes more manageable. Once the smaller tasks are planned, they can be arranged in a logical sequence that will lead to the successful construction of the house.

Each step of the solution must be planned so that its task is clear, unambiguous and manageable. To develop this plan often means "playing computer" with pencil and paper. By thinking like the computer and tracing the steps it would follow, a solution to the problem can usually be reached. The programmer can then translate these actions into the instructions that will make up the computer program.

A common mistake of programmers is to begin writing "code" (the term "code" is used to define the instructions that make up a program) before the problem and its solution are understood and planned. This frequently results in a program that must be changed by adding or deleting lines until the desired output is achieved. The consequence of this approach is a program that is a "mish-mash" of statements which do not flow logically from one statement to another. For example, too many IF ... THEN and GOTO statements added to a program can confuse the order in which instructions are to be carried out. With the orderly flow of instructions destroyed, the logic of the program is difficult to follow, not only by other programmers but also by the author of the program. Without a clearly defined and logical sequence, correcting errors in a program becomes difficult if not impossible. Therefore, a good programmer should plan a program as thoroughly as possible before approaching the computer.

If the planning has been done properly, the program will be well organized with an orderly flow of instructions. When the time comes to begin writing the program code, it is important that the code be written with a visible structure that shows the organization and order of the activities that the program will carry out. To give the program a visible structure the following techniques should be used:

1. Use REMs at the beginning of the program to explain what the program does and what the important variables represent. REMs can also be placed throughout the program to explain what parts of the program do.
2. Use separate blocks of line numbers for any subroutines. For example, if a routine has 15 lines that run from line number 100 to number 250, begin the next subroutine at line number 300. Use REMs to identify and explain what each subroutine does.

Planning a Real Program

To demonstrate the proper planning of a program, we will plan and write a game program that will place a space ship on the screen and give the game player 3 chances to shoot it down. The ship will look like this:

The ship's location on the screen will be chosen at random. The player will shoot it down by entering the number of lines down from the top of the screen and the number of spaces to the right of the left margin where the player thinks the ship is. The messages to the player that input the guesses will be printed near the bottom of the screen. The program will end when either the ship is hit or the player has had 3 shots without a hit. The screen should look like the following:

The first thing that must be done in planning a program is to have a clear understanding of what the program is to do. With a firm idea of what the program is to do in mind, a plan can be developed that will break the program down into separate parts. A first step in making this plan is to list the actions that the computer must carry out to accomplish the goal of the program. Our example program must:

1. Choose randomly a number of lines down and a number of spaces to the right to print the ship.
2. Move the cursor to the proper location and print the ship on the screen.
3. Input the player's guess. This will begin on the 21st line down from the top of the screen so that it will be out of the way of the area on the screen where the ship might be.
4. Move the cursor to print a shot on the screen.
5. Check to see if the shot is a miss or a hit.
6. If it is a hit move the cursor to blow up the ship.
7. Repeat steps 2-5 three times if a miss.

When these steps are studied carefully, one task that is common to steps 2, 3, 4 and 6 is that they require the cursor to be moved around the screen so that specific objects can be printed on the screen. This means another task that will be performed has been recognized and must be added to the list of tasks that the program must do in order to complete the program. In this case, this part of the program will be a subroutine that will move the cursor to a specific point on the screen each time something must be printed.

At this point it is a good idea to assign names to the variables that will be used and to use these variable names to make the plan more specific. The following table lists each variable name and its job in the program:

VARIABLE NAME	TASK
D	How many lines down to move the cursor
R	How many spaces right to move the cursor
A	Random down location at start
B	Random number of spaces to the right at start
X	Player's guess for number down
Y	Player's guess for number to the right
S	Loop variable to count shots remaining

The next step is to consider each of the major parts of the program as a separate subroutine that can be planned on its own. A plan can also be designed for the main section of the program that will control the order in which the subroutines will be called into operation. An outline for the program might look like this:

MAIN SECTION

Choose 2 random numbers as variables A and B
FOR S = 3 to 1 STEP−1 (start with 3 shots)
   GOSUB to move cursor and print ship
   GOSUB to move cursor and input guesses as variables X and Y
   GOSUB to move cursor and print shot on the screen
   GOSUB to check for a miss or a hit
NEXT S
When no hit print a sorry message.
END

LIST OF SUBROUTINES

- Subroutine to move cursor down and to the right to proper place to print.
- Subroutine to print the ship.
- Subroutine to input guesses (variables X and Y).
- Subroutine to place shot on screen according to guess.
- Subroutine to check for miss or hit (compare variable X to variable A and variable Y to variable B)
  —If a miss, repeat.
  —If a hit, blow up ship and end program.

Putting the Pieces Together

We now have a plan for the program which outlines the tasks that must be performed. With this plan in mind, the pieces of the program are now ready to be written one at a time.

The first part to be written is the main section of the program that will control the order in which the other parts will be used. Looking at our outline, we see that the main section has four tasks to be accomplished besides calling the subroutines. Lets look at those tasks in more detail:

1. Pick random numbers to assign to variable A and variable B. These will decide the location of the ship. To make the game a little tougher, variable A must be picked from within the range 5-20 and variable B within the range 5-35.
2. Use a loop to repeat the action of the program up to 3 times. GOSUBs within the loop will call subroutines into operation when they are needed.
3. Since completing the loop 3 times means no hit was made, print a message that says the player missed.
4. The section must close with an END statement to keep the first subroutine from being run by accident.

This is the code for the main section of the program. Notice how it follows the four steps of the plan for this section:

```
1   REM   D=LINES DOWN
2   REM   R=SPACES RIGHT
3   REM   A=LOCATION DOWN
4   REM   B=LOCATION RIGHT
5   REM   X=DOWN GUESS
6   REM   Y=RIGHT GUESS
```

```
7   REM
8   REM   *** MAIN BODY ***
9   REM
10  HOME
20  LET A =  INT (13 *  RND (1) + 5)
30  LET B =  INT (30 *  RND (1) + 5)
40  FOR S = 3 TO 1 STEP  - 1
45  IF S = 3 THEN 60
50  GOSUB 200: REM   MOVE CURSOR
60  GOSUB 300: REM   PRINT SHIP
70  GOSUB 400: REM GUESS SHIP'S LOCATION
80  GOSUB 500: REM   PLACE SHOT ON SCREEN
90  GOSUB 600: REM   CHECK FOR MISS OR HIT
100 NEXT S
110 PRINT "TOUGH LUCK SPACE JOCKEY!"
120 PRINT "YOU MISSED YOUR CHANCE."
130 END
140 REM    *** END OF MAIN BODY ***
150 REM
```

Now the plan and code for each subroutine can be written. Since the subroutine that moves the cursor is called from four other subroutines we will write it first and put it at the top of the list of subroutines. This routine which can begin at line number 200 will carry out the same instructions as the cursor movement routine used in program 8.4.

The subroutine uses HTAB and VTAB to move to the proper position on the screen. The code that will translate this plan into instructions for the computer to follow is:

```
190 REM
200 REM   *** MOVE CURSOR DOWN & RIGHT ***
210 VTAB D: HTAB R
220 RETURN
230 REM   *** END OF MOVE CURSOR ***
240 REM
```

The next subroutine is the one that will print the ship on the screen. This routine must:

1. Move the cursor to point where the ship will be printed. (Use the subroutine at line 200 to move the cursor down a number of lines equal to the value of variable A and to the right a number of spaces equal to the value of variable B.)
2. Print the space ship. The ship will use the characters <, * and >.
3. Return to the main section.

The code for this subroutine which begins at line 300 should look like this:

```
300 REM  *** PRINT SHIP ***
310 LET D = A
320 LET R = B
330 GOSUB 200
340 PRINT "<**>"
350 RETURN
360 REM  *** END OF PRINT SHIP ***
370 REM
```

The subroutine to input the player's guesses begins on line 400. It is longer than most of the subroutines but it is not difficult to plan because of the planning that has already been done has given this subroutine a well defined task to perform:

1. Move the cursor down to the 18th line (Use the subroutine 200).
2. Tell how many shots are left.
3. Input variable X as the guess for the number of lines down. (Allow only numbers between 1 and 18).
4. Input variable Y as the guess for the number of spaces to the right. (Allow only numbers between 0 and 39 because TAB counts the 40 space width of the screen from 0 to 39).
5. Return to the main section for the next subroutine.

The translation of these instructions into the program code begins at line 400:

```
400 REM  *** GUESS SHIP'S LOCATION ***
410 LET D = 20
420 LET R = 1
430 GOSUB 200
440 PRINT "YOU HAVE "S" SHOT(S) LEFT."
450 INPUT "HOW MANY DOWN (1-18)? ";X
460 IF X < 1 OR X > 18 THEN 450
470 INPUT "TO THE RIGHT (0-39)? ";Y
480 IF Y < 0 OR Y > 39 THEN 470
490 RETURN
491 REM  *** END OF GUESS LOCATION ***
492 REM
```

With the guess made, the next step is to plan the routine that will place the shot on the screen. Placing the shot on the screen will give the player an opportunity to see how accurate the guesses were and to make corrections on the next try. This routine is very similar to the routine that prints the ship on the screen:

1. Assign variable D the value of variable X and assign variable R the value of variable Y.
2. Move the cursor to the place the player guessed. (Use the subroutine at 200).
3. Print an asterisk to represent the shot.

4. Wait for a few seconds and then clear the screen. (Clearing the screen will prepare the screen for either a new guess or the results of a hit.)
5. Return to the main section for the next subroutine.

The translation of these steps into code begins at line 500:

```
500  REM   *** PLACE SHOT ON SCREEN ***
510  LET D = X
520  LET R = Y
530  GOSUB 200: REM   MOVE CURSOR
540  PRINT "*"
550  FOR W = 1 TO 300
560  NEXT W
570  HOME
580  RETURN
590  REM   *** END OF PLACE SHOT ***
595  REM
```

With a shot taken at the ship, the last thing to be done is to check for a miss or a hit:

1. Compare variables X and A to see if the player's down guess and the ship's down location are the same. If they are not equal, go back for another shot.
2. Compare the value of variable Y to the value of variable B to see if the player's guess of the number of spaces to the right is correct. Since the ship is four characters long, not only Y=B+1, but Y=B+2 and Y=B+3 must be compared as well. If none of these are true, then go back for another shot.
3. Move the cursor to the location of the ship and print a message saying it has blown up.
4. Wait for a while and then print a message saying the player is a good shot.
5. End the program.

The plan for this subroutine translates into the following code that begins at line 600:

```
600  REM   *** CHECK FOR A MISS OR A HIT ***
610  IF A < > X THEN   RETURN
620  IF Y < > B AND Y < > B + 1 AND Y < > B + 2 AND
     Y < > B + 3 THEN   RETURN
630  REM   *** BLOW UP AND END PROGRAM ***
640  LET D = A
650  LET R = B
660  GOSUB 200
670  PRINT "BLAMO!"
680  FOR W = 1 TO 300
690  NEXT W
700  HOME
710  PRINT "GOOD SHOOTING SPACE ACE."
720  END
```

Program 8.7

A listing of our entire game program is now possible and it would look this:

```
1   REM   D=LINES DOWN
2   REM   R=SPACES RIGHT
3   REM   A=LOCATION DOWN
4   REM   B=LOCATION RIGHT
5   REM   X=DOWN GUESS
6   REM   Y=RIGHT GUESS
7   REM
8   REM   *** MAIN BODY ***
9   REM
10  HOME
20  LET A =  INT (13 * RND (1) + 5)
30  LET B =  INT (30 * RND (1) + 5)
40  FOR S = 3 TO 1 STEP  - 1
45  IF S = 3 THEN 60
50  GOSUB 200: REM   MOVE CURSOR
60  GOSUB 300: REM   PRINT SHIP
70  GOSUB 400: REM GUESS SHIP'S LOCATION
80  GOSUB 500: REM   PLACE SHOT ON SCREEN
90  GOSUB 600: REM   CHECK FOR MISS OR HIT
100 NEXT S
110 PRINT "TOUGH LUCK SPACE JOCKEY!"
120 PRINT "YOU MISSED YOUR CHANCE."
130 END
140 REM  *** END OF MAIN BODY ***
150 REM
200 REM  *** MOVE CURSOR DOWN & RIGHT ***
210 VTAB D: HTAB R
220 RETURN
230 REM  *** END OF MOVE CURSOR ***
240 REM
300 REM  *** PRINT SHIP ***
310 LET D = A
320 LET R = B
330 GOSUB 200
340 PRINT "<**>"
350 RETURN
360 REM  *** END OF PRINT SHIP ***
370 REM
400 REM  *** GUESS SHIP'S LOCATION ***
410 LET D = 20
420 LET R = 1
430 GOSUB 200
440 PRINT "YOU HAVE "S" SHOT(S) LEFT."
450 INPUT "HOW MANY DOWN (1-18)? ";X
460 IF X < 1 OR X > 18 THEN 450
470 INPUT "TO THE RIGHT (0-39)? ";Y
480 IF Y < 0 OR Y > 39 THEN 470
490 RETURN
491 REM  *** END OF GUESS LOCATION ***
492 REM
500 REM  *** PLACE SHOT ON SCREEN ***
```

```
510    LET D = X
520    LET R = Y
530    GOSUB 200
540    PRINT "*"
550    FOR W = 1 TO 300
560    NEXT W
570    HOME
580    RETURN
590    REM  *** END OF PLACE SHOT ***
595    REM
600    REM  *** CHECK FOR A MISS OR A HIT ***
610    IF A < > X THEN  RETURN
620    IF Y < > B AND Y < > B + 1 AND Y < > B + 2
AND Y < > B + 3 THEN  RETURN
630    REM  *** BLOW UP AND END PROGRAM ***
640    LET D = A
650    LET R = B
660    GOSUB 200
670    PRINT "BLAMO!"
680    FOR W = 1 TO 300
690    NEXT W
700    HOME
710    PRINT "GOOD SHOOTING SPACE ACE."
720    END
```

Debugging

Debugging is the process of locating errors or "bugs" in a program and then correcting them. The best way to avoid bugs is to plan a program carefully. However, even the most carefully planned and written program will often contain errors. Debugging is much easier though, when a program has been broken down into well-defined subroutines as our example was. Since each subroutine carries out a specific task it is much easier to locate the error and correct it. There are two basic types of errors that will cause a program to work improperly.

Run Time Errors

Run time errors, which cause the computer to halt the run of a program, are found by the computer during the run of a program. Run time errors are usually of two types. One type is created when a statement is typed improperly:

10 REED X, Y

should be

10 READ X, Y

A second type of run time error is caused by an instruction that tells the computer to carry out a task that is not in agreement with the computer's rules of operation. For example,

10 READ A$, B
20 DATA 35, SMITH

Review

5. Find the run time error in the following program and correct it:

```
10 INPUT A
20 FOR J = 10 TO 1
30 LET C = A * J
40 NEXT J
```

6. There is an error in the following program that will cause the program to halt. Find it and correct it:

```
10 HOME
20 FOR J = 1 TO 20
30 LET K = K + 1
40 PRINT J * K
50 NEXT K
```

Logic Errors

If the program does not break any of BASIC's rules, the computer will accept the program and run it. However, that does not mean that the output of the program will be what the programmer intended. A wise observer of people and their use of computers once said that computers always do what you tell them to do, which is not always what you want them to do. Errors that cause the computer's output to be different from what is expected are called logic errors and are the most difficult to detect. These errors often result from a programmer's incorrect analysis of the task a program is to carry out. This then leads to the programmer's planning a sequence of instructions that is incorrect or leaves out an important instruction.

Program 8.8

Harry Hacker wrote this program for his older sister Henrietta who sells left-handed skyhooks. This program keeps track of the number of sky hooks she has left after she fills an order. She began with 145 hooks:

```
1  REM   H = NUMBER OF HOOKS
2  REM   N = NUMBER OF HOOKS IN ORDER
3  REM   A$ = YOUR ANSWER
10 HOME
20 INPUT "HOOKS IN ORDER? ";N
30 LET H = 145
40 LET H = H - N
50 PRINT "HOOKS NOW ON HAND "H
60 INPUT "ANOTHER ORDER (YES/NO) ? ";A$
70 IF A$ < > "YES" THEN END
80 PRINT
90 GOTO 10
```

```
]RUN
HOOKS IN ORDER? 45
HOOKS NOW ON HAND 100
ANOTHER ORDER (YES/NO) ? YES

HOOKS IN ORDER? 30
HOOKS NOW ON HAND 115
ANOTHER ORDER (YES/NO) ? NO
```

The program seems to work, but the output is not correct. Needless to say, Henrietta is not happy with Harry's work. She knows she cannot have more hooks left after filling the second order than she had after filling the first order. Harry has made a logic error. Line 30, which sets the initial or beginning value of variable H, is out of sequence. The computer will keep resetting the value of variable H to 145 each time the program is repeated rather than keep variable H equal to the result of variable H minus the value of variable N.

Review

7. Find the logic error in the following program and correct it.

```
10 FOR J = 0 TO 10
20 LET A = J / 2
30 IF A = INT(J / 2) THEN 10
40 PRINT A
50 NEXT J
```

8. There is a logic error in this program also. Find it and correct it:

```
10 READ A,B
20 IF A = - 99 THEN 80
30 PRINT
40 PRINT A * B
50 LET C = C + (A * B)
60 LET C = 0
70 GOTO 10
80 PRINT C
90 DATA 4, 8, 5, 10
100 DATA 6, 12, -99, -99
```

Hand Tracing

One way to create confidence in a program's output is to trace the results of a program by hand using test data. This is called hand tracing. If working the calculations by hand produces the same results as the program, then the programmer can be confident that the program works at least for the data that is being tested.

Program 8.9

This program assigns variable N a value using READ and is then supposed to calculate and print the sum of the first N integers. For example, if variable N=5 the sum should equal 1+2+3+4+5 or 15:

```
10   HOME
20   READ N
30   FOR C = 1 TO N
40   LET S = S + C
50   NEXT C
60   PRINT "THE NUMBER OF INTEGERS = "N
70   PRINT "THE SUM OF THOSE INTEGERS = "S
80   PRINT
90   GOTO 20
100  DATA  3,5,10

]RUN
THE NUMBER OF INTEGERS = 3
THE SUM OF THOSE INTEGERS = 6

THE NUMBER OF INTEGERS = 5
THE SUM OF THOSE INTEGERS = 21

THE NUMBER OF INTEGERS = 10
THE SUM OF THOSE INTEGERS = 76


?OUT OF DATA ERROR IN 20
```

If the output for this program is checked by hand for N = 3, S = 6 (1+2+3) is a correct answer. However, if the programmer relied only on this test data, then a serious logic error is overlooked. A problem with the test data technique is that the data chosen for the test may bypass the bug. A test by hand using N=5, has S=15 (1+2+3+4+5) as the result. This does not agree with the output of the program. It is now obvious that there is a bug somewhere in the program.

The problem now is to find the place in the program where the error occurs. One way to do this is to "play computer" with the program. In fact, if this done as part of the planning of the program, errors like this can most often be avoided in the first place. This method of debugging is commonly called *hand tracing*.

To find this program's bug, the programmer must make a table that shows each variable in the program. Then the programmer must trace the value of each variable line-by-line recording the value of each variable when a line is executed:

Line	N	C	S
10	0	0	0
20	3	0	0
30	3	1	0
40	3	1	1
50	3	2	1
40	3	2	3
50	3	3	3
50	3	3	6
60-70			(Print 3, 6)
20	5	3	6
30	5	1	6
50	5	1	7 (Error! S should be 1)

At each line of the hand tracing the current value of each variable is written down. The program begins at line 10 with each of the variables having a value of 0 because the program has not yet assigned a value to any of the variables. A value is not changed unless there is a statement in the program that instructs the computer to change that value. The error begins to become apparent when the computer is told to go back to line 20. Variable N is assigned a new value so the program can calculate the sum of the first 5 integers. On line 30, variable C is reassigned a value of 1 by FOR C = 1 TO N. However, when the computer executes line 40 to begin calculating the new sum, variable S still has its old value of 6. The computer was never given an instruction to set the value of variable S back to 0 so the program began calculating the sum of the first 5 integers by adding 1 to 6.

STOP and CONTinue

Halting or breaking a program on purpose at certain points in a program is also a useful debugging technique. STOP is very similar to the END statement, but unlike the END, STOP tells the programmer the line number where the break in the program occurred. Also, a program halted by a STOP instruction can be resumed at the point of the interruption by typing CONT, which is an abbreviation for continue. Breaking a program in this way becomes a useful debugging tool because the programmer can then look at the current value of any of the program's variables by using immediate mode to tell the computer to print the value of a variable on the screen.

Program 8.10

A STOP statement is added to Program 8.9 to test the results of the hand tracing:

```
10  HOME
20  READ N
30  FOR C = 1 TO N
35  IF S > 6 THEN  STOP
40  LET S = S + C
50  NEXT C
60  PRINT "THE NUMBER OF INTEGERS = "N
70  PRINT "THE SUM OF THOSE INTEGERS = "S
80  PRINT
```

```
 90  GOTO 20
100   DATA  3,5,10

]RUN
THE NUMBER OF INTEGERS = 3
THE SUM OF THOSE INTEGERS = 6


BREAK IN 35
]PRINT N,C,S
5                  2                  7

]CONT

BREAK IN 35
]PRINT N,C,S
5                  3                  9
```

When the program tries to calculate the value of the first 5 integers, the IF . . . THEN on line 35 becomes true. The STOP command produces the BREAK IN 35 message and halts the program. The programmer then types PRINT and the names of the 3 variables in question (N, C, and S). When RETURN is pressed, the values of those variables appear on the screen. Typing CONT tells the computer to continue the program from the next statement. This again produces the incorrect output and again forces a BREAK IN 35 message. However, now the programmer can be sure that the bug in the program is caused by not setting the value of variable S back to 0.

This error can be corrected by adding an instruction to set variable S back to 0 and by changing the GOTO in line 90 so that it sends the computer to this new instruction:

15 LET S = 0
90 GOTO 15

Now a run of the program produces the correct results:

```
THE NUMBER OF INTEGERS = 3
THE SUM OF THOSE INTEGERS = 6

THE NUMBER OF INTEGERS = 5
THE SUM OF THOSE INTEGERS = 15

THE NUMBER OF INTEGERS = 10
THE SUM OF THOSE INTEGERS = 55


?OUT OF DATA ERROR IN 20
```

Since it is no longer necessary, the IF . . . THEN statement on line 35 can be deleted from the program by typing the line number and pressing RETURN.

Review

9. Janet wrote this program to calculate the areas and perimeters of several rectangles. Hand trace the program to make sure that it will produce the correct output:

```
10 FOR F = 1 TO 3
20 READ L, W
30 LET P = (2 * L) + (2 * W)
40 LET A = L * W
50 PRINT A, P
60 NEXT F
70 DATA 5, 3, 7, 9, 8, 8
```

EXERCISES

1. Write a program that displays the following output on the screen. Use a subroutine to print the word "PART" and the correct number:

   ```
   PART 1
   ******************************************
   PART 2
   !            !            !            !
   PART 3
   ABABABABABABABABABABABABABABABABABABABABABA
   ```

2. Janet's Girl Scout Troop is having a carnival to raise money for charity. Her group's booth is awarding a ball, a balloon, a toy car or a candy bar as prizes. She has decided to have the computer pick the prize so no one will be able to get angry with her because he or she wanted something else. Write a program that picks a random number from 1 to 4 and uses ON . . . GOTO to print the prize that is to be received:

   ```
   RUN
   YOUR PRIZE IS A CANDY BAR.
   PRESS P & RETURN FOR ANOTHER PRIZE?
   ```

3. Write a program that allows a user to select either addition or subtraction. The program should then randomly select 2 numbers between 1 and 100 that will be added or subtracted:

   ```
   RUN
   SELECT THE MATH OPERATION YOU WISH DONE:
   1 — ADDITION
   2 — SUBTRACTION

   TYPE 1 OR 2 AND RETURN? 2

   90 − 45 = 45
   ```

4. What will be the exact output of the following program?

```
10   READ X
20   ON X GOTO 30,50,70,90,110,130,150
30   PRINT "MERRILY ";
40   GOTO 10
50   PRINT "ROW, ";
60   GOTO 10
70   PRINT "YOUR BOAT"
80   GOTO 10
90   PRINT "GENTLY DOWN THE STREAM"
100  GOTO 10
110  PRINT "LIFE IS BUT A DREAM"
120  GOTO 10
130  PRINT
140  GOTO 10
150  END
170  DATA  2,2,2,3,4,1,1,1,1,1,6,5,7
```

5. Give Amanda's little brother something to try for in his multiplication review program. Add a subroutine to this program that puts his name in the center of the screen and then flashes his name and the word CORRECT on and off each time he gets a problem right. This is how the program works now:

RUN
TYPE YOUR NAME? HARVEY

OKAY HARVEY HERE ARE 5 MULTIPLICATION FACTS FOR YOU.

10 * 3 = ? 30
CORRECT!

12 * 7 = ? 74
TRY AGAIN.

12 * 7 = ?

6. What is the output of this program? Make your prediction then type it in and run it:

```
10   HOME
20   PRINT "AREA CALCULATOR - SELECT FIGURE"
30   PRINT "1. RECTANGLE"
40   PRINT "2. RIGHT TRIANGLE"
50   INPUT "TYPE 1 OR 2: ";F
60   PRINT
70   INPUT "ENTER THE HEIGHT (WIDTH)? ";H
80   INPUT "ENTER THE BASE (LENGTH)? ";B
90   PRINT
100  ON F GOSUB 200,300
110  PRINT "THE AREA IS "A" SQUARE UNITS"
120  END
```

```
200  LET A = B * H
210  RETURN
300  LET A = .5 * H * B
310  RETURN
```

7. Bjorn Rich needs help balancing his Swiss Bank account because his mail often arrives late at his isolated mountain top ski lodge. His program needs two subroutines, one for deposits and one for withdrawals. Don't forget to give Bjorn a way out of the program when he is finished with his balancing act.

```
RUN
1) WITHDRAWAL
2) DEPOSIT
3) EXIT PROGRAM

TYPE 1, 2, OR 3? 2

AMOUNT TO DEPOSIT?  500
YOUR BALANCE IS $500

1) WITHDRAWAL
2) DEPOSIT
3) EXIT PROGRAM

TYPE 1, 2, OR 3? 1

AMOUNT TO WITHDRAW  600
WOW! THAT WILL BOUNCE OVER MY HEAD.
TOO MUCH!
AMOUNT TO WITHDRAW 275
YOUR BALANCE IS $ 225

1) WITHDRAWAL
2) DEPOSIT
3) EXIT PROGRAM

TYPE 1, 2, OR 3? 3
```

8. Can you figure out what is happening to the mouse in the following program. Will he find his lunch or will he find that he is lunch? Type it in and run it to check your prediction:

```
10    HOME
20    PRINT "THE MOUSE IS IN THE MAZE"
30    GOSUB 100
40    PRINT "SIMPLY AMAZING!"
50    END
100   PRINT "IN ROOM 1"
110   LET X =  INT (2 *  RND (1) + 1)
120   ON X GOTO 200,300
200   PRINT "IN ROOM 2"
210   LET X =  INT (2 *  RND (1) + 1)
220   ON X GOTO 100,300
300   PRINT "IN ROOM 3"
310   LET X =  INT (3 *  RND (1) + 1)
320   ON X GOTO 100,200,400
400   PRINT "IN ROOM 4"
410   LET X =  INT (3 *  RND (1) + 1)
420   ON X GOTO 300,500,600
500   PRINT "IN ROOM 5"
510   PRINT "THE CHEESE IS THE MOUSE'S LUNCH!"
520   RETURN
600   PRINT "IN ROOM 6"
610   PRINT "THE MOUSE IS THE CAT'S LUNCH!"
620   RETURN
```

9. Harry Hacker and Joe Kolodnigork are tired of flipping baseball cards the old-fashioned way and wish to use the computer to flip for them. The game is played like this: the player who starts flips one of his baseball cards. This card will land with either the player's picture facing up or down. The second player then flips one of his baseball cards. In order to win the other player's card, the landing position (face up or down) of his card must match the position of the first player's card. If the second player fails to match the first player's flip, the first player wins. The winner of each round gets to flip first. Help Joe and Harry out by writing a plan for this program. All they should have to do is tell the computer how many cards they each have to start and who goes first.

10. Each of the following programs contains a run time error. In each case identify and correct the error(s):

(A) 10 READ A, B, C, D
    20 LET E = (A * B) + C + D
    30 PRINT E
    40 END
    50 DATA 2, 34, 5

(B) 10 INPUT "ENTER YOUR AGE";A
    20 IF A < 5 OR > 19 THEN 40
    30 INPUT "WHAT'S YOUR FAVORITE TV SHOW";S$
    40 IF A > 16 THEN PRINT "TO YOUNG TO DRIVE"
    50 IF S$ = "MASH" THEN PRINT "THAT'S MY FAVORITE TOO!"

(C) 10 FOR J = 10 TO 1
    20 PRINT TAB (J) "*****"
    30 NEXT J

(D) 10 INPUT "HOW MANY TIMES TO ADD 2" T
    20 FOR C = 1 TO T
    30 LET S = S + 2
    40 NEXT T
    50 PRINT S

(E) 10 PRINT "NAME" TAB(20) "BATTING AVG."
    20 READ N$, B
    30 IF N$ = "ZZZ" THEN END
    40 PRINT N$ TAB(20) B
    50 GOTO 10
    60 DATA FRED, .354, JANET, .253, HARRY, .187,
            JOE, .500, ZZZ, 0

(F) 10 FOR X = 1 TO 26
    20 LET A$ = A$ + X
    30 NEXT X
    40 PRINT A$
    50 END

11. The crime fighting business is getting a bit expensive these days so Batman is trying to keep track of the cost of catching crooks. However, he is not happy with the program that the Boy Wonder has written for the Bat Computer because the Bat Books don't balance. See if you can find the bug in this bat's belfry and correct the program for the Boy Blunder:

```
10    HOME
20    READ C
30    PRINT "TOTAL CRIMEFIGHTING COSTS $ "C
40    PRINT "CROOK" TAB( 15)"JAIL TERM"
60    FOR C = 1 TO 4
70    READ C$,J
80    PRINT C$ TAB( 15)J
```

```
90  NEXT C
100 PRINT "AVERAGE COST PER CROOK $ "C / 4
110 END
120 DATA 112134.79, CAT WOMAN, 20, RIDDLER, 35,
PENGUIN, 15, JOKER, 99
```

12. The following programs have logic errors. (The programs run but the output is not what is expected.) Find and correct the errors:

   (A) 10 READ A, B, C
       20 IF A = −99 THEN END
       30 PRINT A + B + C
       40 GOTO 20
       50 DATA 1, 3, 5, 7, 9, 11, −99, −99, −99

   (B) 10 FOR X = 1 TO 10
       20 IF X > 5 THEN 50
       30 PRINT X "IS GREATER THAN 5."
       40 GOTO 60
       50 PRINT X "IS LESS THAN 5."
       60 NEXT X
       70 END

   (C) PRINT "STRING BUILDER"
       20 INPUT "HOW MANY CHARACTERS IN THE STRING";L
       30 FOR W = 1 TO L
       40 INPUT "TYPE A CHARACTER";C$
       50 LET W$ = W$ + C$
       60 NEXT W
       70 PRINT
       80 PRINT W$
       90 INPUT "TYPE Y TO BUILD ANOTHER";A$
       100 IF A$ = "YES" THEN 20

13. Trace the following program by hand to predict its output:

```
10   HOME
20   PRINT "GRADE AVERAGER"
30   READ N
40   PRINT "THERE WERE "N" SCORES TO AVERAGE."
50   PRINT
60   FOR A = 1 TO N
70   READ S
80   PRINT "SCORE "A" = "S
90   LET T = T + S
100  NEXT A
110  LET M = T / N
120  PRINT "THE AVERAGE WAS "M
130  END
140  DATA 5,75,89,99,84,91
```

14. Design a program that will allow the user to pick one of three math operations: addition (numbers from 1-100), subtraction (numbers from 1-100), or multiplication (numbers from 1-12). The program user will then be given 5 problems. For each correct answer award 20 points. Take away 5 points for each incorrect answer. If the player gets a right answer print 1 of these 3 reward messages:

- SMART PENCIL YOU'VE GOT THERE!
- A MARVELOUS MATHEMATICIAN.
- IS THIS MATH MAGIC?

Print the player's score after completing 5 problems. Once you have written a plan and an outline, write the program itself.

NESTED LOOPS AND SUBSCRIPTED VARIABLES 9

DIM
RESTORE
GET
VAL ( )

DIM
RESTORE
GET
VAL ( )

Nested Loops and Subscripted Variables 9-1

The FOR... NEXT loop is an important tool in programming. It makes it easy for the programmer to tell the computer to carry out a series of instructions a specific number of times. This chapter will further explain how loops can be used to carry out programming tasks. Another important part of programming is the use of variables. We have seen that there are both numeric and string variables, and that LET, INPUT and READ-DATA are instructions that assign a value to a variable. However, there are tasks that the simple variables we have used so far cannot do easily. In this chapter, therefore, we will look at a more complex type of variable that will increase a program's ability to store and use data.

Nested Loops

The FOR... NEXT loop was explained in Chapter 5. To further increase the usefulness of these instructions, loops can be placed or nested within other loops. For example:

```
10 FOR J = 1 TO 10
20 FOR K = 1 TO 5
30 NEXT K
40 NEXT J
```

To be properly nested, a loop must be entirely within another loop. The beginning and the end of different loops must never overlap. For example, the following arrangement of loops is not allowed:

```
10 FOR J = 1 TO 10
20 FOR K = 1 TO 5
30 NEXT J
40 NEXT K
```

These two loops overlap because the end of the first loop, NEXT J, comes before the end of the second loop, NEXT K. If this sample program were run, it would produce a

?NEXT WITHOUT FOR ERROR IN 40

Program 9.1

This program uses two nested loops to print the multiplication table from 1 * 5 and 1 * 6 to 5 * 5 and 5 * 6. The outer loop uses variable name X as a loop counter to count from 1 to 5. The value of variable X is then used as the first factor each time a new multiplication fact is calculated. The inner loop uses variable name Y to produce the number by which the value of variable X will be multiplied each time the inner loop is repeated. Remember, the counter variable of a loop does not have to begin with 1:

```
10  FOR X = 1 TO 5
20  FOR Y = 5 TO 6
30  LET Z = X * Y
40  PRINT X" * "Y" = "Z,
50  NEXT Y
60  PRINT
70  NEXT X

]RUN
1 * 5 = 5        1 * 6 = 6
2 * 5 = 10       2 * 6 = 12
3 * 5 = 15       3 * 6 = 18
4 * 5 = 20       4 * 6 = 24
5 * 5 = 25       5 * 6 = 30
```

- **Line 10:** Variable X in this FOR...TO statement begins the loop with a value of 1. The loop will continue until variable X is greater than 5. Variable X will also be used as the first factor each time a multiplication fact is calculated.
- **Line 20:** Variable Y begins with a value of 5. The loops will end when variable Y has a value of 6.
- **Line 30:** This statement multiplies the current value of variable X by the current value of variable Y and assigns that value to variable Z.
- **Line 40:** This PRINT statement displays the current values of variables X, Y and Z and the proper math symbols. The comma at the end of the statement arranges the output in two neat columns.
- **Line 50:** The NEXT Y statement marks the end of the inner loop.
- **Line 60:** This PRINT statement cancels the effect of the comma on line 40 and moves the cursor down to the next line.
- **Line 70:** The NEXT X statement marks the end of the outer loop.

Line 30 multiplies the value of variables X and Y to determine the value of variable Z. The first time the outer loop is repeated variable X has a value of 1 and variable Y has a value of 5, so variable Z has a value of 5. After line 40 prints the equation, the inner loop is repeated and variable X still has a value of 1, but now variable Y has a value of 6. Therefore, the next time line 30 calculates the value of variable Z it is assigned a value of 6. The inner loop is now finished since the value of variable Y has reached its end value of 6. The outer loop now increases the value of variable X to 2 and the inner loop is repeated. Each time the inner loop is repeated in this way, the value of variable Y is reset to 5 by the FOR Y = 5 TO 6 instruction on line 20. With variable Y reset to 5, the calculations on line 30 are made using the new value of variable X.

Program 9.2

This program nests 3 loops to calculate and print all the possible combinations of quarters, dimes and nickels that add up to fifty cents:

```
10   PRINT "QUARTERS","DIMES","NICKELS"
20   FOR Q = 0 TO 2
30   FOR D = 0 TO 5
40   FOR N = 0 TO 10
50   IF (Q * 25) + (D * 10) + (N * 5) = 50 THEN PRINT Q,D,N
60   NEXT N
70   NEXT D
80   NEXT Q

]RUN
```

QUARTERS	DIMES	NICKELS
0	0	10
0	1	8
0	2	6
0	3	4
0	4	2
0	5	0
1	0	5
1	1	3
1	2	1
2	0	0

In this program variable Q represents the number of quarters, variable D the number of dimes and variable N the number of nickels. The start and end values of the loops are determined by the maximum and minimum number of each coin that adds up to 50 cents. For example, there can be as few as 0 quarters or as many as 2. Likewise, there might be as few as 0 dimes or as many as 5, and there might be as few as 0 nickels or as many as 10. Because the loops are nested this way, line 50 is able to check *all* the possible combinations of coins that *might* add up to 50. However, only those combinations that equal 50 are printed. The output shows clearly how the outermost loop does not increase the value of variable Q until the value of variable D in the middle loop reaches 5, and the middle loop does not increase the value of variable D until the value of variable N in the inner-most loop reaches 10. Each time the number of dimes and nickels is checked by repeating the middle and inner loops, the value of variable D and the value of variable N are reset to 0 by FOR D = 0 TO 5 on line 30 and by FOR N = 0 TO 10 on line 40.

Review

1. Write a program that uses nested loops to produce the following output:

```
OUTER LOOP = 1
INNER = 1  INNER = 2  INNER = 3  INNER = 4
OUTER LOOP = 2
INNER = 1  INNER = 2  INNER = 3  INNER = 4
OUTER LOOP = 3
INNER = 1  INNER = 2  INNER = 3  INNER = 4
```

2. Predict the output of the following program. Check your prediction by typing the program in and running it:

```
10  FOR A = 1 TO 10
20  PRINT "+";
30  FOR B = 1 TO 10
40  PRINT "*";
50  NEXT B
60  PRINT "+"
70  NEXT A
```

The Need for Array Variables

In Chapter 2, we learned that each time a variable is assigned a new value, the old value is erased and lost forever. However, there are many situations where a programmer would like to recall one or more of a variable's previous values. For example, if a girl named Helen planned and wrote a program that allowed her to calculate the batting averages of her friends on her softball team, she would have the program ask for the name of each teammate, the number of times each batted and the number of hits. To work properly, the program should print the name and average of each of those team members. Helen did not want to use READ and DATA statements to store the data because the number of averages the program had to calculate could change from game to game, as would the names of the team mates and the number of at bats and hits for each. She thought that using INPUT statements would be a better way to enter the data. Helen's plan for this program made the program seem simple enough:

First: Input the following data:
  a. number of teammates to calculate averages for
  b. the name of each teammate
  c. the number of times each was at bat
  d. the number of hits each teammate had

Second: Calculate the batting average by dividing the number of hits by the number of times at bat.

Third: Display the following data:
  a. the name of each teammate
  b. the batting average

When Helen looked at the 3 steps of her plan, she realized that she needed 2 loops. One loop would input the data and calculate each average. A second loop would print the results of the calculations and the name of each teammate.

Program 9.3

This is the program Helen wrote. Notice how the output is not quite what Helen had in mind in her plan:

```
1   REM T = NUMBER OF TEAMMATES
2   REM N$ = NAME OF TEAMMATE
3   REM B = TIMES AT BAT
4   REM H = NUMBER OF HITS
5   REM A = BATTING AVERAGE
10  HOME
20  INPUT "HOW MANY TEAMMATES TO CALCULATE ? ";T
30  PRINT
40  FOR J = 1 TO T
50  INPUT "TEAMMATE'S NAME ";N$
60  INPUT "TIMES AT BAT ";B
70  INPUT "NUMBER OF HITS ";H
80  LET A = H / B
90  PRINT
100 NEXT J
110 HOME
120 PRINT "NAME" TAB( 15)"AVERAGE"
130 FOR J = 1 TO T
140 PRINT N$; TAB( 15);A
150 NEXT J

]RUN
HOW MANY TEAMMATES TO CALCULATE ? 3

TEAMMATE'S NAME MARY ANNE
TIMES AT BAT 6
NUMBER OF HITS 2

TEAMMATE'S NAME JEAN
TIMES AT BAT 4
NUMBER OF HITS 3

TEAMMATE'S NAME HELEN
TIMES AT BAT 6
NUMBER OF HITS 3

NAME           AVERAGE
HELEN          .5
HELEN          .5
HELEN          .5
```

Helen's plan was a good one, but it did not work the way she wanted it to because of the way simple variables are stored in the computer's memory. If we compare the way variables are stored in the computer's memory to mail boxes, as was done in Chapter 2, the actions of the computer in working with variable names N$, B, H and A would look like this during the run of the program:

	N$	B	H	A
1st repetition of the loop	MARYANNE	6	2	.333333333
2nd repetition	JEAN	4	3	.75
3rd repetition	HELEN	6	3	.5

Each variable uses only one box whose contents are constantly being changed. When the computer executes the loop that prints the names and averages on the screen, variables N$ and A contain only the values they had after the third repetition of the loop. All of their earlier values were lost.

Arrays: Variables with Many Boxes

An array uses a type of variable that allows the computer to employ more than one memory box as a place to store the variable's values. An array is made up of numbered memory boxes that store either numeric or string data. To use an array instead of a simple variable, a programmer must tell the computer the name of the array and which of the boxes the programmer wants to use. In a program, an array variable looks like this:

$$X(N)$$

Array Name   (Subscript Number)

The array name is the name by which all the memory boxes that are part of an array are known. Each individual box within an array is called a subscripted variable. The subscript is the number within the parentheses which tells the computer which of the boxes that make up the array the programmer wants the computer to use.

Continuing to use the idea of memory boxes, an array with 3 subscripted variables storing the numbers 7, 5 and 10 would look like this:

N(1)	N(2)	N(3)
7	5	10

It is important to realize that the subscript number is the number of the box not the value stored within the box. For example, the array described here is a list of numbers named N( ) and the 3rd item on the list, subscripted variable N(3), has a value of 10.

The subscripted variables that make up an array are used much like simple variables. For instance, there can be both numeric or string subscripted variables. Also, subscripted variables are assigned values by using LET, INPUT, and READ statements in the same way that simple variables are assigned values. When using subscripted variables in a program, the subscript number can be an integer, a variable or the result of an arithmetic expression. For example, N(5), N(X) and N(X+3) are all possible subscripted variable names.

Program 9.4

This is how Helen used arrays to make her batting average program work exactly as she had planned it:

```
1   REM T = NUMBER OF TEAMMATES
2   REM N$() = NAME OF TEAMMATE
3   REM B = TIMES AT BAT
4   REM H = NUMBER OF HITS
5   REM A = BATTING AVERAGE
10  HOME
20  INPUT "HOW MANY TEAMMATES TO CALCULATE? ";T
30  PRINT
40  FOR J = 1 TO T
50  INPUT "TEAMMATE'S NAME? ";N$(J)
60  INPUT "TIMES AT BAT? ";B
70  INPUT "NUMBER OF HITS? ";H
80  LET A(J) = H / B
90  PRINT
100  NEXT J
110  HOME
120  PRINT "NAME" TAB( 15)"AVERAGE"
130  FOR J = 1 TO T
140  PRINT N$(J); TAB( 15);A(J)
150  NEXT J

]
]RUN
HOW MANY TEAMMATES TO CALCULATE? 3

TEAMMATE'S NAME? MARY ANNE
TIMES AT BAT? 6
NUMBER OF HITS? 2

TEAMMATE'S NAME? JEAN
TIMES AT BAT? 4
NUMBER OF HITS? 3

TEAMMATE'S NAME? HELEN
TIMES AT BAT? 6
NUMBER OF HITS? 3

NAME            AVERAGE
MARY ANNE       .333333333
JEAN            .75
HELEN           .5
```

Helen's program is still made up of two loops, one following the other. In the first loop, 3 names are input and a batting average calculated for each name. The loop counter, variable J, was used to keep track of the subscript values for each of the subscripted variables that made up the arrays N$(J) and A(J). When the value of variable J was 1, variable N$(1) was assigned the name MARY ANNE. Variable A(1) was assigned a value equal to 2/6, which is .333333333:

N$(1)   A(1)

| MARYANNE | | .333333333 |

When variable J was equal to 2, N$(2) was assigned JEAN as its value, and variable A(2) was assigned the result of ¾, which is .75, as its value:

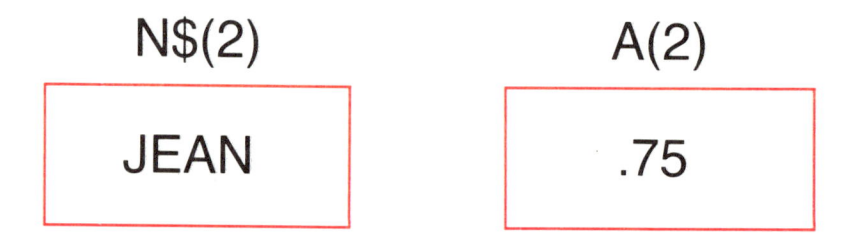

N$(2)   A(2)

| JEAN | | .75 |

When variable J was equal to 3, N$(3) was assigned HELEN as its value, and variable A(3) was assigned the result of 3/6, which is .5, as its value:

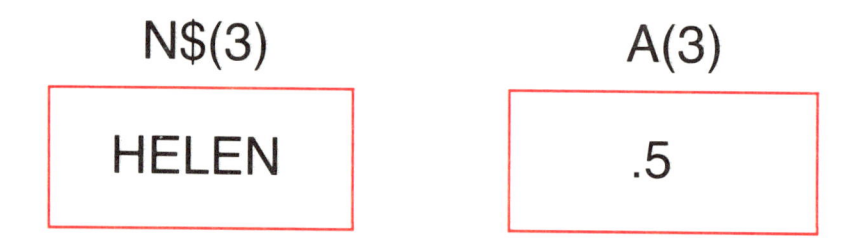

N$(3)   A(3)

| HELEN | | .5 |

The second loop prints each of the subscripted variables that make up the arrays N$(J) and A(J). Because each array is made up of 3 separate boxes (subscripted variables) whose contents are assigned a single value, each time the loop is repeated the contents of a different box (subscripted variable) are printed on the screen.

The subscripted variables that make up an array can be used in exactly the same ways that simple values are used. Likewise, their values can be replaced by new values. When a subscripted variable's value is replaced by a new value, the old value is lost just as the value of a simple value is lost when it is replaced by a new value.

Program 9.5

This program uses an array with 4 subscripted variables to show how subscripted variables are used in the same way that simple variables are used. Notice the difference between the subscript number and the value that a subscripted variable represents:

```
10   LET L(1) = 7
20   LET L(2) = 5
30   LET L(3) = 4
40   PRINT "L(1)= "L(1),"L(2)= "L(2)
45   PRINT "L(3)= "L(3),"L(4)= "L(4)
50   PRINT "L(1+2)= "L(1 + 2)
60   PRINT "L(1) + L(2)= "L(1) + L(2)
70   LET L(4) = L(2) + L(3)
80   PRINT "L(4)= "L(4)
90   LET L(1) = L(2) - L(3)
100  PRINT "NOW L(1)= "L(1)

]RUN
L(1)= 7              L(2)= 5
L(3)= 4              L(4)= 0
L(1+2)= 4
L(1) + L(2)= 12
L(4)= 9
NOW L(1)= 1
```

- **Lines 10-30:** Three of the subscripted variables that make up the array L( ) are each assigned their value by separate LET statements.

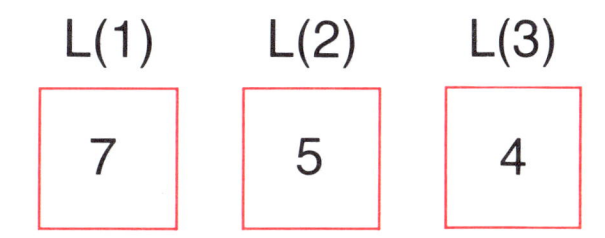

L(1)	L(2)	L(3)
7	5	4

- **Line 40:** The contents of each of the four subscripted variables that make up the array are printed on the screen. Since variable L(4) has not been assigned a value, its value is given as 0 by the computer.
- **Line 50:** 1 is added to 2 to get 3. The computer then prints the contents of subscripted variable L(3) which is 4. Note that the computer did not add the values of variables L(1) and L(2).
- **Line 60:** Variable L(1), which has a value of 7, and variable L(2), which has a value of 5, are added to get 12.

The subscript is only the number of the box in which a value is stored and should not be confused with the value stored in the box. If the value of the subscript is changed, the computer looks in a different box.

- **Line 70:** Subscripted variable L(4) is assigned a new value by adding the contents of subscripted variables L(2) and L(3). The result of this operation gives variable L(4) a value of 9.
- **Line 80:** The value of subscripted variable L(4) is printed on the screen.

- **Line 90:** Subscripted variable L(1) is given a new value. Its old value of 7 is replaced by the new value of 1 after the computer subtracts the value of subscripted variable L(3), which is 4, from the value of subscripted variable L(2), which is 5.
- **Line 100:** The new value of subscripted variable L(1) is printed on the screen.

Subscripted variables allow a programmer to store and recall the past values of the variables that make up an array, but as lines 70 and 90 demonstrate, subscripted variables still function in the same way that simple variables function. A programmer can carry out math operations with them, assign them a value or change their values at any time.

Review

3. Write a program that picks 10 random numbers from 1 to 100 and stores them in an array of subscripted variables. After the numbers are picked and stored, have the computer print each of the numbers and the name of the subscripted variable that stores it:

   ```
   RUN
   L(1) = 27        L(2) = 13
   L(3) = 45        L(4) = 43
   L(5) = 27        L(6) = 34
   L(7) = 2         L(8) = 22
   L(9) = 17        L(10) = 98
   ```

4. Using subscripted variables, write a program in which 3 numbers are entered. Then have the computer type them back in reverse order.

   ```
   RUN
   ENTER A NUMBER? 4
   ENTER A NUMBER? 6
   ENTER A NUMBER? 1

   1
   6
   4
   ```

5. Write a program that enters 7 words from the keyboard. Then have the computer randomly select 4 of the words and write them as a sentence. The sentence need not make any sense and words may be repeated:

   ```
   RUN
   ENTER A WORD? JACK
   ENTER A WORD? AND
   ENTER A WORD? JILL
   ENTER A WORD? WENT
   ENTER A WORD? UP
   ENTER A WORD? THE
   ENTER A WORD? HILL

   UP WENT THE HILL.
   ```

DIMensioning an Array

Without any special instructions the computer will allow a subscripted variable to have subscript values ranging from 0 to 10. That means a list of as many as 11 boxes can be set aside as part of an array:

| A(0) | A(1) | A(2) | A(3) | A(4) | A(5) | A(6) | A(7) | A(8) | A(9) | A(10) |

If an array will need subscript values greater than 10, the computer must be told what the DIMensions of the array are. This is done by using a DIM statement. The format for a DIM statement is:

    10 DIM <variable name> (<dimension>)

In a program a DIM statement for a string array named N$( ) with subscript values up to 100 would look like this:

    20 DIM N$(100)

The dimension value may be a number or a variable. For example:

    10 LET L = 100
    20 DIM N$(L)

will dimension an array that is equivalent to the variable in line 20 above.

If the array N$(L) were storing people's names and a programmer also wanted to store their ages, another array would have to be dimensioned. It could be dimensioned in a separate statement on a different line, or the above statement could be rewritten like this:

    10 LET L = 100
    20 DIM N$(L), A(L)

If a programmer asks the computer to dimension an array and there is not enough space available in the computer's memory for the array, the following error message will appear and the run of the program will be halted:

    ?OUT OF MEMORY ERROR

A program must DIMension an array before the program tries to use any of the subscripted variables that make up the array. Also, the program must not use the subscript values that are higher than the number to which an array has been dimensioned. To help keep these two rules in mind, it is good programming style to place DIM statements near the beginning of a program. This helps to make clear what arrays are being used in a program as well as what the dimensioned length of each array is.

Program 9.6

In order to better organize his time, Joe Kolodnigork asked his sister Josephine to computerize the customer list of his lawn mowing service. He currently has 12 customers and wants to be able to ask the computer to tell him which lawns to mow depending on the day of the week. He also wants the program to tell him how much to charge each customer:

```
1    REM   N$(C) = NAMES
2    REM   D$(C) = DAY TO CUT
3    REM   P(C) = PRICE TO CHARGE
10   HOME
20   READ C
30   DIM N$(C),D$(C),P(C)
40   FOR J = 1 TO C
50   READ N$(J),D$(J),P(J)
60   NEXT J
70   PRINT "WHAT DAY IS TODAY?"
80   INPUT "(M, TU, W, TH, F OR SA): ";A$
90   PRINT
100  IF A$ <  > "M" AND A$ <  > "TU" AND A$
     <  > "W" AND A$ <  > "TH" AND
     A$ <  > "F" AND A$ <  > "SA" THEN 80
110  PRINT "NAME","CHARGE"
120  FOR T = 1 TO C
130  IF D$(T) = A$ THEN  PRINT N$(T),"$ "P(T)
140  NEXT T
150  PRINT "THAT'S IT FOR TODAY."
200  REM   NUMBER OF CUSTOMERS
210  DATA  12
220  REM NAME,DAY TO CUT, CHARGE
230  DATA HACKER,M,15,JONES,F,12,JOHNSTON,TH,18
240  DATA SMITH,SA,25,BREWSTER,W,20,ZAHARCHUK,TH,21
250  DATA BIDWELL,SA,22,MURPHY,W,7,DINGLE,TU,12
260  DATA NILSON,M,23,WANG,TH,9,WHITE,SA,27

]RUN
WHAT DAY IS TODAY?
(M, TU, W, TH, F OR SA): W

NAME                CHARGE
BREWSTER            $ 20
MURPHY              $ 7
THAT'S IT FOR TODAY.
```

- **Line 20:** Variable C is the number of customers that Joe has. The variable C can now be used to DIM the arrays that will store the name, day to cut and price to charge each customer.
- **Line 30:** Since Joe has more than 10 customers, the arrays that store his customer information will have subscript values greater than 10 so the arrays must be dimensioned. The variable C is the number of N$( ) and D$( ), and P( ) boxes created in the computer's memory. N$(J) stores the customer's name, D$(J) stores the day of the week that the customer's lawn is to be mowed and P(J) stores the price that this customer is to be charged.

- **Lines 40-60:** The loop that reads the names, days of the week, and prices to charge from the data statements and assigns the data to the correct array. The loop counter, variable J, is used to change the subscript values each time the loop is repeated. For instance, when variable J is 1, variable N$(J) = HACKER, variable D$(J) = M for Monday and variable P(J) = 15.
- **Lines 70-100:** These lines input the day of the week for which information is needed. If the data entered for the day of the week is not correct, line 100 uses an IF . . . THEN with AND to send the computer back to line 80.
- **Line 110:** This line prints headings for the two columns of data that will be displayed. One column is titled NAME and the other column CHARGE. A comma is used to separate the columns on the screen.
- **Lines 120-140:** This loop searches through all the D$(T) subscripted variables for a match to the day entered as variable A$. When one of these subscripted variables has a value that is the same as the value of variable A$, the customer's name, variable N$(T), and the price to charge them, variable P(T), are printed on the screen.

```
RUN
WHAT DAY IS TODAY?
(M, TU, W, TH, F OR SA)? W

NAME              CHARGE
BREWSTER          $ 20
MURPHY            $ 7
THAT'S IT FOR TODAY.
```

In the run shown above the value input as variable A$ was "W". The condition on line 130, IF A$ = D$(T), was not true until the loop had been repeated 5 times. When variable J had a value of 5, variable A$ did equal D$(5) because variable D$(5) is a "W". This made the condition on line 130 true, so variable N$(5) which is BREWSTER and variable P(5) which is 20 were printed on the screen. When the loop made its eighth repetition, the condition on line 130 was true again because D$(8) is also a "W." Therefore, variable N$(8), which is MURPHY, and varible P(8), which is 7, were also printed on the screen.

- **Line 150:** This message tells Joe that all the data for the day requested has been displayed.
- **Lines 200-210:** A REM and DATA statement to show that the data item in line 210 is the number of customers. If Joe gets more customers, he can make the program read the new information by changing only this number and by adding the proper data.
- **Line 220:** A REM statement that shows that the data is arranged by name, day of the week and price so that Joe can easily add or delete customers.
- **Lines 230-260:** The data that will be used by the program.

Review

6. Even though the National League has won more All-Star games than the American League, Harry Hacker is a fan of the American League baseball teams. This program is supposed to input the name of a city and give the name of the team that plays in that city or say if there is no American League team in that city. Find and correct the error in this program:

```
1    REM    C$() = THE NAME OF THE CITIES
2    REM    T$() = THE TEAM NAMES
3    REM    N$ = NAME OF CITY TO LOOK FOR
10   HOME
20   FOR S = 1 TO 14
30   READ C$(S),T$(S)
40   NEXT S
50   INPUT "TYPE IN THE NAME OF A CITY ? ";N$
60   FOR S = 1 TO 14
70   IF C$(S) = N$ THEN  PRINT C$(S);"    ";T$(S): GOTO 50
80   NEXT S
90   INPUT "ANOTHER CITY TO CHECK (YES/NO) ? ";A$
100   IF A$ = "YES" THEN  PRINT : GOTO 50
110  END
200  DATA DETROIT,TIGERS,BOSTON,RED SOX
210  DATA BALTIMORE,ORIOLES,TORONTO,BLUE JAYS
220  DATA MILWAUKEE,BREWERS,NEW YORK,YANKEES
230  DATA CLEVELAND,INDIANS,CALIFORNIA,ANGELS
240  DATA OAKLAND,A'S,CHICAGO,WHITE SOX
250  DATA KANSAS CITY,ROYALS,TEXAS,RANGERS
260  DATA SEATTLE,MARINERS,MINNESOTA,TWINS
```

7. Write a program that picks 12 random numbers from 1 to 100. Then print those numbers vertically and horizontally.

```
]RUN
3
13
99
13
99
71
99
80
29
72
76
10
3 13 99 13 99 71 99 80 29 72 76 10
```

Longer Variable Names

In explaining simple and array variables it has been previously explained that a variable name can be a letter, a letter and a digit, or two letters. This means that N, L$, L1, C1$, CL,and BB$ are legal variable names as are L(1), X$(1), Z1(1), R1$(1), WW(1) and GB$(1). Actually, a variable name can be up to 255 characters in length. Therefore, ALPHABET, MILK, BREAD, and CALC12 are all allowable variable names. However, there are some problems that can arise when longer variable names are used.

The major problem is that the computer recognizes only the first two letters of a variable name. This means that SNACK and SNUB mean the same to the computer since the computer only considers the letters SN. This may cause a logic error that will not halt the program but can cause the output of the program to be incorrect. In fact, in a longer program an error like this might not be noticed at all.

Another problem is caused by the possibility that the computer will confuse longer variable names with BASIC statements. For example,

FORTUNE, MOTOR, CANDY and DIMWIT are all unacceptable variable names because they contain a BASIC statement:

> **FOR**TUNE contains FOR
> MOT**OR** contains OR
> C**AND**Y contains AND
> **DIM**WIT contains DIM

All BASIC commands and statements are reserved words on the computer. Variable names that contain any of these reserved words will cause a run time error. The program will be halted by a SYNTAX ERROR message. However, this can be a difficult error to find since the variable name is a normal English word that does not look as if it has anything wrong with it.

Longer variable names can be useful, especially in identifying what a variable represents in the program. However, because of the problems mentioned here, longer variable names should be used cautiously.

Review

8. By what name will the computer recognize the following variables:

   A.) ACCOUNT01
   B.) ACCOUNT02
   C.) SUPERMAN$
   D.) SPY$
   E.) SPOT$

9. Harry Hacker is being hassled by his big brother who owes Harry money. Harry's brother will use any excuse to keep from paying, and poor Harry cannot figure out why his program that keeps track of the amount of the loan does not work. Help out Harry by finding the errors in this program and then type in and run the corrected program:

   ```
   10 INPUT"ENTER NEW LOAN AMOUNT $";LOAN1
   20 READ LOAN
   30 LOAN = LOAN + LOAN1
   40 PRINT "YOU OWE $" LO
   ```

10. In which of the following statements are the variable names illegal and why?

   A.) DIM DRAGON$(25)
   B.) LET COUNT = COUNT + 1
   C.) LET AVERAGE = TOTAL / ITEMS
   D.) IF STIFF(1) = OWE THEN GOSUB 1000
   E.) ON SMELL GOSUB 100, 200, 300

Program 9.7

This program demonstrates the use of subscripted variables to create 15 "words". The words are made by choosing from 1 to 7 letters at random from an array. The words may be real but they may also be nonsense words:

```
1    REM    A$(26) = AN ARRAY FOR LETTERS OF ALPHABET
2    REM    R = RANDOM LENGTH OF EACH WORD
3    REM    P = RANDOM SUBSCRIPT FOR LETTER
4    REM    W$ = THE WORD THAT IS BUILT
10   HOME
20   DIM A$(26)
30   FOR A = 1 TO 26
40   READ A$(A)
50   NEXT A
60   FOR W = 1 TO 15
70   LET R =   INT (7 * RND (1) + 1)
80   FOR L = 1 TO R
90   LET P =   INT (26 * RND (1) + 1)
100  LET W$ = W$ + A$(P)
110  NEXT L
120  PRINT W$
130  LET W$ = ""
140  NEXT W
200  DATA A,B,C,D,E,F,G,H,I,J,K,L,M
210  DATA N,O,P,Q,R,S,T,U,V,W,X,Y,Z
```

```
]RUN
CAUOQYO
VDVWVP
KW
DHV
V
XLADZ
Z
ZUHST
W
BGVXTG
LEDA
TQNCF
FR
PTLF
JKJGDQ
```

- **Lines 1-4:** These REM statements identify the important variables that are used in the program.
- **Line 20:** This line tells the computer the DIMension of the array that will store the 26 subscripted variables that make up the alphabet.
- **Lines 30-50:** This loop reads one letter at a time from the data statements and places each letter in one of the 26 subscripted variables that are part of the array A$(A). When variable A=1, then A$(1) equals "A"; when A=2, then A$(2) equals "B" all the way up to A=26 and A$(26) equals "Z". Notice that there is no confusion between using A$( ) as the array name and A as the subscript variable.
- **Line 60:** The beginning of the outer loop of two nested loops. This loop counts the number of words (15) that will be created.
- **Line 70:** Assigns variable R a random number from 1 to 7. This will be the length of the next word that the program will create.
- **Line 80:** This is the inner loop of the nested loops. It picks the letters and builds the word. When a word has been built by repeating this loop a number of times equal to the value of variable R, this loop ends and the outer loop continues.
- **Line 90:** Picks a random number from 1 to 26. This number will be the subscript number of a letter of the alphabet that will be used to make the word.
- **Line 100:** This statement builds the word. String variable W$ begins with no value. It is a null string (" ") that contains no characters. Each time the loop is repeated the letter that is stored in the subscripted variable A$(P) is added to variable W$. If the number picked for variable P is 10, then A$(10), which is the letter J, will be made part of variable W$. If variable P is a 5, then the letter E will be added to variable W$ because A$(5)="E".
- **Line 110:** NEXT L signals the end of the inner loop. The loop will be repeated until variable L is greater than the random number picked as variable R.
- **Line 120:** Prints variable W$, which is the word, on the screen.
- **Line 130:** Erases the word that is currently stored in variable W$ so that the next word made will start with no letters. Variable W$ is erased and initialized by making it equal to a null string which is done by placing two quotation marks side by side with nothing between them.
- **Line 140:** NEXT W tells the computer that a word has been built and that the outer loop can begin another repetition. The loop will continue to repeat until the value of variable W is greater than 15.

RESTORE

At times it is necessary to have a program read the same data more than once. The RESTORE statement tells the computer to go back to the first DATA statement in the program and begin reading from the first item of data. The RESTORE statement uses the following format:

110 RESTORE

After executing this statement, the computer is ready to reuse the data from the beginning.

Program 9.8

RESTORE is used in this program to allow a list of names and phone numbers to be read and re-read:

```
10   PRINT "PHONE LIST"
20   INPUT "TYPE NAME TO FIND? ";S$
30   FOR J = 1 TO 5
40   READ N$,P$
50   IF N$ = S$ THEN  PRINT N$,P$: GOTO 80
60   NEXT J
70   PRINT S$" NOT FOUND"
80   PRINT
90   INPUT "TYPE 'YES' TO SEARCH AGAIN? ";A$
100  IF A$ < > "YES" THEN  END
110  RESTORE
120  PRINT : GOTO 20
130  DATA BOB,555-1234,MIKE,555-3232
140  DATA BRUCE,555-6831,RALPH,555-9823
150  DATA ROBBIE,555-5432

]RUN
PHONE LIST
TYPE NAME TO FIND? RALPH
RALPH              555-9823

TYPE 'YES' TO SEARCH AGAIN? YES

TYPE NAME TO FIND? ROB
ROB NOT FOUND

TYPE 'YES' TO SEARCH AGAIN? NO
```

On line 90 the user is asked if the phone list is to be searched again. If the answer is yes, RESTORE on line 110 tells the computer to go back to the first DATA statement. When line 120 sends the computer back to line 20 to input a new name to search for, the computer will start the search for that name with the first name, Bob, in the first DATA statement. If RESTORE were not used the search would start with Robbie, the name following Ralph, rather than from the beginning.

Review

11. Write a program that uses the following data to search for and print the grades each student received in each math class this semester. The output should look like this:

    RUN
    TYPE END TO EXIT THE PROGRAM.

    NAME? HARRY HACKER
    GRADES: 78 87 65 79 90

    NAME? JOE KOLODNIGORK
    GRADES: 60 80 75 77 89

    NAME? JOHN DOE
    STUDENT JOHN DOE NOT FOUND

    NAME? END

Use the following data in your program.

NAME	GRADES
Joe Kolodnigork	60, 80, 75, 77, 89
Diana Prince	88, 90, 93, 89, 92
Harry Hacker	78, 87, 65, 79, 90
Al K. Seltzer	67, 78, 88, 98, 99
Rhoda Dendron	85, 87, 84, 89, 90

GET

The GET statement is used to input data one digit or character at a time. Its format in a program is:

GET <variable name>

When the computer executes a GET statement, the computer checks to see what key has been pressed on the keyboard. The computer GETs that character or digit and assigns it to the variable that is part of the GET statement. Much like the INPUT statement, the GET statement waits for the user to enter data from the keyboard. However, it is not necessary to hit the RETURN key because a RETURN is supplied by the GET.

It is good programming style to make a program as simple and easy to use as possible so that people who do not understand how a computer works can use it. One way in which GET can be used to do this is by giving a user a "menu" of choices from which to pick what the computer will do next:

CHOOSE THE TYPE OF PROBLEM TO REVIEW:

1. ADDITION
2. SUBTRACTION
3. MULTIPLICATION
4. DIVISION

TYPE THE NUMBER OF YOUR SELECTION:

Another method is to give the program user yes or no decisions to make and have the computer wait until the proper key is pressed:

TYPE Y FOR YES OR N FOR NO.

Using a GET statement simplifies these inputs by allowing a single keystroke to tell the computer what to do next.

Program 9.9

Program 8.5 allowed a user to choose 1 of 3 movie reviews to read but used INPUT statements to enter the user's selections. In this version of the program, GET is used to simplify the way that choices are input by the user:

```
1   REM   N = YOUR CHOICE OF MOVIE
2   REM   A$ = YOUR CHOICE TO SEE ANOTHER REVIEW
10  HOME
20  PRINT "SELECT A MOVIE REVIEW:"
```

```
30   PRINT "1 - STAR WARS"
40   PRINT "2 - THE EMPIRE STRIKES BACK"
50   PRINT "3 - RETURN OF THE JEDI"
60   PRINT : PRINT "CHOOSE THE REVIEW BY NUMBER."
70   PRINT "TYPE 1, 2, OR 3: ";
80   GET N
90   PRINT N
100  IF N < 0 OR N > 3 THEN 70
110  ON N GOSUB 200,300,400
120  PRINT : PRINT "ANOTHER REVIEW"
130  PRINT "Y OR N: ";
140  GET A$
150  PRINT A$
160  IF A$ = "Y" THEN 10
170  IF A$ = "N" THEN   END
180  GOTO 130
190  REM
195  REM
200  REM   *** STAR WARS ***
210  PRINT "LUKE BATTLES THE EMPIRE,"
220  PRINT "RESCUES THE PRINCESS,"
230  PRINT "DESTROYS THE DEATH STAR AND"
240  PRINT "GETS HIS PICTURE ON BURGER KING"
250  PRINT "GLASSES."
260  RETURN
270  REM   *** END STAR WARS ***
280  REM
290  REM
300  REM   *** THE EMPIRE STRIKES BACK ***
310  PRINT "THE REBEL ALLIANCE IS TEMPORARILY"
320  PRINT "SET BACK AND HAN IS CAPTURED"
330  PRINT "AND FROZEN."
340  RETURN
350  REM   *** END EMPIRE STRIKES BACK ***
360  REM
370  REM
400  REM   *** RETURN OF THE JEDI ***
410  PRINT "LUKE LEARNS HIS REAL"
420  PRINT "IDENTITY AND THE EMPIRE IS"
430  PRINT "DEFEATED. "
440  RETURN
450  REM   *** END RETURN OF THE JEDI ***

]RUN
SELECT A MOVIE REVIEW:
1 - STAR WARS
2 - THE EMPIRE STRIKES BACK
3 - RETURN OF THE JEDI

CHOOSE THE REVIEW BY NUMBER.
TYPE 1, 2, OR 3: 2
THE REBEL ALLIANCE IS TEMPORARILY
SET BACK AND HAN IS CAPTURED
AND FROZEN.

ANOTHER REVIEW
Y OR N: N
```

- **Lines 20-60:** These lines are the menu.
- **Line 70:** This line tells the user which key to press to make a selection. The semicolon at the end of the line keeps the cursor on the line to print the number selected by the user.
- **Line 80:** This GET statement tells the computer to assign variable name N the value of the next key pressed.
- **Line 90:** The computer is told to print the value of variable N. Though it is not necessary to print the number that was selected, it is good programming style to do so.
- **Line 100:** The value of variable N is checked to make sure that it is within the correct range.
- **Line 140:** The computer is told to assign the value of the next key pressed to string variable A$.
- **Line 150:** The value of variable A$ is printed on the screen. This enables the user to see whether the computer has correctly received the instructions that the user intended.
- **Line 160:** If the key pressed is the Y key, the computer branches to line 10 to repeat the program.
- **Line 170:** If the key pressed is the N key, the program ends.
- **Line 180:** If the user presses any key other than Y or N, the program goes back to line 130 and repeats the instruction to enter a Y or an N. This is good programming style because it prevents a program from being ended by accidentally pressing the wrong key.

VAL( )

It is often useful to change the string character or characters for a number into their numeric value. This is done by assigning a numeric variable the VAL( ) of the string characters:

LET A = VAL (<string>)

The string that is within the parentheses can be a string variable or a string of characters within quotation marks:

LET A = VAL(A$)
LET B = VAL("23")

VAL( ) will convert all combinations of the characters 0-9 into numeric values. The first non-numeric character that the computer encounters will cause the conversion of characters to numbers to halt. A string that begins with a non-numeric character will be given a value of 0:

PRINT VAL("1234")
1234

PRINT VAL("2") + VAL("3")
5

PRINT VAL("007 JAMES BOND")
7

PRINT VAL("TWO")
0

An important use for VAL( ) is preventing the accidental input of incorrect data that halts a program with an error message. SYNTAX ERRORS with GET and errors caused by a user typing a non-numeric character when the computer is expecting numbers as data such as the REENTER with INPUT can be eliminated by using a string variable to input all data. After the data is entered as a string, the string variable can be changed into its numeric value by using VAL( ). The following examples show how this technique can be used with INPUT or GET in a program:

```
50 INPUT"TYPE A NUMBER"; N$
60 LET N = VAL(N$)
```

OR

```
80 GET A$ :
90 LET A = VAL(A$)
```

It is good programming style to prevent errors by using "preventive programming" techniques like this whenever possible.

Program 9.10

This is a number guessing game that allows the user to select a range of random numbers and then gives the player an unlimited number of chances to guess the number. By using VAL( ) to check all input, the program has been made more user friendly since it anticipates the user entering the wrong type of data.

```
1   REM   L = LEVEL OF DIFFICULTY
2   REM   B = THE HIGHEST NUMBER TO PICK
3   REM   N = NUMBER PICKED BY THE COMPUTER
4   REM   G = USER'S GUESS
10  HOME
20  PRINT "SELECT THE DIFFICULTY LEVEL"
30  PRINT "1. NUMBERS FROM 1 TO 10"
40  PRINT "2. NUMBERS FROM 1 TO 50"
50  PRINT "3. NUMBERS FROM 1 TO 100"
60  PRINT "4. NUMBERS FROM 1 TO 500"
70  PRINT "5. NUMBERS FROM 1 TO 1000"
80  PRINT : PRINT "TYPE 1, 2, 3, 4, OR 5: ";
90  GET L$
100 PRINT L$
110 LET L = VAL (L$)
120 IF L < 1 OR L > 5 THEN 80
130 IF L = 1 THEN LET B = 10: GOTO 180
140 IF L = 2 THEN LET B = 50: GOTO 180
150 IF L = 3 THEN LET B = 100: GOTO 180
160 IF L = 4 THEN LET B = 500: GOTO 180
170 LET B = 1000
180 LET N = INT (B * RND (1) + 1)
190 PRINT : INPUT "TYPE YOUR GUESS? ";G$
200 LET G = VAL (G$)
210 IF G = N THEN 240
220 IF G < N THEN PRINT "TOO LOW  GUESS AGAIN": GOTO 190
230 IF G > N THEN PRINT "TOO HIGH GUESS AGAIN": GOTO 190
240 PRINT "YOU GUESSED IT!"
250 END
```

```
]RUN
SELECT THE DIFFICULTY LEVEL
1. NUMBERS FROM 1 TO 10
2. NUMBERS FROM 1 TO 50
3. NUMBERS FROM 1 TO 100
4. NUMBERS FROM 1 TO 500
5. NUMBERS FROM 1 TO 1000

TYPE 1, 2, 3, 4, OR 5: 2

TYPE YOUR GUESS? 50
TOO HIGH GUESS AGAIN

TYPE YOUR GUESS? 25
TOO LOW  GUESS AGAIN

TYPE YOUR GUESS? 37
TOO LOW  GUESS AGAIN

TYPE YOUR GUESS? 43
TOO LOW  GUESS AGAIN

TYPE YOUR GUESS? 47
TOO LOW  GUESS AGAIN

TYPE YOUR GUESS? 49
YOU GUESSED IT!
```

- **Line 110:** The character input by GET L$ is converted into a number and assigned to variable L.
- **Line 120:** The value of variable L is checked to make sure that it is within the range of values that the program needs. If variable L is not within the proper range, the program goes back to line 80 and repeats the input.
- **Lines 130-170:** Depending on the value of variable L, variable B is given its value. Notice how the colons allow GOTO 180 to be included on lines 130,140,150 and 160. In this way, line 170 does not need an IF . . . THEN because the computer will get to this line only when variable L is equal to 5.
- **Line 190:** The number guessed is input as a string variable G$.
- **Line 200:** Variable G is assigned a value equal to VAL (G$).
- **Lines 210-230:** The value of variable G is compared to the value of the computer's number variable N. If variable G equals variable N, the program branches to line 240 where YOU GUESSED MY NUMBER is printed and the program ends.

Review

12. Predict the output of each of the following VAL( ) instructions. Check your predictions by using immediate mode:

   a. PRINT VAL("12.34")   b. PRINT VAL("123CAT456")
   c. PRINT VAL("-76")   d. PRINT VAL("ONE23")

13. Christine's nephew can't make the happy birthday message she sent him in a computer program work. Look at a listing of the program and a run of it below. Correct the program using GET and VAL so that this problem will not repeat itself:

LIST
10 INPUT "HOW OLD ARE YOU?";A
20 PRINT "HAPPY BIRTHDAY TO YOU"
30 PRINT "ALL GOOD SEVENS GO STRAIGHT TO HEAVEN."

RUN
HOW OLD ARE YOU? SEVEN
?REDO FROM START
HOW OLD ARE YOU?

Program 9.11

This program uses VAL( ), GET, and RESTORE to search DATA statements in which baseball player's uniform numbers, names and batting averages are stored. When a player's uniform number is input, the appropriate name and batting average is printed.

```
10   HOME
20   INPUT "PLAYER'S NUMBER PLEASE: ";A$
30   LET A = VAL (A$)
40   RESTORE
50   FOR I = 1 TO 10
60   READ N,N$,B
70   IF A = N THEN 110
80   NEXT I
90   PRINT "PLAYER # "A" NOT FOUND": PRINT
100  GOTO 120
110  PRINT N$,B: PRINT
120  PRINT "DO YOU WANT ANOTHER ? ";
130  GET A$
140  PRINT A$
150  IF A$ = "Y" THEN 20
160  DATA 22,SNYDER,.387,44,NILSON,.295
170  DATA 14,TIBBETTS,.358,6,SMALL,.201
180  DATA 13,ZAHARCHUK,.275,86,DINGLE,.123
190  DATA 19,WANG,.264,1,BIDWELL,.392
200  DATA 16,PRESLEY,.393,34,DECKEL,.168
210  END

]RUN
PLAYER'S NUMBER PLEASE: 13
ZAHARCHUK        .275

DO YOU WANT ANOTHER ? Y
PLAYER'S NUMBER PLEASE: 6
SMALL            .201

DO YOU WANT ANOTHER ? Y
PLAYER'S NUMBER PLEASE: 12
PLAYER # 12 NOT FOUND

DO YOU WANT ANOTHER ? N
```

- **Line 10:** Clears the screen.
- **Line 20:** Inputs the jersey number of the player you want to find.
- **Line 30:** Gives variable A the numeric value of variable A$.
- **Line 40:** Allows the user to access the data from the top of the list.
- **Line 50:** Starts the loop which will search the data.
- **Line 60:** Reads in the number, name and batting average of the next player in the list.
- **Line 70:** If the player's number matches the number just read in, the loop is exited.
- **Line 80:** Completes the loop started in line 60.
- **Line 90:** If the loop has been completed without a match, then the appropriate message is printed.
- **Line 110:** The player's name and batting average are output when a match is made.
- **Line 120-150:** This routine asks the user whether he or she wants to try again. A GET is used to accept the answer.
- **Line 160-200:** DATA used for the READ in line 60.

Conclusion

Now that you have worked your way through this text you should be familiar with the fundamentals of BASIC. This knowledge will enable you to discover and take advantage of the versatility of the computer. Your ability to design your own programs means that you are less dependent upon commercial software and that you can now use the computer to suit your purposes.

More important, your experience with this text has introduced you to new problem solving techniques and improved your ability to analyze, plan and organize. You've learned that the computer will not accept sloppy, illogical thinking, and inevitably, you have improved your capacity for rigorous, disciplined thought. In short, this text has helped you become a better thinker.

Finally, with the help of this text you have acquired a skilled familiarity with the world of computers that is rapidly changing the way we live. You will find that there is a demand in society for the very skills that this text has sought to teach you, and therefore you are among the fortunate who can confront our increasingly computerized world with confidence.

EXERCISES

1. Use two nested loops to have the computer print a rectangle with 8 lines and 20 asterisks in each line:

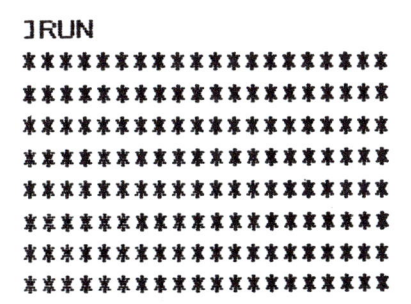

   ```
   ]RUN
   ********************
   ********************
   ********************
   ********************
   ********************
   ********************
   ********************
   ********************
   ```

2. Predict the output of the following program and check by typing it in and running it. Rerun the program after deleting line 50 to see how the output changes:

   ```
   10  FOR J = 1 TO 5
   20  FOR K = 1 TO ((2 * J) - 1)
   30  PRINT "*";
   40  NEXT K
   50  PRINT
   60  NEXT J
   ```

3. Use nested loops to draw the following right triangle:

   ```
   ]RUN
   *
   **
   ***
   ****
   *****
   ******
   *******
   ********
   ```

4. Reverse the direction of the triangle so that it looks like this:

   ```
   ]RUN
   ********
   *******
   ******
   *****
   ****
   ***
   **
   *
   ```

5. Use two nested loops to draw the following triangle:

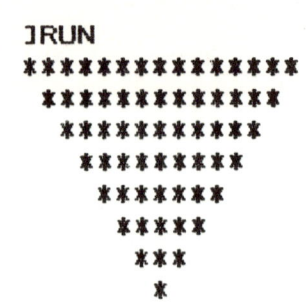

```
]RUN
***************
*************
***********
*********
*******
*****
***
*
```

6. Use nested loops to reverse the direction of the triangle so that it looks like this:

```
]RUN
       *
      ***
     *****
    *******
   *********
  ***********
 *************
***************
```

7. Write a program in which you enter the values for the array X(J) using the statement FOR J = 1 TO 6. Then print the values of both variable J and the subscripted variables of the array, but print the values in 2 groups. The first group will use 1, 3, and 5 as values of variable J and the second group will use 2, 4 and 6 as the values of variable J:

```
]RUN
TYPE A NUMBER? 7
TYPE A NUMBER? 4
TYPE A NUMBER? 3
TYPE A NUMBER? 8
TYPE A NUMBER? 9
TYPE A NUMBER? 2
J = 1      X( 1 ) = 7
J = 3      X( 3 ) = 3
J = 5      X( 5 ) = 9
J = 2      X( 2 ) = 4
J = 4      X( 4 ) = 8
J = 6      X( 6 ) = 2
```

8. Write a program in which you enter 15 letters of the alphabet (not necessarily) different. Then print all letters in reverse order as a single block of letters:

```
]RUN
TYPE A LETTER? A
TYPE A LETTER? W
TYPE A LETTER? S
TYPE A LETTER? E
TYPE A LETTER? F
TYPE A LETTER? T
TYPE A LETTER? G
TYPE A LETTER? Y
TYPE A LETTER? H
TYPE A LETTER? U
TYPE A LETTER? J
TYPE A LETTER? G
TYPE A LETTER? R
TYPE A LETTER? E
TYPE A LETTER? G
GERGJUHYGTFESWA
```

9. As part of her initiation into the local computer club, Erin had to play computer and predict the output of the following programs. See how you would do on the same test and then check your predictions by running each program.

(A) 10 FOR L = 1 TO 3
    20 FOR N = 5 TO 6
    30 PRINT L, N
    40 NEXT N
    50 NEXT L

(B) 10 FOR X = 10 TO 15 STEP 2
    20 FOR Y = 15 TO 10 STEP −2
    30 IF Y = X THEN 100
    40 IF X < Y THEN PRINT X
    50 IF X > Y THEN PRINT Y
    60 NEXT Y
    70 NEXT X
    80 END

(C) 10 FOR S = 0 TO 10
    20 READ A(S)
    30 NEXT S
    40 PRINT A(0), A(3), A(7), A(10)
    50 DATA 23, 12, 45, 2, 87, 34, 89, 17, 2, 35, 70, 63

10. This is another problem Erin had to do for her initiation. See if you can pass the test too and predict the output of the following program. Then type it in to check your prediction:

```
10   FOR R = 1 TO 5
20   READ N$(R),A(R),B(R)
30   M(R) = (A(R) + B(R)) / 2
40   NEXT R
50   PRINT "NAME" TAB( 15)"QUIZ 1" TAB( 22)"QUIZ 2"
TAB( 30)"AVERAGE"
```

```
60    FOR C = 1 TO 5
70    PRINT N$(C); TAB( 15);A(C); TAB( 22);B(C);
TAB( 30);M(C)
80    NEXT C
90    DATA SUE,85,73,JOE,81,89
100   DATA MIKE,78,63,MARY,98,75
110   DATA ALLISA,100,95
```

11. Harry and Joe want to find out how many random numbers between 1 and 100 the computer can pick before it repeats itself.
    a.) Their program has a few errors. Correct the errors so the program will produce the following output:

```
10   FOR X = 1 TO 100
20   REM *** PICK A RANDOM NUMBER ***
30   LET N(X) = INT (100 * RND (1) + 1)
40   REM *** LOOP THRU ALL EARLIER NUMBERS ***
50   FOR Y = 1 TO (X - 1)
60   REM *** CHECK FOR DUPLICATES ***
70   IF N(Y) < > N(X) THEN 150
80   NEXT Y
90   NEXT X
110  END
150  REM *** HOW MANY AND THE NUMBERS ***
160  PRINT "DUPLICATE AFTER "X" NUMBERS."
170  FOR J = 1 TO X
180  PRINT N(J)" ";
190  NEXT J
```

b.) The first time they wrote the program they wrote line 60 this way:

60 FOR Y = 1 TO 100

This first instruction does not work. Harry claimed to have an inspiration from Spiderman that led them to the correct instruction. What was the real reason that their first line did not work?

12. Write a program that reads the name, street address and phone number of 5 people into 3 arrays: N$(X), A$(X) and P$(X). The program user then enters a name and the program prints the name, address and phone number of that person. If the name is not there, have the program print PERSON NOT FOUND.

    RUN
    ENTER NAME? SPIDERMAN

    12 WEB HEAD LANE
    555-9999

    ENTER NAME? SUPERMAN

    PERSON NOT FOUND.

    ENTER NAME?

13. For Penny's computer club initiation, she had to predict the output of the following program. Can you do it also? Type the program in and run it to check your prediction.

```
10   READ B1,B2,B3,B4,B5,B6
20   FOR X = 1 TO 6
30   READ B(X)
40   NEXT X
50   PRINT "B4= "B4" BUT B(4)= "B(4)
60   PRINT B1 + B2 + B3,
70   PRINT B(1) + B(2) + B(3),B(1 + 2 + 3)
80   DATA  3,7,4,1,8,12
90   DATA  14,42,69,86,12,111
```

14. Sue and Ellen have decided to "kill two birds with one stone" by writing a program that will quiz them on the capitals of the countries of Western Europe for their Social Studies class and help them practice their programming. The program will begin by asking if they want to match the capital to the country or the country to the capital:

ENTER NUMBER OF YOUR SELECTION:

1) COMPUTER GIVES COUNTRY YOU GIVE CAPITAL.
2) COMPUTER GIVES CAPITAL YOU GIVE COUNTRY.

If they get an answer wrong, they want the program to tell them the right answer. The data for this program is:

COUNTRY	CAPITAL
United Kingdom	London
Ireland	Dublin
France	Paris
Spain	Madrid
Portugal	Lisbon
Italy	Rome
Greece	Athens
Belgium	Brussels
Netherlands	Amsterdam
Luxembourg	Luxembourg
West Germany	Bonn
Austria	Vienna
Switzerland	Bern

See if you can do as well as they hope to do by planning and writing the same program. Do not forget to use subroutines to break the program down into smaller parts that do only one job at a time.

15. Fred, Harry, Wendy, Penny and Joe are members of the Bulletin Board Committee of their computer club. Each of them is supposed to have a day of the week when it is his or her job to check the computer bulletin board for messages. Write a program that will allow the user to enter a day of the week and be told whose day it is to check the bulletin board for messages:

    RUN
    BULLETIN BOARD SCHEDULE

    FOR WHAT DAY : ? TUESDAY
    ON TUESDAY FRED HAS BULLETIN BOARD DUTY.
    TYPE YES TO CHECK ANOTHER DAY? NO

Program Data

NAME	DUTY DAY
FRED	TUESDAY
HARRY	THURSDAY
WENDY	WEDNESDAY
PENNY	FRIDAY
JOE	MONDAY

16. Wendy and Joe were quite surprised to find the computer club's computer running one day. They thought nothing of it at first and began to type away on a program they had in mind. Everything seemed to be working fine, but they soon found that someone had played a trick on them and left a program running on the computer. What does this program that they found do?

```
10   HOME : PRINT "  WELCOME TO THE MYSTERY WRITER"
20   PRINT "PRESS ANY KEY TO TYPE ON THE SCREEN"
30   PRINT "PRESS * TO QUIT THE PROGRAM"
40   PRINT "PRESS RETURN FOR A NEW LINE."
50   GET A$
60   PRINT A$;
70   IF A$ = "*" THEN  PRINT "DONE": END
80   GOTO 50
```

17. Harry Hacker has decided to write a program that stores an inventory of all his comic books. All he has to do is tell the computer which type of comic book, and the computer will tell him how many of that type he has. Harry is tired of REDO FROM START and SYNTAX ERROR messages when he enters the wrong kind of data. Show Harry how to enter his data with a single key stroke and without caring whether he hits a wrong key by accident:

    RUN
    SELECT A NUMBER:

    1. SPIDERMAN
    2. BATMAN
    3. SUPERMAN
    4. GI JOE

    TYPE 1,2,3 OR 4 : 1

    YOU HAVE 37 SPIDERMAN COMICS.

APPENDIX A

Proper Care of Equipment

Diskettes should not be stored near any device which produces heat or a strong magnetic field such as a television set or computer monitor.

Making a New Diskette Operational, INIT

It is necessary to initialize, or "format", a new diskette before the computer can use it for the first time. First, the Disk Operating System (DOS) must be loaded into the computer from some previously initialized diskette, such as the System Master provided by the manufacturer. This is done by inserting the diskette in drive 1 and turning on the computer. The diskette to be initialized should then be substituted for the diskette in the drive. Type NEW and then enter a "greeting program". A greeting program is a program stored on the disk that the computer will run automatically when it is turned on with the diskette in the drive. A short example is shown here:

```
10  REM   GREETING PROGRAM
20  PRINT "HOMEWORK DISKETTE"
30  PRINT "INITIALIZED BY"
40  PRINT "MICHAEL BIDWELL"
50  PRINT "SEPTEMBER 27, 1984"
60  END
```

After the greeting program has been entered, the INIT command is used to initialize the diskette and save the greeting program on it. Its format is:

INIT <program name>

The greeting program will be saved under the name specified. For example:

INIT HELLO

will instruct the computer to initialize the diskette in the drive and store the program currently in memory on the diskette with the name HELLO.

SAVE

The SAVE command is used to store a program on a diskette. Its format is:

SAVE <program name>

For example:

SAVE TAXES

will save the program currently in memory on the diskette and give it the name TAXES. If there is already a program on the diskette with that name, the new program will replace it, thereby destroying the original.

The program name may be up to thirty characters long. The first character may not be a digit.

LOAD

Programs previously stored on a diskette can be recalled using the LOAD command. Its format is:

LOAD <program name>

For example:

LOAD TAXES

will load the program TAXES into memory from the diskette. Any program previously in memory will be replaced. It is important to note that this procedure does not remove the program from the diskette. An exact copy of the program is made and placed in the computer's memory.

CATALOG

Typing the command CATALOG in immediate mode produces a list of all the programs and files on a diskette:

```
]CATALOG

DISK VOLUME 254

*A 003 HELLO
 I 003 APPLESOFT
*B 006 LOADER.OBJ0
*B 042 FPBASIC
*B 042 INTBASIC
 A 003 MASTER
*B 009 MASTER CREATE
 I 009 COPY
*B 003 COPY.OBJ0
 A 009 COPYA
 B 003 CHAIN
*A 014 RENUMBER
*A 003 FILEM
 B 020 FID
*A 003 CONVERT13
 B 027 MUFFIN
*A 003 START13
*B 007 BOOT13
*A 004 SLOT#

]
```

The catalog is displayed in four columns. If the first column contains an asterisk, the program or file has been locked to prevent accidental removal. If no asterisk is present, it is unlocked. (A description of the commands LOCK and UNLOCK is presented later in this appendix.) The second column contains a single letter identifying the type of program or file listed. An A signifies a program written in Applesoft. An I signifies a program written in Integer BASIC. A T signifies a data file, and a B signifies a file or program in machine code. The number in the third column indicates the number of sectors the program or file takes up on the diskette. The minimum is two. The fourth column contains the name of the program or file.

RENAME

The RENAME command is used to change the name of a program or file that has been stored on a diskette. Its format is:

RENAME <old name>, <new name>

For example:

RENAME TAXES,IRS

will give the program TAXES on the diskette the new name IRS.

DELETE

Unwanted programs and files are removed from a diskette with the DELETE command. Its format is:

DELETE <program or file name>

For example:

DELETE IRS

will remove the program IRS from the diskette in the drive.

LOCK and UNLOCK

The LOCK command is used to prevent a program or file from being removed accidentally from a diskette. Its format is:

LOCK <program or file name>

For example:

LOCK TAXES

will lock the program TAXES stored on the diskette. A subsequent attempt to rename or delete it will result in the error message FILE LOCKED.

Locked programs or files can be unlocked with the command UNLOCK. Its format is:

UNLOCK <program or file name>

For example:

UNLOCK TAXES

will unlock the program TAXES. Once a program or file has been unlocked, it can be renamed or deleted.

Multiple Drive Systems

When you are using a system that has more than one diskette drive, it is often necessary to specify which drive you want to use. This is done by using an expanded syntax for the commands in this appendix. The expanded format is,

$$<command>,D<d>$$

where d is the number of the desired drive. For example:

$$CATALOG,D2$$

will produce a list of the programs and files stored on the diskette in drive 2. Similarly,

$$SAVE\ TAXES,D1$$

will instruct the computer to save the program currently in memory under the name TAXES on the diskette drive 1. When no drive is explicitly specified with a command, the computer will use the drive that was last specified with a command. When the computer is first turned on, it uses drive 1 until otherwise specified.

GLOSSARY

algorithm: a precise, step-by-step description of a method for solving a problem.

accumulator: a variable that changes its value each time its assignment statement is repeated, thus collecting a total. The change in its value may vary each time it is repeated.

array: subscripted set of variables that stores related values.

assign: to give a variable a value.

BASIC: a popular computer language. It is an acronym for Beginner's All-Purpose Symbolic Instruction Code.

branch: a change in the direction of the flow of instructions in a program.

bug: an error in either the design or the coding of a program.

character string: a sequence of letters, number and/or special characters such as punctuation marks.

code: the instructions that make up a program.

coding: the process of writing "code," or instructions, that the computer can understand.

command: an instruction to the computer in a language the computer understands.

conditional branch: a change in the flow of the program from one part to another based on a comparison.

constant: a variable value that remains unchanged throughout a program.

counter: a variable that changes its value by a specific amount each time it is repeated, therefore keeping a count of the occurrences of an event.

cursor: a special symbol used by the computer to show where the next character will be printed on the screen.

debugging: the process of finding and removing "bugs", or errors, in a program.

edit: to make changes in a program.

execute: to carry out the commands and instructions of a program.

E notation: called scientific notation, a way of expressing very large or very small numbers by indicating the number or places to the left or right the decimal point should be moved.

exponent: a number indicating how many times a number should be multiplied by itself, i.e., $2 \uparrow 2 = 2 * 2, 2 \uparrow 3 = 2 * 2 * 2$.

flag: when a condition equals this specified value, the program branches to a different section of the program. Usually used with the IF . . . THEN statement.

format: the way in which instructions are laid out.

home: the starting position of the cursor at the top left hand corner of the screen.

immediate mode: the mode in which the computer executes commands and instructions immediately when the RETURN key is pressed.

initialize: to assign a variable a value equal to the value it must have at the beginning of a program or subroutine.

input: the act of entering data into the computer.

integer: a whole number or the whole number part of a mixed number.

line number: the number in front of each line of code that is used to place each line of instructions in its order of execution within the program.

loop: a section of a program designed to be executed repeatedly.

nested loop: a loop placed entirely within another loop.

numeric variable: a variable that is assigned number values.

order of operations: the order in which the computer will carry out math operations beginning with exponents, then multiplication and division, and finally addition and subtraction.

output: data or information displayed by the computer on a device such as the screen or a printer.

program: a series of instructions that tells the computer what operations to carry out and in what order to perform them.

program line: one line of code in a program. Each line is preceded by a line number.

random number: a number picked by chance.

reserved word: a word, such as PRINT or FOR, that is part of the language of the computer and therefore cannot be used as part of a variable name.

scrolling: the upward and downward movement of output on the computer's display screen.

statement: all the elements that combined carry out an instruction, i.e., a PRINT instruction can be followed by quotation marks, variable names, semicolons, commas, etc., to make an entire PRINT statement.

string: a sequence of letters, numbers and/or special characters such as punctuation marks.

string variable: a variable that has a string as its value.

structured program: a program that is designed so that its parts and how they work are obvious to anyone reading the program.

subroutine: a section of a program that executes a specific task and is called by a GOSUB and exited by a RETURN.

subscript: the number used to identify each of the individual variables that make up an array.

subscripted variable: one of the numbered variables that make up an array.

syntax: the correct rules, or "grammar", with which a programming language is used.

variable: a name used to represent a value that is stored in the memory of the computer. This value can be changed.

SUMMARY OF BASIC INSTRUCTIONS

AND: used in IF ... THEN statements when more than one condition is to be checked.

CATALOG: a DOS command for producing a list of files and programs stored on a diskette.

CLEAR: a command used to free space in the computer's memory taken up by unneeded variables.

COLOR: a graphics command for setting the color to be used with low-resolution graphics.

CONT: causes execution of a program to resume after it has been stopped by CONTROL-C, STOP or END.

DATA: the statement used to signify a list of data that is part of a program.

DELETE: a DOS command for removing a program or file from a diskette.

DIM: the command for setting the size of, and reserving space for a subscripted variable.

DOS: the disk operating system.

END: halts the execution of a program.

FLASH: causes the computer to print flashing characters on the display.

FOR ... TO: used to define the beginning and range of a loop.

GET: used to input a single character from the keyboard without striking the RETURN key.

GOSUB: instructs the computer to jump to a subroutine starting at the specified line.

GOTO: instructs the computer to jump to a specified line in a program.

GR: a graphics command that causes the computer to enter the low-resolution graphics mode.

HCOLOR: a graphics command for setting the color to be used with high-resolution graphics.

HGR: a graphics command that causes the computer to enter the high-resolution graphics mode.

HGR2: same as HGR.

HLIN: a graphics command used for drawing lines in the low-resolution graphics mode.

HOME: clears the screen and moves the cursor to the upper left-hand corner of the screen.

HPLOT: a graphics command for plotting dots in the high-resolution graphics mode.

HTAB: moves the cursor to the right or left on the screen.

IF ... THEN: instructs the computer to take a specific course of action if a condition is found to be true.

INPUT: a command used for entering data into the computer.

INT: a mathematical function that returns the integer portion of the floating point number.

INVERSE: causes the computer to print characters as black on white.

LIST: displays the lines of a program in memory.

LOAD: a DOS command for recalling a program previously stored on a diskette.

NEW: removes the program currently in the memory so that a new one can be entered.

NEXT: indicates the end of a loop started with a FOR ... TO.

NORMAL: causes the computer to print characters as white on black.

ON ... GOSUB: causes program execution to jump to one of several subroutines depending on the value of an expression.

ON ... GOTO: causes program execution to jump to one of several program lines depending on the value of an expression.

OR: used in IF ... THEN statements to compare more than one condition at a time. If any condition is true, the comparison is true.

PLOT: a graphics command for plotting points in low-resolution graphics mode.

PRINT: causes the computer to display information on the screen or printer.

READ: takes data from a DATA statement and assigns it to a specific variable.

REM: signifies that what follows is a comment by the programmer, not a command to be executed by the computer.

RESTORE: allows data in a program to be read again starting at the beginning of the data.

RETURN: used at the end of a subroutine, it sends program execution back to the point where the subroutine was called from.

RND: a function that returns a random number greater than or equal to 0 and less than 1.

RUN: starts execution of a program.

SAVE: a DOS command that instructs the computer to save the program in memory on a diskette under the name specified.

STOP: halts program execution.

TAB: moves the cursor to the right on the display.

TEXT: a graphics command that causes the computer to leave the graphics mode it is in and return to the regular display mode.

VAL: a function that returns the numeric value of a string composed of numeric characters.

VLIN: a graphics command that draws a vertical line in the low-resolution graphics mode.

VTAB: moves the cursor up or down on the screen.

REVIEW ANSWERS

CHAPTER ONE

1. ```
   ]PRINT 2 + 5
   7

   ]PRINT 6 - 3
   3

   ]PRINT 5 * 3
   15

   ]PRINT 15 / 3
   5
   ```

2. ```
   ]PRINT "I AM 5 FEET TALL."
   I AM 5 FEET TALL.
   ```

3. ```
   ]PRLNT "LOOK MA! NO HANDS."

   ?SYNTAX ERROR
   ```

4. ```
   ]PRINT "LOOK MA! NO HANDS."
   LOOK MA! NO HANDS.
   ```

5. ```
   ]RUN
   MY COMPUTER IS
   A CHIP OFF THE OLD
   BLOCK!
   ```

6. ```
   ]RUN
   1368
   351


   ]RUN
   12 COOKIES MAKE A DOZEN.
   ```

8.]RUN
    8 EQUALS 8
    40 + 20 = 60

9.]RUN
    TED DECKEL

10.]RUN
    TED DECKEL
    MY COMPUTER LIKES ME

11.]RUN
    SCREEN EDITING
    CAN BE FUN
    IT SAVES WORK

12. 10   PRINT "SCREEN EDITING"
    20   PRINT "CAN BE FUN"
    25   PRINT "AND"
    30   PRINT "IT SAVES WORK"

13. 25   PRINT "AND"
    30   PRINT "IT SAVES WORK"

CHAPTER TWO

1.]RUN
    100

2. 10   LET B = 45
    20   LET C = 15
    30   PRINT B - C

    ]RUN
    30

4. 10   LET B = 64
    20   LET A = 32
    30   LET C = A + B
    40   PRINT C

    ]RUN
    96

5.]RUN
    GO FOR BROKE

6. 10 LET A$ = "COMPUTER"
    20 LET B = 64
    30 PRINT A$
    40 PRINT B

7. 10 LET N$ = "WONDERFUL WENDY"
    20 LET P$ = "PROGRAMMER"
    30 PRINT N$" ACE COMPUTER "P$

8. 10 LET X = 25
    20 LET Y = 50
    30 PRINT "THE PRODUCT OF "X" AND "Y" IS "X * Y
    40 PRINT X" * "Y" = "X * Y

9. 10 INPUT A
    20 INPUT B
    30 PRINT A" + "B" = "A + B

10. 10 INPUT A
    20 PRINT "10 * "A" = "10 * A

11. 10 INPUT N$
    20 PRINT "HI! "N$

12. 10 INPUT "TYPE A NUMBER? ";N
    20 PRINT "12 + "N" = "12 + N
    30 PRINT "12 * "N" = "12 * N

13. 10 INPUT "WHAT IS YOUR NAME? ";A$
    20 INPUT "WHAT IS YOUR FRIEND'S NAME? ";B$
    30 PRINT B$" IS A FRIEND OF "A$

CHAPTER THREE

1. 10 PRINT "YOUR NAME HERE"
    20 GOTO 10

R-4   Review Answers

2.]RUN
    *** ***** ***** ***** ***** ***** ***** ***** ***** **
    BREAK IN 10

3. 10   LET C = C + 2
    20   PRINT C
    30   GOTO 10

4. 10   INPUT "WHAT IS N? ";N
    20   PRINT "12 + "N" = "12 + N
    30   PRINT "12 * "N" = "12 * N
    40   GOTO 10

5. 10   INPUT "WHAT IS YOUR NAME? ";A$
    20   INPUT "WHAT IS YOUR FRIEND'S NAME? ";B$
    30   PRINT A$" IS A FRIEND OF "B$
    40   GOTO 10

6.]RUN
    MILEAGE CALCULATOR
    ENTER MILES RUN EACH DAY.
    ONE DAY'S MILEAGE: 2
    TOTAL MILES = 2

    ONE DAY'S MILEAGE: 3
    TOTAL MILES = 5

    ONE DAY'S MILEAGE: 3
    TOTAL MILES = 8

    ONE DAY'S MILEAGE: 2
    TOTAL MILES = 10

    ONE DAY'S MILEAGE: 5
    TOTAL MILES = 15

    ONE DAY'S MILEAGE:

    BREAK IN 30

7. 70   GOTO 30

8. 10   READ X
    20   READ Y
    30   PRINT X" - "Y" = "X - Y
    40   DATA 5, 3

9.  ```
    10  READ S$
    20  PRINT "A "S$" IS MY FAVORITE SNACK"
    30  READ D$
    40  PRINT "A "D$" IS MY FAVORITE DRINK"
    50  DATA HAMBURGER, COKE
    ```

10. ```
    10  PRINT "MY FAVORITE TEAMS:"
    20  READ T$
    30  PRINT T$
    40  GOTO 20
    50  DATA BOSTON RED SOX
    60  DATA NEW ENGLAND PATRIOTS
    70  DATA NEW YORK GIANTS
    ```

11. ```
    10  READ A
    20  PRINT A
    30  GOTO 10
    40  DATA 2, 4, 6, 8, 10
    ```

12. ```
    ]RUN
    SECRET AGENT FILE

    ?SYNTAX ERROR IN 60
    ```

13. ```
    ]RUN
    *** **           ****              *** ###
    ```

14. ```
    10  PRINT "MONSTER","DESCRIPTION"
    15  PRINT
    20  READ M$,A1$,A2$,A3$
    30  PRINT M$,A1$" "A2$" "A3$
    40  GOTO 20
    50  DATA  GODZILLA, GREEN, SCALY, UGLY
    60  DATA  KING KONG, BIG, BROWN, HAIRY
    ```

CHAPTER FOUR

1.  ```
    10  INPUT "ENTER PASSWORD PLEASE? ";P$
    20  IF P$ = "AVIATRIX" THEN 60
    30  PRINT "SORRY CHARLIE"
    40  PRINT
    50  GOTO 10
    60  PRINT "YOU'RE THE BOSS"
    ```
    ```

2. 10 INPUT "TYPE A NUMBER? ";N
    20 IF N = 25 THEN 100
    30 IF N > 25 THEN 70
    40 PRINT "TOO SMALL"
    50 PRINT
    60 GOTO 10
    70 PRINT "TOO LARGE"
    80 PRINT
    90 GOTO 10
    100 PRINT "JUST RIGHT"
    110 PRINT
    120 GOTO 10

3. 10 INPUT "ENTER FIRST NUMBER? ";A
    20 INPUT "ENTER SECOND NUMBER? ";B
    30 IF A < B THEN 70
    40 PRINT B
    50 PRINT A
    60 GOTO 10
    70 PRINT A
    80 PRINT B
    90 GOTO 10

4. 10 INPUT "ENTER A LAST NAME? ";A$
    20 INPUT "ENTER ANOTHER NAME? ";B$
    30 IF A$ < B$ THEN 70
    40 PRINT B$
    50 PRINT A$
    60 GOTO 90
    70 PRINT A$
    80 PRINT B$
    90 PRINT
    100 INPUT "TWO MORE NAMES TO COMPARE? ";Y$
    110 IF Y$ = "YES" THEN 10
    120 PRINT "BYE."

5. 10 LET C = C + 1
    20 PRINT C" ";
    30 IF C < 10 THEN 10
    40 PRINT
    50 PRINT "ALL DONE."

6. 10 READ N
    20 IF N = - 99 THEN 50
    30 LET S = S + N
    40 GOTO 10
    50 PRINT "THE SUM IS "S
    60 DATA 26, 37, 42, 65, 89
    70 DATA 234, 567, -99

7.  ```
    10  INPUT "ENTER A NUMBER? ";N
    20  IF N > 25 AND N < 50 THEN 50
    30  PRINT " "N" IS OUT OF RANGE"
    40  GOTO 10
    50  PRINT " "N" IS BETWEEN 25 AND 50"
    60  GOTO 10
    ```

8.  ```
    10  INPUT "TYPE A WORD? ";N$
    20  IF N$ < "GARBAGE" OR N$ > "TRASH" THEN 50
    30  PRINT "NO"
    40  GOTO 10
    50  PRINT "YES"
    60  GOTO 10
    ```

CHAPTER FIVE

1.  ```
    10  FOR X = 1 TO 10
    20  PRINT X" ";
    30  NEXT X
    ```

2.  ```
    10  FOR X = 1 TO 20
    20  PRINT "LOOP THE LOOP!"
    30  NEXT X
    ```

3.  ```
    ]RUN
    5 6 7 8 9 10
    THE SUM OF ALL NUMBERS FROM 5 TO 10
    IS 45
    ```

4.  ```
    50  NEXT J
    ```

5.  ```
    10  INPUT "STEP VALUE? ";N
    20  FOR S = 10 TO 30 STEP N
    30  PRINT " "S;
    40  NEXT S
    ```

6.  ```
    ]RUN
    FROM 0 TO 100 BY 5
    0 5 10 15 20 25 30 35 40 45 50 55 60 65 70 75 80 85 90 95 100
    LOOP COMPLETED J = 105

    ]RUN
    FROM 0 TO 100 BY 10
    0 10 20 30 40 50 60 70 80 90 100
    LOOP COMPLETED J = 110
    ```

Review Answers

7.]RUN
    0 7 14 21 28 35
    THE FINAL VALUE OF B IS 42

8. 10 FOR X = 20 TO 10 STEP - 2
    20 PRINT X" ";
    30 NEXT X

9. 10 INPUT "STEP VALUE? ";N
    20 FOR X = 30 TO 0 STEP - N
    30 PRINT " "X;
    40 NEXT X

10. 10 PRINT   TAB(20);"THIS"
    20 PRINT   TAB(20);"IS"
    30 PRINT   TAB(20);"TAB"

CHAPTER SIX

1a.]PRINT 6 - 9 / 3
    3

 b.]PRINT 5 * 15 - 5
    70

 c.]PRINT 3 ^ 2 + 1
    10

 d.]PRINT 3 * (5 + 6)
    33

 e.]PRINT 25 / 5 + 3 * 12
    41

 f.]PRINT (13 - 3) / (10 / 2)
    2

    ]PRINT (2 + 1) ^ (8 / 4)
    9

    ]PRINT 3 * (2 + (5 - 2))
    15

2. 30 LET C = (A + B) * 2

3a.   ]PRINT 100 / 8
       12.5

  b.   ]PRINT 22 / 7
       3.14285714

  c.   ]PRINT 5 / 6 - 1 / 8
       .708333333

  d.   ]PRINT 37 / 2
       18.5

  e.   ]PRINT 11 / 3
       3.66666667

4a.   ]PRINT INT(199.99999)
       199

  b.   ]PRINT INT(22 / 7)
       3

  c.   ]PRINT INT(-3.01)
       -4

  d.   ]PRINT INT(.005)
       0

  e.   ]PRINT INT(-.999)
       -1

5.
```
10  FOR I = 1 TO 10
20  LET N =  INT (100 *  RND (1) + 1)
30  PRINT N,
40  NEXT I
```

6.
```
10  LET A =  INT (25 *  RND (1) + 1)
20  LET B =  INT (25 *  RND (1) + 1)
30  PRINT A" + "B" = "A + B
```

7.
```
10  FOR K = 1 TO 15
20  LET N =  INT (11 *  RND (1) + 10)
30  PRINT N
40  NEXT K
```

8.
```
10  LET A =  INT (26 *  RND (1) + 25)
20  LET B =  INT (25 *  RND (1) + 1)
30  PRINT " "A" - "B" = "A - B
```

R-10   Review Answers

9a. .0142

 b. 432100

 c. 456231000

 d. .005

 e. 6708700

 f. .000067896

10.]RUN
     5E-03
     123400
     1.984E-05
     ALL DATA READ

11. 10 LET A = 25.92
     20 LET B = INT (10 * A) * .1
     30 PRINT "25.92 TO THE NEAREST TENTH IS "B

CHAPTER SEVEN

1. 10 HOME
    20 HTAB 18
    30 VTAB 12
    40 PRINT "APPLE"

2. 10 HOME
    20 FOR I = 1 TO 4
    30 READ V,H
    40 VTAB V
    50 HTAB H
    60 PRINT "*";
    70 NEXT I
    80 DATA 3,1,3,40,24,1,24,40

3.  ```
    10   HOME
    20   FLASH
    30   PRINT "UNCLE BILL'S WHAMBURGERS "
    40   PRINT "      WEEKLY SPECIAL       "
    50   PRINT "    REGULAR WHAMBURGER     "
    60   PRINT "       FRIES & DRINK       "
    70   PRINT
    80   PRINT "         ONLY $1.39        "
    90   NORMAL
    100  END
    ```

4.  ```
    10   HOME
    20   INVERSE
    30   PRINT "UNCLE BILL'S WHAMBURGERS "
    40   PRINT "      WEEKLY SPECIAL       "
    50   PRINT "    REGULAR WHAMBURGER     "
    60   PRINT "       FRIES & DRINK       "
    70   PRINT
    75   FLASH
    80   PRINT "         ONLY $1.39        "
    90   NORMAL
    100  END
    ```

5.  ```
    10   GR
    20   COLOR= 3
    30   VLIN 0,10 AT 0
    40   HLIN 0,5 AT 10
    50   END
    ```

6.  ```
    10   GR
    15   COLOR= 9
    20   PLOT 14,25
    30   VLIN 27,33 AT 14
    ```

7.  ```
    10   HGR
    20   FOR I = 1 TO 500
    30   LET H =  INT ( RND (1) * 280)
    40   LET V =  INT ( RND (1) * 160)
    50   LET C =  INT ( RND (1) * 8)
    60   HCOLOR= C
    70   HPLOT H,V
    80   NEXT I
    90   PRINT "STARRY STARRY NIGHT"
    100  END
    ```
    ```

8.
```
10   HGR2
20   HCOLOR= 2
30   FOR A = 0 TO 140 STEP 20
40   HPLOT 0,A TO A,140
50   NEXT A
60   END
```

CHAPTER EIGHT

1.
```
10   INPUT "NAME? ";N$
20   PRINT N$
30   IF N$ = "DONALD" THEN  GOSUB 100
40   PRINT
50   GOTO 10
100   PRINT "------"
110   RETURN
```

2.
```
10   HOME
20   FOR J = 1 TO 10
30   LET A =  INT (12 *  RND (1) + 1)
40   LET B =  INT (12 *  RND (1) + 1)
50   LET C = A * B
60   PRINT A" * "B" = ";
70   INPUT D
80   IF D = C THEN 120
100   NEXT J
110   END
120   LET T =  INT (3 *  RND (1) + 1)
130   ON T GOSUB 150,170,190
140   GOTO 100
150   PRINT "GOOD SHOW!"
160   RETURN
170   PRINT "SUPER EFFORT!"
180   RETURN
190   PRINT "RIGHT ON!"
200   RETURN
```

3.
```
10   INPUT "WHAT IS YOUR INPUT (0-3) ? ";A
20   ON A + 1 GOSUB 100,200,300,400
30   END
100  PRINT "SPIDERMAN IS A ZERO!"
110  RETURN
200  PRINT "J. JONA JAMSON IS A GEM."
210  RETURN
300  PRINT "SPIDY IS ALL SPUN OUT."
310  RETURN
400  PRINT "SPIDERS SHOULD BE SQUASHED."
410  RETURN
```

4.
```
10   FOR C = 1 TO 5
20   LET S =  INT (4 * RND (1) + 1)
30   LET A =  INT (13 * RND (1) + 1)
40   PRINT "CARD "C" IS THE "A" OF ";
50   ON S GOTO 80,100,120,140
60   NEXT C
70   END
80   PRINT "HEARTS"
90   GOTO 60
100  PRINT "CLUBS"
110  GOTO 60
120  PRINT "SPADES"
130  GOTO 60
140  PRINT "DIAMONDS"
150  GOTO 60
```

5.
```
10   INPUT A
20   FOR J = 10 TO 1 STEP  - 1
30   LET C = A * J
40   NEXT J
```

6.
```
10   HOME
20   FOR J = 1 TO 20
30   LET K = K + 1
40   PRINT J * K
50   NEXT J
```

7.
```
10   FOR J = 0 TO 10
20   LET A = J / 2
30   IF A =  INT (J / 2) THEN 50
40   PRINT A
50   NEXT J
```

R-14   Review Answers

8.
```
10   READ A,B
20   IF A = -99 THEN 80
30   PRINT
40   PRINT A * B
50   LET C = C + (A * B)
70   GOTO 10
80   PRINT C
90   DATA 4, 8, 5, 10
100  DATA 6, 12, -99, -99
```

9.

Line	F	L	W	P	T
10	1				
20		5	3		
30				16	
40			15		
50					31
60	2				
20		7	9		
30				32	
40			63		
50					126
60	3				
20		8	8		
30				32	
40			64		
50					222
60	4				

CHAPTER NINE

1.
```
10  FOR O = 1 TO 3
20  PRINT "OUTER LOOP = "O
30  FOR I = 1 TO 4
40  PRINT "INNER = "I" ";
50  NEXT I
60  PRINT
70  NEXT O
```

2.
```
]RUN
+**********+
+**********+
+**********+
+**********+
+**********+
+**********+
+**********+
+**********+
+**********+
+**********+
```

3.
```
10  FOR I = 1 TO 10
20  LET L(I) =  INT (100 * RND (1) + 1)
30  NEXT I
40  FOR I = 1 TO 10
50  PRINT "L("I") = "L(I),
60  NEXT I
```

4.
```
10  FOR I = 1 TO 3
20  INPUT "ENTER A NUMBER? ";N(I)
30  NEXT I
40  FOR I = 3 TO 1 STEP  - 1
50  PRINT N(I)
60  NEXT I
```

R-16 Review Answers

5.
```
10  FOR I = 1 TO 7
20  INPUT "ENTER A WORD? ";W$(I)
30  NEXT I
40  FOR V = 1 TO 4
50  LET R = INT (7 * RND (1) + 1)
60  PRINT W$(R)" ";
70  NEXT V
80  PRINT "."
```

6.
```
15  DIM C$(14),T$(14)
```

7.
```
10   DIM N(12)
20   FOR C = 1 TO 12
30   LET N(C) = INT (100 * RND (1) + 1)
40   NEXT C
50   FOR C = 1 TO 12
60   PRINT N(C)
70   NEXT C
80   FOR C = 1 TO 12
90   PRINT N(C)" ";
100  NEXT C
```

8a. AC

b. AC

c. SU$

d. SP$

e. SP$

9.
```
10  INPUT "ENTER NEW LOAN AMOUNT $";L1
20  READ L2
30  LET L = L1 + L2
40  PRINT "YOU OWE $"L
50  DATA  4.65
```

Review Answers   R-17

10a. 'ON' FROM DRAGON$ IS A RESERVED WORD

b. COUNT IS A LEGAL VARIABLE NAME

c. 'TO' FROM TOTAL IS A RESERVED WORD

d. 'IF' FROM STIFF(1) IS A RESERVED WORD

e. SMELL IS A LEGAL VARIABLE NAME

11.
```
10   PRINT "TYPE END TO EXIT THE PROGRAM."
20   PRINT
30   INPUT "NAME? ";N$
40   IF N$ = "END" THEN   END
50   LET I = 0
60   READ S$,G1,G2,G3,G4,G5
70   LET I = I + 1
80   IF S$ = N$ THEN   PRINT "GRADES: "G1" "G2" "G3" "G4" "G5: GOTO 110
90   IF I < 5 THEN 60
100  PRINT "STUDENT "N$" NOT FOUND"
110  RESTORE
120  GOTO 20
130  DATA JOE KOLODNIGORK,60,80,75,77,89
140  DATA DIANA PRINCE,88,90,93,89,92
150  DATA HARRY HACKER,78,87,65,79,90
160  DATA AL K. SELTZER,67,78,88,98,99
170  DATA RHODA DENDRON,85,87,84,89,90
```

12a.]PRINT VAL("12.34")
12.34

b.]PRINT VAL("123CAT456")
123

c.]PRINT VAL("-76")
-76

d.]PRINT VAL("ONE23")
0

13. 10   PRINT "HOW OLD ARE YOU? ";
     15   GET A$
     16   PRINT A$
     17   LET A =   VAL (A$)
     20   PRINT "HAPPY BIRTHDAY TO YOU"
     30   PRINT "ALL GOOD SEVENS GO STRAIGHT TO HEAVEN."

ODD EXERCISE ANSWERS

CHAPTER ONE

1a.]PRINT 5 + 16
     21

 b.]PRINT 33 - 16
     17

 c.]PRINT 13 * 3
     39

 d.]PRINT 239 * 27
     6453

 e.]PRINT 250 / 5
     50

 f.]PRINT 999 / 11
     90.8181819

3.   10 PRINT "**********"
     20 PRINT "*   *"
     30 PRINT "*   *"
     40 PRINT "*   *"
     50 PRINT "*   *"
     60 PRINT "**********"

5.
```
10   PRINT "   *"
20   PRINT "  * *"
30   PRINT " * * *"
40   PRINT "   *"
50   PRINT "   *"
60   PRINT "   *"
70   PRINT "   *"
80   PRINT "  * *"
90   PRINT "  * *"
100  PRINT " ***"
```

7.
```
10   PRINT 275" * "39" = "275 * 39
```

9.
```
10   PRINT "MILEAGE FOR FIRST WEEK IS "2 + 3 + 5 + 3 + 5
```

11.
```
10   PRINT "OUR CLASS ZOO"
20   PRINT "GERBILS: "5
30   PRINT "MICE: "6
40   PRINT "BIRDS: "3
```

13.
```
10   PRINT "RED MARBLES = "5 + 6
20   PRINT "BLUE MARBLES = "10 + 6
30   PRINT "TOTAL MARBLES = "5 + 6 + 10 + 6
```

15.
```
10   PRINT "ORANGE JUICE $ "1.99 * 2
20   PRINT "MILK $ ".89 * 2
```

CHAPTER TWO

1.
```
]RUN
THE VALUE OF A IS
3
```

3.]RUN
    25
    25

5. 10 LET A = 275
    20 LET B = 39
    30 PRINT A" * "B" = "A * B

7.]RUN
    THE VALUE OF B
    12

9. 10 INPUT "HOW MANY PACKS OF GUM ? ";N
    20 PRINT "THAT WILL BE $"N * .35

11. 10 INPUT "PRICE OF BREAD $";P
    20 INPUT "NUMBER OF LOAVES ?";N
    30 PRINT "COST $"N * P

13. 10 INPUT "HOW MANY BOOKS ? ";N
    20 INPUT "HOW MANY DAYS OVERDUE ? ";D
    30 PRINT "FINES ARE $"D * N * .1

15. 10 INPUT "AMOUNT OWED $";A
    20 INPUT "AMOUNT PAID $";P
    30 PRINT "YOUR CHANGE $"P - A
    40 PRINT "THANK YOU"

CHAPTER THREE

1. 10 LET T = T + 3
    20 PRINT T
    30 GOTO 10

Answers to Odd Numbered Exercises

3.
```
10  LET X = X + 2
20  PRINT "5 * "X - 1" = "5 * (X - 1),"5 * "X" = "5 * X
30  GOTO 10
```

5.
```
10  LET P = 1550
20  PRINT "THE STARTING AMOUNT IS "P
30  INPUT "SUBTRACT? ";S
40  LET P = P - S
50  PRINT "NEW AMOUNT IS "P
60  PRINT
70  GOTO 30
```

7.
```
]RUN
10
20
30
40
50

?OUT OF DATA ERROR IN 10
```

9.
```
]RUN
35
70
17
76

?OUT OF DATA ERROR IN 10
```

11.
```
10  READ A$,A
20  PRINT "NAME: "A$
30  PRINT "GRADE: "A
40  PRINT
50  GOTO 10
60  DATA JOE KOLODNIGORK, 79
70  DATA H. HACKER, 99
80  DATA T. TURKEY, 55
```

13.
```
]RUN
AAA111          222BBB          333     10
```

15.
```
10  READ L,W,U$
20  PRINT "LENGTH "L" "U$
30  PRINT "WIDTH "W" "U$
40  PRINT "AREA= "L * W" SQUARE "U$
50  PRINT
60  GOTO 10
70  DATA 5, 4, INCHES
80  DATA 6, 10, CENTIMETERS
90  DATA 15, 5, METERS
```

CHAPTER FOUR

1.
```
10  INPUT "HOW OLD ARE YOU? ";A
20  IF A = > 16 THEN 50
30  PRINT "YOU MUST WAIT "16 - A" YEARS TO DRIVE."
40  GOTO 10
50  PRINT "YOU ARE OLD ENOUGH TO DRIVE A CAR."
60  GOTO 10
```

3.
```
10  INPUT "TYPE A WORD? ";X$
20  IF X$ = "BIGWOW" THEN 50
30  PRINT "??????"
40  GOTO 10
50  PRINT "!!!!!!"
```

5.
```
10  READ A
20  LET T = T + A
30  IF A < > .3 THEN 10
40  PRINT "TOTAL AMOUNT BORROWED =$";T
50  DATA 1.25,.50,.50,.20,.30
```

7.
```
10  PRINT "**********"
20  LET R = R + 1
30  IF R < > 5 THEN 10
```

9.
```
10   PRINT "SPEEDY SUBTRACTION PROGRAM"
20   INPUT "ENTER LARGER NUMBER? ";A
30   INPUT "ENTER SMALLER NUMBER? ";B
35   IF A < B THEN 100
40   PRINT A" - "B" = "A - B
50   PRINT
60   GOTO 20
100  PRINT
110  PRINT "NO WAY!"
120  PRINT "ENTER THE LARGER NUMBER FIRST!"
130  GOTO 50
```

11.
```
20   IF L$ > "G" AND L$ < "P" THEN 50
```

13.
```
10   INPUT "ENTER A NUMBER? ";X
20   IF X > 75 OR X < 50 THEN 50
30   PRINT "BETWEEN"
40   GOTO 10
50   PRINT "NOT BETWEEN"
60   GOTO 10
```

15.
```
10   PRINT "  *"
20   PRINT " ***"
30   PRINT "*****"
40   PRINT "  *"
50   PRINT "  *"
60   PRINT "  *"
70   PRINT "  *"
80   PRINT " ***"
90   PRINT " ***"
100  PRINT " ***"
110  LET C = C + 1
120  PRINT
130  IF C < > 25 THEN 10
```

17.
```
10   INPUT "HOURS WORKED: ";H
20   INPUT "HOURLY WAGE $ ";W
30   IF H < 40 THEN 60
40   LET S = 40 * W + (H - 40) * (W * 2)
50   GOTO 70
60   LET S = H * W
70   PRINT "THE WEEKLY WAGE IS $ ";S
```

19.
```
10   READ A$,P
20   IF A$ = "END" THEN 150
30   IF P > 75 THEN 10
40   PRINT
50   PRINT "DEAR "A$","
60   PRINT "    I AM SORRY THAT I MUST FIRE YOU."
70   PRINT "YOU HAVE BEEN SUCH A FINE EMPLOYEE"
80   PRINT "WITH A PRODUCTION RATING OF "P"."
90   PRINT "    I AM SURE THAT YOU WILL HAVE NO"
100  PRINT "TROUBLE FINDING ANOTHER JOB."
110  PRINT   TAB( 20);"SINCERELY,"
120  PRINT
130  PRINT   TAB( 20);"SIMON LEE GREE"
140  GOTO 10
150  END
160  DATA   HOWE,92,OAKLEY,70
170  DATA   ANDERSON,96,WOLLY,88
180  DATA   GOERZ,74,END,-99
```

21.
```
10   INPUT "HOW MANY TIMES TO PRINT TEST? ";T
20   LET L = 0
30   LET L = L + 1
40   PRINT "TESTING"
50   IF L < > T THEN 30
60   PRINT
70   PRINT "TEST OVER. "L" TESTINGS PRINTED"
80   INPUT "TYPE YES TO RUN ANOTHER TEST? ";Y$
90   IF Y$ = "YES" THEN 10
```

CHAPTER FIVE

1.
```
10   FOR I = 1 TO 7
20   PRINT "*********"
30   NEXT I
```

3.
```
10   PRINT "*****"
20   FOR I = 1 TO 6
30   PRINT " ***"
40   NEXT I
50   PRINT "*****"
```

5.
```
5   FOR V = 1 TO 25
10  PRINT "  *"
20  PRINT " ***"
30  PRINT "*****"
40  PRINT "  *"
50  PRINT "  *"
60  PRINT "  *"
70  PRINT "  *"
80  PRINT " ***"
90  PRINT " ***"
100 PRINT " ***"
110 PRINT
120 NEXT V
```

7.
```
10  FOR I = 10 TO 97 STEP 3
20  PRINT I" ";
30  NEXT I
```

9.
```
10  PRINT TAB( 10);"**********"
20  FOR I = 1 TO 5
30  PRINT TAB( 10);"*        *"
40  NEXT I
50  PRINT TAB( 10);"**********"
```

11.
```
10  FOR L = 1 TO 6
20  PRINT TAB( 7 - L)"*****"
30  NEXT L
```

13.
```
]RUN
ITEM                COST

CANDY             $ 5.59
ICE CREAM         $ 2.55
CAKE              $ 7.65
SODA              $ 2.99
FAVORS            $ 2.99
-----------------------------
TOTAL COST:       $ 21.77
```

15.
```
10   PRINT "THE FIRST 8 PRESIDENTS:"
20   INPUT "DATA FOR WHICH PRESIDENT? ";N$
30   LET C = 0
40   LET C = C + 1
50   IF C = 9 THEN 230
60   READ P$,S$,T
70   IF N$ < > P$ THEN 40
80   PRINT
90   PRINT "NUMBER: "C
100  PRINT "NAME: "P$
110  PRINT "STATE: "S$
120  PRINT "TERM: "T" YEARS"
130  PRINT
140  END
150  DATA  GEORGE WASHINGTON,VIRGINIA,8
160  DATA  JOHN ADAMS,MASSACHUSETTS,4
170  DATA  THOMAS JEFFERSON,VIRGINIA,8
180  DATA  JAMES MADISON,VIRGINIA,8
190  DATA  JAMES MONROE,VIRGINIA,8
200  DATA  JOHN QUINCY ADAMS,MASSACHUSETTS,4
210  DATA  ANDREW JACKSON,SOUTH CAROLINA,8
220  DATA  MARTIN VAN BUREN,NEW YORK,4
230  PRINT
240  PRINT N$" NOT ON THIS LIST"
250  END
```

CHAPTER SIX

1a.
```
]PRINT 33 - 5 + 16
44

]PRINT 3 * 2 + 2 * 3
12

]PRINT 33 - (5 + 16)
12

]PRINT 3 * (2 + 2) * (3 + 2)
60

]PRINT (25 + 30) / 25 + 3
5.2

]PRINT ((10 + 5) / 3) + 2 * 15
35
```

```
]PRINT 15 / 3 + 2
7

]PRINT (10 + 5) / (5 - 2)
5

]PRINT 2 ^ 3
8

]PRINT 2^ (2 + 1)
8
```

3.
```
30  LET P = 2 * (L + W)

]RUN
ENTER WIDTH: 3
ENTER LENGTH: 4
THE PERIMETER IS 14
```

5.
```
150 GOTO 70

]RUN
EVEN NUMBER TESTER
ENTER A NUMBER: 16
16 IS EVEN.
ANOTHER NUMBER TO TEST? NO
```

7.
```
45  IF N / C < > P THEN LET P = P + 1
```

9a.
```
10  PRINT "FLIPPING"
20  FOR C = 1 TO 100
30  IF RND (1) < .5 THEN 60
40  LET H = H + 1
50  GOTO 70
60  LET T = T + 1
70  NEXT C
80  PRINT "HEADS = "H
90  PRINT "TAILS = "T
```

9b.
```
10    PRINT "WHICH WILL WIN HEADS (H) OR TAILS (T)? "
20    INPUT "ENTER YOUR GUESS? ";G$
30    PRINT
40    IF G$ = "H" THEN 70
50    LET Y$ = "TAILS"
60    GOTO 80
70    LET Y$ = "HEADS"
80    PRINT "FLIPPING"
90    FOR C = 1 TO 100
100   IF RND (1) < .5 THEN 130
110   LET H = H + 1
120   GOTO 140
130   LET T = T + 1
140   NEXT C
150   PRINT "HEADS = "H
160   PRINT "TAILS = "T
170   IF H = T THEN 250
180   IF H < T THEN 210
190   LET W$ = "HEADS"
200   GOTO 230
210   LET W$ = "TAILS"
220   PRINT W$" WON!"
230   PRINT "YOU PICKED "Y$
240   END
250   PRINT "IT'S A TIE; NO ONE WINS"
```

11.
```
10    INPUT "ENTER THE NUMBER OF INCHES ? ";I
20    LET C = I * 2.54
30    PRINT
40    PRINT I" INCHES = "C" CENTIMETERS"
```

13.
```
10    INPUT "ENTER BASE IN METERS: ";B
20    INPUT "ENTER HEIGHT IN METERS: ";H
30    LET A = .5 * B * H
40    PRINT "AREA = "A" SQUARE METERS"
50    PRINT
60    INPUT "ANOTHER TRIANGLE TO COMPUTE? ";Y$
70    IF Y$ = "YES" THEN 10
```

15.
```
10    FOR M = 1 TO 7
20    READ N,D
30    LET R =   INT (N / D * 1000 + .5)
40    PRINT N"/"D" OF A METER = "R" MILLIMETERS"
50    NEXT M
60    DATA  1,4,1,3,1,2,5,8,2,3,3,4,7,8
```

CHAPTER SEVEN

1.
```
10   HOME
20   FOR I = 1 TO 5
30   HTAB I
40   PRINT "*"
50   NEXT I
60   FOR I = 4 TO 1 STEP  - 1
70   HTAB I
80   PRINT "*"
90   NEXT I
100  END
```

3.
```
5    HOME
10   GR
20   COLOR= 2
30   HLIN 0,39 AT 0
40   HLIN 0,39 AT 39
50   VLIN 0,39 AT 0
60   VLIN 0,39 AT 39
70   END
```

5.
```
10   HOME
20   GR
30   FOR X = 0 TO 15
40   COLOR= X
50   VLIN 0,39 AT (X + 3) * 2
60   VLIN 0,39 AT (X + 3.5) * 2
70   NEXT X
80   END
```

7.
```
10   HOME
20   GR
30   FOR X = 0 TO 39
40   COLOR= 1
50   PLOT 10,X
60   COLOR= 0
70   PLOT 10,X
80   NEXT X
```

9.
```
10  HOME
20  HGR2
30  FOR I = 1 TO 7
40  HCOLOR= I
50  LET J = I * 10
60  HPLOT 0,J TO 279,J
70  NEXT I
```

11.
```
10  HOME
20  HGR
30  HCOLOR= 2
40  HPLOT 250,20 TO 250,110 TO 130,110 TO 250,20
50  END
```

13.
```
10  HOME
20  HGR
30  HCOLOR= 6
40  HPLOT 10,10 TO 130,110 TO 130,10
50  HPLOT  TO 70,10 TO 70,110
60  HPLOT  TO 10,110 TO 10,10
70  END
```

15.
```
10   HGR
20   HCOLOR= 5
30   HPLOT 125,0 TO 153,0 TO 153,30 TO 125,30 TO 125,0
40   HPLOT 119,50 TO 159,50 TO 159,110 TO 119,110 TO 119,50
50   HPLOT 139,30 TO 139,50
60   HPLOT 75,55 TO 119,55
70   HPLOT 159,55 TO 204,55
80   HPLOT 109,159 TO 139,110 TO 169,159
90   HPLOT 139,5 TO 139,15
100  HPLOT 132,20 TO 146,20
110  HPLOT 133,7
120  HPLOT 145,7
130  HPLOT 129,60 TO 149,60
140  HPLOT 139,60 TO 139,85
```

CHAPTER EIGHT

1.
```
10   LET X = 1
20   GOSUB 100
30   PRINT "****************************************"
40   LET X = 2
50   GOSUB 100
60   PRINT "!              !              !              !"
70   LET X = 3
80   GOSUB 100
90   FOR T = 1 TO 18: PRINT "AB";: NEXT T
91   PRINT "A"
92   END
100  PRINT "PART "X
110  RETURN
```

3.
```
10   PRINT "SELECT THE MATH OPERATION YOU WISH DONE:"
20   PRINT
30   PRINT "1 - ADDITION"
40   PRINT "2 - SUBTRACTION"
50   PRINT
60   INPUT "TYPE 1 OR 2 AND RETURN? ";T
70   LET A =  INT (100 *  RND (1) + 1)
80   LET B =  INT (100 *  RND (1) + 1)
90   ON T GOSUB 200,300
100  PRINT
110  PRINT A" "S$" "B" = "S
120  END
200  REM   *** ADDITION ***
210  LET S = A + B
220  LET S$ = "+"
230  RETURN
300  REM    *** SUBTRACTION ***
310  LET S = A - B
320  LET S$ = "-"
330  RETURN
```

5.
```
10   INPUT "TYPE YOUR NAME? ";N$
20   PRINT
30   PRINT "OKAY "N$" HERE ARE 5 MULTIPLICATION FACTS FOR YOU."
40   FOR F = 1 TO 5
50   LET A =  INT (15 *  RND (1) + 1)
60   LET B =  INT (15 *  RND (1) + 1)
70   LET S = A * B
80   PRINT A" * "B" = ";
90   INPUT U
100  IF U < > S THEN  PRINT "TRY AGAIN.": PRINT : GOTO 80
110  PRINT
120  GOSUB 200
130  PRINT
140  NEXT F
150  END
200  PRINT  TAB( 10);
210  FLASH
220  PRINT "CORRECT! "N$
230  NORMAL
240  RETURN
```

7.
```
10   PRINT "1) WITHDRAWAL"
20   PRINT "2) DEPOSIT"
30   PRINT "3) EXIT PROGRAM"
40   PRINT
50   INPUT "TYPE 1, 2 OR 3? ";T
60   ON T GOSUB 200,300,110
70   PRINT
80   PRINT "YOUR BALANCE IS $"B
90   PRINT
100  GOTO 10
110  END
200  REM  *** WITHDRAWAL ***
210  INPUT "AMOUNT TO WITHDRAW? ";A
215  IF B - A < 0 THEN  PRINT "WOW! THAT WILL BOUNCE O
     VER MY HEAD.": PRINT "TOO MUCH!": GOTO 210
220  LET B = B - A
230  RETURN
300  REM  *** DEPOSIT ***
310  INPUT "AMOUNT TO DEPOSIT? ";D
320  LET B = B + D
330  RETURN
```

9. **Main body**

   1. Use INPUT statements to
      a. Find out how many cards Harry has at the start.
      b. Find out how many cards Joe has at the start.
      c. Find out who is to go first.

   2. If Harry goes first, GOSUB subroutine Harry Flips First.

   3. If Joe goes first, GOSUB subroutine Joe Flips First.

   4. Determine the winner of the round.
      a. Increase the winner of the round's number of cards by 1.
      b. Decrease the loser of the round's number of cards by 1.
      c. The winner goes first in the next round.

   5. Print out the results of the round.

   6. Go back and start at step 2.

   Subroutines:

   Harry Flips First
      1. Flip Harry's card and print the result (UP or DOWN).
      2. Flip Joe's card and print the result (UP or DOWN).
      3. RETURN to main body.

   Joe Flips First
      1. Flip Joe's card and print the result (UP or DOWN).
      2. Flip Harry's card and print the result (UP or DOWN).
      3. RETURN to main body.

11.
```
20   READ B
30   PRINT "TOTAL CRIMEFIGHTING COSTS $ "B
100  PRINT "AVERAGE COST PER CROOK $ "B / 4
```

13.

Line	N	A	S	T	M
20	5				
50		1			
60			75		
80				75	
90		2			
60			89		
80				164	
90		3			
60			99		
80				263	
90		4			
60			84		
80				347	
90		5			
60			91		
80				438	
90		6			
100					87.6

CHAPTER NINE

1.
```
10  FOR O = 1 TO 8
20  FOR I = 1 TO 20
30  PRINT "*";
40  NEXT I
50  PRINT
60  NEXT O
```

E-18   Answers to Odd Numbered Exercises

3.
```
10  FOR J = 1 TO 8
20  FOR Y = 1 TO J
30  PRINT "*";
40  NEXT Y
50  PRINT
60  NEXT J
```

5.
```
10  FOR J = 1 TO 8
20  PRINT  TAB( J);
30  FOR I = 1 TO (9 - J) * 2 - 1
40  PRINT "*";
50  NEXT I
60  PRINT
70  NEXT J
```

7.
```
10  FOR J = 1 TO 6
20  INPUT "TYPE A NUMBER? ";X(J)
30  NEXT J
40  FOR K = 1 TO 6
50  READ X
60  PRINT "J = "X"    X( "X" ) = "X(X)
70  NEXT K
80  DATA  1,3,5,2,4,6
```

9a.]RUN

    1   5
    1   6
    2   5
    2   6
    3   5
    3   6

b.]RUN

    10
    10
    10
    12
    12
    11
    14
    13
    11

c.]RUN

    23   2
    17   70

11.
```
1   DIM N(100)
10  FOR X = 1 TO 100
20  REM  *** PICK A RANDOM NUMBER ***
30  LET N(X) =  INT (100 *  RND (1) + 1)
40  REM *** LOOP THRU ALL EARLIER NUMBERS ***
45  IF X = 1 THEN 90
50  FOR Y = 1 TO (X - 1)
60  REM *** CHECK FOR DUPLICATES ***
70  IF N(Y) = N(X) THEN 150
80  NEXT Y
90  NEXT X
110 END
150 REM *** HOW MANY AND THE NUMBERS ***
160 PRINT "DUPLICATE AFTER "X" NUMBERS."
170 FOR J = 1 TO X
180 PRINT N(J)" ";
190 NEXT J
```

13.
```
]RUN
B4= 1 BUT B(4)= 86
14              125              111
```

15.
```
10  HOME
20  PRINT "BULLETIN BOARD SCHEDULE"
30  PRINT
40  INPUT "FOR WHAT DAY : ? ";D$
50  LET I = 0
60  RESTORE
70  LET I = I + 1
80  READ T$,N$
90  IF D$ = T$ THEN 150
100  IF I < 5 THEN 70
110  PRINT "THAT DAY IS NOT ON MY LIST."
120  INPUT "TYPE YES TO CHECK ANOTHER DAY? ";Y$
130  IF Y$ < > "YES" THEN  END
140  GOTO 30
150  PRINT "ON "D$" "N$" HAS BULLETIN BOARD DUTY."
160  GOTO 120
170  DATA TUESDAY,FRED,THURSDAY,HARRY
180  DATA WEDNESDAY,WENDY,FRIDAY,PENNY
190  DATA MONDAY,JOE
```

17.
```
10   PRINT "SELECT A NUMBER:"
20   PRINT
30   FOR K = 1 TO 4
40   READ C$,C
50   PRINT K". "C$
60   NEXT K
70   RESTORE
80   PRINT
90   PRINT "TYPE 1, 2, 3, OR 4 : ";
100  GET A$
110  PRINT A$
120  LET A = VAL (A$)
130  IF A < 1 OR A > 4 THEN 80
140  FOR N = 1 TO A
150  READ C$,C
160  NEXT N
170  PRINT
180  PRINT "YOU HAVE "C" "C$" COMICS."
190  DATA SPIDERMAN,37,BATMAN,12
200  DATA SUPERMAN,15,GI JOE,4
```

INDEX

Accumulator	3-6	High-Resolution Graphics	7-9
AND	4-10	HLIN	7-6
Arrays	9-4	HOME	7-1
BASIC	1-1	HPLOT	7-10
CATALOG	A-2	HTAB	7-1
COLOR	7-6	IF . . . THEN	4-1
Color Chart, High-Resolution	7-10	Immediate Mode	1-2
Color Chart, Low-Resolution	7-6	INIT	A-1
Comparing Numeric Values	4-1	INPUT	2-9
Comparing Strings	4-2	INVERSE	7-3
Conditional Statements	4-1	Line Numbering	1-4
CONT	8-25	LIST	1-7
Correcting Errors	1-8	LOAD	A-2
Counter	3-3	LOCK	A-3
Cursor Movement (In Editing)	1-1	Logic Errors	8-22
Cursor Movement (In a Program)	7-2	Loops	3-2
DATA	3-8	Low-Resolution Graphics	7-1
Debugging	8-21	Multiple Statement Lines	8-1
DELETE	A-3	Need for Arrays	9-4
DIM	9-11	Nested FOR . . . NEXT Loops	9-1
Diskette Directories	A-2	NEW	1-1
Diskette Formatting	A-1	NEXT	5-1
Errors, Correcting	1-8	NORMAL	7-3
Errors, Logic	8-22	Null Strings	9-18
Errors, REENTER	2-12	Numeric Variables	2-1
Errors, Rounding	6-10	ON . . . GOSUB	8-10
Errors, Run Time	8-21	ON . . . GOTO	8-12
Errors, SYNTAX	1-3	OR	4-10
Extended Use of the IF . . . THEN Statement	4-4	Order of Operations	6-1
Extended Variable Names	9-14	Planning a Program	8-13
FLASH	7-3	PLOT	7-6
FOR . . . TO . . . STEP	5-6	PRINT	1-2
Formatting Diskettes	A-1	PRINT Formatting	3-12
GET	9-19	PRINT TAB	5-8
GOSUB	8-3	PRINT Zones	3-12
GOTO	3-1	Program Structuring Rules	8-14
GR	7-5	Quotation Marks	1-3
Graphics, High-Resolution	7-9	Raising to a Power	6-2
Graphics, Low-Resolution	7-5	Random Numbers	6-7
Hand Tracing	8-23	READ	3-8
HCOLOR	7-10	REM	2-14
		RENAME	A-3
		RESTORE	9-17

RETURN	8-3	Subscripted Variables	9-6
RND	6-7	TAB	5-8
Rounding Errors	6-10	TEXT	7-5
RUN	1-5	Tracing	8-23
Run Time Errors	8-21	Unacceptable Variable Names	9-14
SAVE	A-1	UNLOCK	A-3
Scientific Notation	6-11	VAL	9-21
Screen Dimensions (Text)	7-1	Variables	2-1
Screen Dimensions		Variables, Longer Names	9-14
(High-Resolution Graphics)	7-9	Variables, Names	2-1
Screen Dimensions		Variables, Numeric	2-1
(Low-Resolution Graphics)	7-5	Variables, String	2-4
STEP	5-4	Variables, Subscripted	9-6
STOP	8-25	VTAB	7-1
String Variables	2-4	VLIN	7-7
Structuring a Program	8-13	What is a Variable	2-1
Subroutines	8-2	Zones, Printing	3-12
Subscripts	9-6		

INTERACTIVE COLLEGE
OF TECHNOLOGY
MEDIA CENTER
MAIN CAMPUS

005.4
Pres   Presley, Bruce
        A Beginner's Guide to the
        Apple

005.4
Pres   Presley, Bruce
        A Beginner's Guide to the
        Apple

DATE	ISSUED TO

005.4
Pres   Presley, Bruce
        A Beginner's Guide to the
        Apple